The Collected Poetry of W. H. Auden

THE
COLLECTED
POETRY OF
W. H. AUDEN

RANDOM HOUSE · NEW YORK

Manufactured in the United States of America
by Kingsport Press, Inc. Kingsport, Tennessee

Whether conditioned by God, or their neural structure, still
All men have this common creed, account for it as you will:—
The Truth is one and incapable of contradiction;
All knowledge that conflicts with itself is Poetic Fiction.

Preface

IN the eyes of every author, I fancy, his own past work falls into four classes. First, the pure rubbish which he regrets ever having conceived; second—for him the most painful—the good ideas which his incompetence or impatience prevented from coming to much (*The Orators* seems to me such a case of the fair notion fatally injured); third, the pieces he has nothing against except their lack of importance; these must inevitably form the bulk of any collection since, were he to limit it to the fourth class alone, to those poems for which he is honestly grateful, his volume would be too depressingly slim.

W. H. A.

CONTENTS

ix

x

Part I

POEMS

Musée des Beaux Arts

About suffering they were never wrong,
The Old Masters: how well they understood
Its human position; how it takes place
While someone else is eating or opening a window or just
    walking dully along;
How, when the aged are reverently, passionately waiting
For the miraculous birth, there always must be
Children who did not specially want it to happen, skating
On a pond at the edge of the wood:
They never forgot
That even the dreadful martyrdom must run its course
Anyhow in a corner, some untidy spot
Where the dogs go on with their doggy life and the
    torturer's horse
Scratches its innocent behind on a tree.

In Brueghel's *Icarus*, for instance: how everything turns away
Quite leisurely from the disaster; the ploughman may
Have heard the splash, the forsaken cry,
But for him it was not an important failure; the sun shone
As it had to on the white legs disappearing into the green
Water; and the expensive delicate ship that must have seen
Something amazing, a boy falling out of the sky,
Had somewhere to get to and sailed calmly on.

In War Time *
(For Caroline Newton)

Abruptly mounting her ramshackle wheel,
Fortune has pedalled furiously away;
The sobbing mess is on our hands today.

* The poems marked by asterisks are published for the first time in book
form.

3

Those accidental terrors, Famine, Flood,
Were never trained to diagnose or heal
Nightmares that are intentional and real.

Nor lust nor gravity can preach an aim
To minds disordered by a lucid dread
Of seeking peace by going off one's head.

Nor will the living waters whistle; though
Diviners cut their throats to prove their claim,
The desert remains arid all the same.

If augurs take up flying to fulfill
The doom they prophesy, it must be so;
The herons have no modern sign for No.

If nothing can upset but total war
The massive fancy of the heathen will
That solitude is something you can kill,

If we are right to choose our suffering
And be tormented by an Either-Or,
The right to fail that is worth dying for,

If so, the sweets of victory are rum:
A pride of earthly cities premising
The Inner Life as socially the thing,

Where, even to the lawyers, Law is what,
For better or for worse, our vows become
When no one whom we need is looking, Home

A sort of honour, not a building site,
Wherever we are, when, if we chose, we might
Be somewhere else, yet trust that we have
        chosen right.

Two's Company

Again in conversations
Speaking of fear
And throwing off reserve
The voice is nearer
But no clearer
Than first love
Than boys' imaginations.

For every news
Means pairing off in twos and twos
Another I, another You
Each knowing what to do
But of no use.

Never stronger
But younger and younger
Saying good-bye but coming back, for fear
Is over there
And the centre of anger
Is out of danger.

The Composer

All the others translate: the painter sketches
A visible world to love or reject;
Rummaging into his living, the poet fetches
The images out that hurt and connect.

From Life to Art by painstaking adaption,
Relying on us to cover the rift;
Only your notes are pure contraption,
Only your song is an absolute gift.

Pour out your presence, O delight, cascading
The falls of the knee and the weirs of the spine,
Our climate of silence and doubt invading;

You alone, alone, O imaginary song,
Are unable to say an existence is wrong,
And pour out your forgiveness like a wine.

Voltaire at Ferney

Almost happy now, he looked at his estate.
An exile making watches glanced up as he passed,
And went on working; where a hospital was rising fast
A joiner touched his cap; an agent came to tell
Some of the trees he'd planned were progressing well.
The white alps glittered. It was summer. He was very great.

Far off in Paris, where his enemies
Whispered that he was wicked, in an upright chair
A blind old woman longed for death and letters. He would write
"Nothing is better than life." But was it? Yes, the fight
Against the false and the unfair
Was always worth it. So was gardening. Civilise.

Cajoling, scolding, scheming, cleverest of them all,
He'd led the other children in a holy war
Against the infamous grown-ups; and, like a child, been sly
And humble when there was occasion for
The two-faced answer or the plain protective lie,
But patient like a peasant waited for their fall.

And never doubted, like D'Alembert, he would win:
Only Pascal was a great enemy, the rest
Were rats already poisoned; there was much, though, to be done,

And only himself to count upon.
Dear Diderot was dull but did his best;
Rousseau, he'd always known, would blubber and give in.

So, like a sentinel, he could not sleep. The night was full
　　of wrong,
Earthquakes and executions. Soon he would be dead,
And still all over Europe stood the horrible nurses
Itching to boil their children. Only his verses
Perhaps could stop them: He must go on working. Overhead
The uncomplaining stars composed their lucid song.

Journey to Iceland

And the traveller hopes: "Let me be far from any
Physician"; and the ports have names for the sea,
　　The citiless, the corroding, the sorrow;
　　And North means to all: "Reject."

And the great plains are forever where the cold fish is hunted,
And everywhere; the light birds flicker and flaunt;
　　Under the scolding flag the lover
　　Of islands may see at last,

Faintly, his limited hope, as he nears the glitter
Of glaciers, the sterile immature mountains intense
　　In the abnormal day of this world, and a river's
　　Fan-like polyp of sand.

Then let the good citizen here find natural marvels:
A horse-shoe ravine, an issue of steam from a cleft
　　In the rock, and rocks, and waterfalls brushing the
　　Rocks, and among the rocks birds.

7

And the student of prose and conduct places to visit:
The site of a church where a bishop was put in a bag,
    The bath of a great historian, the fort where
    An outlaw dreaded the dark;

Remember the doomed man thrown by his horse and crying,
"Beautiful is the hillside, I will not go,"
    The old woman confessing, "He that I loved the
    Best, to him I was worst."

For Europe is absent: this is an island and therefore
A refuge, where the fast affections of its dead may be bought
    By those whose dreams accuse them of being
    Spitefully alive, and the pale

From too much passion of kissing feel pure in its deserts.
Can they? For the world is, and the present, and the lie.
    The narrow bridge over the torrent,
    And the small farm under the crag

Are the natural setting for the jealousies of a province;
And the weak vow of fidelity is formed by the cairn;
    And within the indigenous figure on horseback
    On the bridle path down by the lake

The blood moves also by crooked and furtive inches,
Asks all our questions: "Where is the homage? When
    Shall justice be done? O who is against me?
    Why am I always alone?"

No, our time has no favourite suburb; no local features
Are those of the young for whom all wish to care;
    The promise is only a promise, the fabulous
    Country impartially far.

Tears fall in all the rivers. Again the driver
Pulls on his gloves and in a blinding snowstorm starts
    Upon his deadly journey, and again the writer
    Runs howling to his art.

Gare du Midi

A nondescript express in from the South,
Crowds round the ticket barrier, a face
To welcome which the mayor has not contrived
Bugles or braid: something about the mouth
Distracts the stray look with alarm and pity.
Snow is falling. Clutching a little case,
He walks out briskly to infect a city
Whose terrible future may have just arrived.

The Labyrinth

Anthropos apteros for days
Walked whistling round and round the Maze,
Relying happily upon
His temperament for getting on.

The hundredth time he sighted, though,
A bush he left an hour ago,
He halted where four alleys crossed,
And recognised that he was lost.

"Where am I? Metaphysics says
No question can be asked unless
It has an answer, so I can
Assume this maze has got a plan.

If theologians are correct,
A Plan implies an Architect:
A God-built maze would be, I'm sure,
The Universe in miniature.

Are data from the world of Sense,
In that case, valid evidence?
What in the universe I know
Can give directions how to go?

All Mathematics would suggest
A steady straight line as the best,
But left and right alternately
Is consonant with History.

Aesthetics, though, believes all Art
Intends to gratify the Heart:
Rejecting disciplines like these,
Must I, then, go which way I please?

Such reasoning is only true
If we accept the classic view,
Which we have no right to assert,
According to the Introvert.

His absolute pre-supposition
Is—Man creates his own condition:
This maze was not divinely built,
But is secreted by my guilt.

The centre that I cannot find
Is known to my Unconscious Mind;
I have no reason to despair
Because I am already there.

My problem is how *not* to will;
They move most quickly who stand still;
I'm only lost until I see
I'm lost because I want to be.

If this should fail, perhaps I should,
As certain educators would,
Content myself with the conclusion;
In theory there is no solution.

All statements about what I feel,
Like I-am-lost, are quite unreal:
My knowledge ends where it began;
A hedge is taller than a man."

Anthropos apteros, perplexed
To know which turning to take next,
Looked up and wished he were the bird
To whom such doubts must seem absurd.

Kairos and Logos *

I

Around them boomed the rhetoric of time,
The smells and furniture of the known world
Where conscience worshipped an aesthetic order
And what was unsuccessful was condemned;
And, at the centre of its vast self-love,
The emperor and his pleasures, dreading death.

In lovely verse that military order,
Transferring its obsession onto time,
Besieged the body and cuckolded love;

Puzzling the boys of an athletic world,
These only feared another kind of Death
To which the time-obsessed are all condemned.

Night and the rivers sang a chthonic love,
Destroyer of cities and the daylight order,
But seemed to them weak arguments for death;
The apple tree that cannot measure time
Might taste the apple yet not be condemned;
They, to enjoy it, must renounce the world.

Friendly to what the sensual call death,
Placing their lives below the dogs who love
Their fallen masters and are not condemned,
They came to life within a dying order;
Outside the sunshine of its civil world
The savage waited their appointed time.

Its brilliant self-assertions were condemned
To interest the forest and draw death
On aqueducts and learning; yet the world,
Through them, had witnessed, when predestined love
Fell like a daring meteor into time,
The condescension of eternal order.

So, sown in little clumps about the world,
The fair, the faithful and the uncondemned
Broke out spontaneously all over time,
Setting against the random facts of death
A ground and possibility of order,
Against defeat the certainty of love.

And never, like its own, condemned the world
Or hated time, but sang until their death:
"O Thou who lovest, set its love in order."

II

Quite suddenly her dream became a word:
There stood the unicorn, declaring—"Child";
She kissed her dolls good-bye and one by one
Embraced the faithful roses in the garden,
Waved for the last time to her mother's home,
And tiptoed out into the silent forest.

And seemed the lucky, the predestined one
For whom the stones made way without a word;
And sparrows fought to make her feel at home,
And winds restrained their storms before the child;
And all the children of that mother-forest
Were told to let her treat it as her garden.

Till she forgot that she was not at home
Where she was loved, of course, by everyone,
Could always tell the rose-bush—"Be a forest."
Or make dolls guess when she had thought a word,
Or play at being Mother in the garden
And have importance as her only child.

So, scampering like a sparrow through the forest,
She piled up stones, pretending they were Home,
Called the wild roses that she picked "My Garden,"
Made any wind she chose the Naughty One,
Talked to herself as to a doll, a child
Whose mother-magic knew the Magic Word.

And took the earth for granted as her garden:
Till the day came the children of the forest
Ceased to regard or treat her as a child;
The roses frowned at her untidy home,

The sparrows laughed when she misspelt a word,
Winds cried: "A mother should behave like one."

Frightened and cruel like a guilty child,
She shouted all the roses from her garden,
And threw stones at the winds: without a word
The unicorn slipped off into the forest
Like an offended doll, and one by one
The sparrows flew back to her mother's home.

Of course the forest overran her garden,
Yet, though, like everyone, she lost her home,
The Word still nursed Its motherhood, Its child.

III

If one could name the father of these things,
They would not happen to decide one's fate:
He woke one morning and the verbal truth
He went to bed with was no longer there;
The years of reading fell away; his eyes
Beheld the weights and contours of the earth.

One must be passive to conceive the truth:
The bright and brutal surfaces of things
Awaited the decision of his eyes,
These pretty girls, to be embraced by fate
And mother all the objects of the earth;
The fatherhood of knowledge stood out there.

One notices, if one will trust one's eyes,
The shadow cast by language upon truth:
He saw his rôle as father to an earth
Whose speechless, separate, and ambiguous things
Married at his decision; he was there
To show a lucid passion for their fate.

One has good reason to award the earth
The dog-like dumb devotion of the eyes;
Death, love, dishonour are predicted there,
Her arbitrary moments are the truth:
No, he was not the father of his fate;
The power of decision lay with things.

To know, one must decide what is not there,
Where sickness is, and nothing: all that earth
Presented was a challenge to his fate
To father dreams of talking oaks, of eyes
In walls, catastrophes, sins, poems, things
Whose possibilities excluded truth.

What one expects is not, of course, one's fate:
When he had finished looking at them, there
Were helpless images instead of things
That had looked so decided; instead of earth
His fatherless creation; instead of truth
The luckiest convention of his eyes:

That saw himself there with an exile's eyes,
Missing his Father, a thing of earth
On whose decision hung the fate of truth.

IV

Castle and crown are faded clean away,
The fountain sinks into a level silence;
What kingdom can be reached by the occasions
That climb the broken ladders of our lives?
We are imprisoned in unbounded spaces,
Defined by an indefinite confusion.

We should have wept before for these occasions,
We should have given what is snatched away;

O columns, acrobats of cheering spaces,
O songs that were the royal wives of silence,
Now you are art and part of our confusion;
We are at loggerheads with our own lives.

The order of the macrocosmic spaces,
The outward calm of their remote occasions,
Has lost all interest in our confusion;
Our inner regimen has given way;
The subatomic gulfs confront our lives
With the cold stare of their eternal silence.

Where are the kings who routed all confusion,
The bearded gods who shepherded the spaces,
The merchants who poured gold into our lives?
Where the historic routes, the great occasions?
Laurel and language wither into silence;
The nymphs and oracles have fled away.

And cold and absence echo on our lives:
"We are your conscience of your own confusion
That made a stricken widow of the silence
And weeping orphans of the unarmed spaces,
That laid time waste behind you, stole away
The birthright of innumerable occasions."

O blessing of reproach. O proof that silence
And condemnation presuppose our lives:
We are not lost but only run away,
The authors and the powers of confusion;
We are the promise of unborn occasions;
Our presence is required by all the spaces.

The flora of our lives could guide occasions
Without confusion on their frisking way
Through all the silences and all the spaces.

Who's Who

A shilling life will give you all the facts:
How Father beat him, how he ran away,
What were the struggles of his youth, what acts
Made him the greatest figure of his day:
Of how he fought, fished, hunted, worked all night,
Though giddy, climbed new mountains; named a sea:
Some of the last researchers even write
Love made him weep his pints like you and me.

With all his honours on, he sighed for one
Who, say astonished critics, lived at home;
Did little jobs about the house with skill
And nothing else; could whistle; would sit still
Or potter round the garden; answered some
Of his long marvellous letters but kept none.

His Excellency

As it is, plenty;
As it's admitted
The children happy
And the car, the car
That goes so far,
And the wife devoted:
To this as it is,
To the work and the banks
Let his thinning hair
And his hauteur
Give thanks, give thanks.

All that was thought
As like as not is not;

When nothing was enough
But love, but love,
And the rough future
Of an intransigeant nature,
And the betraying smile,
Betraying, but a smile:
That that is not, is not;
Forget, forget.

Let him not cease to praise,
Then, his spacious days;
Yes, and the success
Let him bless, let him bless:
Let him see in this
The profit larger
And the sin venial
Lest he see as it is
The loss as major
And final, final.

Macao

A weed from Catholic Europe, it took root
Between the yellow mountains and the sea,
And bore these gay stone houses like a fruit,
And grew on China imperceptibly.

Rococo images of Saint and Saviour
Promise her gamblers fortunes when they die;
Churches beside the brothels testify
That faith can pardon natural behaviour.

This city of indulgence need not fear
The major sins by which the heart is killed,
And governments and men are torn to pieces:

18

Religious clocks will strike; the childish vices
Will safeguard the low virtues of the child;
And nothing serious can happen here.

This One

Before this loved one
Was that one and that one
A family
And history
And ghost's adversity
Whose pleasing name
Was neighbourly shame.
Before this last one
Was much to be done,
Frontiers to cross
As clothes grew worse
And coins to pass
In a cheaper house
Before this last one
Before this loved one.

Face that the sun
Is supple on
May stir but here
Is no new year;
This gratitude for gifts is less
Than the old loss;
Touching is shaking hands
On mortgaged lands;
And smiling of
This gracious greeting
"Good day. Good luck"
Is no real meeting

19

But instinctive look
A backward love.

Atlantis *

Being set on the idea
  Of getting to Atlantis,
You have discovered of course
  Only the Ship of Fools is
Making the voyage this year,
As gales of abnormal force
  Are predicted, and that you
  Must therefore be ready to
Behave absurdly enough
  To pass for one of The Boys,
At least appearing to love
  Hard liquor, horseplay and noise.

Should storms, as may well happen,
  Drive you to anchor a week
In some old harbour-city
  Of Ionia, then speak
With her witty scholars, men
Who have proved there cannot be
  Such a place as Atlantis:
  Learn their logic, but notice
How its subtlety betrays
  Their enormous simple grief;
Thus they shall teach you the ways
  To doubt that you may believe.

If, later, you run aground
  Among the headlands of Thrace,
Where with torches all night long

A naked barbaric race
Leaps frenziedly to the sound
Of conch and dissonant gong;
　　On that stony savage shore
　　Strip off your clothes and dance, for
Unless you are capable
　　Of forgetting completely
About Atlantis, you will
　　Never finish your journey.

Again, should you come to gay
　　Carthage or Corinth, take part
In their endless gaiety;
　　And if in some bar a tart,
As she strokes your hair, should say
"This is Atlantis, dearie,"
　　Listen with attentiveness
　　To her life-story: unless
You become acquainted now
　　With each refuge that tries to
Counterfeit Atlantis, how
　　Will you recognise the true?

Assuming you beach at last
　　Near Atlantis, and begin
The terrible trek inland
　　Through squalid woods and frozen
Tundras where all are soon lost;
If, forsaken then, you stand,
　　Dismissal everywhere,
　　Stone and snow, silence and air,
O remember the great dead
　　And honour the fate you are,

Travelling and tormented,
  Dialectic and bizarre.

Stagger onward rejoicing;
  And even then if, perhaps
Having actually got
  To the last col, you collapse
With all Atlantis shining
Below you yet you cannot
  Descend, you should still be proud
  Even to have been allowed
Just to peep at Atlantis
  In a poetic vision:
Give thanks and lie down in peace,
  Having seen your salvation.

All the little household gods
  Have started crying, but say
Good-bye now, and put to sea.
  Farewell, my dear, farewell: may
Hermes, master of the roads,
And the four dwarf Kabiri,
  Protect and serve you always;
  And may the Ancient of Days
Provide for all you must do
  His invisible guidance,
Lifting up, dear, upon you
  The light of His countenance.

Make Up Your Mind

Between attention and attention
The first and last decision
Is mortal distraction
Of earth and air,

22

Further and nearer,
The vague wants
Of days and nights,
And personal error;
And the fatigued face,
Taking the strain
Of the horizontal force
And the vertical thrust,
Makes random answer
To the crucial test;
The uncertain flesh
Scraping back chair
For the wrong train,
Falling in slush,
Before a friend's friends
Or shaking hands
With a snub-nosed winner.

The opening window, closing door,
Open, close, but not
To finish or restore;
These wishes get
No further than
The edges of the town,
And leaning asking from the car
Cannot tell us where we are;
While the divided face
Has no grace,
No discretion,
No occupation
But registering
Acreage, mileage,
The easy knowledge
Of the virtuous thing.

Adolescence

By landscape reminded once of his mother's figure
The mountain heights he remembers get bigger and bigger:
With the finest of mapping pens he fondly traces
All the family names on the familiar places.

Among green pastures straying he walks by still waters;
Surely a swan he seems to earth's unwise daughters,
Bending a beautiful head, worshipping not lying,
"Dear" the dear beak in the dear concha crying.

Under the trees the summer bands were playing;
"Dear boy, be brave as these roots," he heard them saying:
Carries the good news gladly to a world in danger,
Is ready to argue, he smiles, with any stranger.

And yet this prophet, homing the day is ended,
Receives odd welcome from the country he so defended:
The band roars "Coward, Coward," in his human fever,
The giantess shuffles nearer, cries "Deceiver."

Always in Trouble

Can speak of trouble, pressure on men
Born all the time, brought forward into light
For warm dark moan.
Though heart fears all heart cries for, rebuffs with mortal beat
Skyfall, the legs sucked under, adder's bite.
That prize held out of reach
Guides the unwilling tread,
The asking breath,
Till on attended bed
Or in untracked dishonour comes to each
His natural death.

We pass our days
Speak, man to men, easy, learning to point
To jump before ladies, to show our scars:
But no
We were mistaken, these faces are not ours.
They smile no more when we smile back:
Eyes, ears, tongue, nostrils bring
News of revolt, inadequate counsel to
An infirm king.

O watcher in the dark, you wake
Our dream of waking, we feel
Your finger on the flesh that has been skinned,
By your bright day
See clear what we were doing, that we were vile.
Your sudden hand
Shall humble great
Pride, break it, wear down to stumps old systems which await
The last transgression of the sea.

As We Like It

Certainly our city with its byres of poverty down to
The river's edge, its cathedral, its engines, its dogs;
  Here is the cosmopolitan cooking
  And the light alloys and the glass.

Built by the conscience-stricken, the weapon-making,
By us. Wild rumours woo and terrify the crowd,
  Woo us. Betrayers thunder at, blackmail
  Us. But where now are They

Who without reproaches showed us what our vanity
    has chosen,

25

Who pursued understanding with patience like a sex,
　　　had unlearnt
　　Our hatred and towards the really better
　　World had turned their face?

Who knows? The peaked and violent faces are exalted,
The feverish prejudiced lives do not care, and lost
　　Their voice in the flutter of bunting, the glittering
　　Brass of our great retreat,

And the malice of death. For the wicked card is dealt and
The sinister tall-hatted botanist stoops at the spring
　　With his insignificant phial and looses
　　The plague on the ignorant town.

Under their shadows the pitiful subalterns are sleeping;
The moon is usual; the necessary lovers touch;
　　The river is alone and the trampled flower;
　　And through years of absolute cold

The planets rush towards Lyra in a lion's charge. Can
Hate so securely bind? Are they dead here? Yes.
　　And the wish to wound has the power. And tomorrow
　　Comes. It's a world. It's a way.

We're Late

　　Clocks cannot tell our time of day
　　For what event to pray
　　Because we have no time, because
　　We have no time until
　　We know what time we fill,
　　Why time is other than time was.

26

Nor can our question satisfy
The answer in the statue's eye:
Only the living ask whose brow
May wear the Roman laurel now;
The dead say only how.

What happens to the living when we die?
Death is not understood by Death; nor You, nor I.

Consider

Consider this and in our time
As the hawk sees it or the helmeted airman:
The clouds rift suddenly—look there
At cigarette-end smouldering on a border
At the first garden party of the year.
Pass on, admire the view of the massif
Through plate-glass windows of the Sport Hotel;
Join there the insufficient units
Dangerous, easy, in furs, in uniform
And constellated at reserved tables
Supplied with feelings by an efficient band
Relayed elsewhere to farmers and their dogs
Sitting in kitchens in the stormy fens.

Long ago, supreme Antagonist,
More powerful than the great northern whale
Ancient and sorry at life's limiting defect,
In Cornwall, Mendip, or the Pennine moor
Your comments on the highborn mining-captains,
Found they no answer, made them wish to die
—Lie since in barrows out of harm.
You talk to your admirers every day
By silted harbours, derelict works,

In strangled orchards, and the silent comb
Where dogs have worried or a bird was shot.
Order the ill that they attack at once:
Visit the ports and, interrupting
The leisurely conversation in the bar
Within a stone's throw of the sunlit water,
Beckon your chosen out. Summon
Those handsome and diseased youngsters, those women
Your solitary agents in the country parishes;
And mobilize the powerful forces latent
In soils that make the farmer brutal
In the infected sinus, and the eyes of stoats.
Then, ready, start your rumour, soft
But horrifying in its capacity to disgust
Which, spreading magnified, shall come to be
A polar peril, a prodigious alarm,
Scattering the people, as torn-up paper
Rags and utensils in a sudden gust,
Seized with immeasurable neurotic dread.

Seekers after happiness, all who follow
The convolutions of your simple wish,
It is later than you think; nearer that day
Far other than that distant afternoon
Amid rustle of frocks and stamping feet
They gave the prizes to the ruined boys.
You cannot be away, then, no
Not though you pack to leave within an hour,
Escaping humming down arterial roads:
The date was yours; the prey to fugues,
Irregular breathing and alternate ascendancies
After some haunted migratory years
To disintegrate on an instant in the explosion of mania
Or lapse for ever into a classic fatigue.

The Secret Agent

Control of the passes was, he saw, the key
To this new district, but who would get it?
He, the trained spy, had walked into the trap
For a bogus guide, seduced with the old tricks.

At Greenhearth was a fine site for a dam
And easy power, had they pushed the rail
Some stations nearer. They ignored his wires.
The bridges were unbuilt and trouble coming.

The street music seemed gracious now to one
For weeks up in the desert. Woken by water
Running away in the dark, he often had
Reproached the night for a companion
Dreamed of already. They would shoot, of course,
Parting easily who were never joined.

In Sickness and in Health *
(For Maurice and Gwen Mandelbaum)

Dear, all benevolence of fingering lips
That does not ask forgiveness is a noise
    At drunken feasts where Sorrow strips
To serve some glittering generalities:
Now, more than ever, we distinctly hear
The dreadful shuffle of a murderous year
And all our senses roaring as the Black
Dog leaps upon the individual back.

Whose sable genius understands too well
What code of famine can administrate
    Those inarticulate wastes where dwell

29

Our howling appetites: dear heart, do not
Think lightly to contrive his overthrow;
O promise nothing, nothing, till you know
The kingdom offered by the love-lorn eyes
A land of condors, sick cattle, and dead flies.

And how contagious is its desolation,
What figures of destruction unawares
    Jump out on Love's imagination
And chase away the castles and the bears;
How warped the mirrors where our worlds are made;
What armies burn up honour, and degrade
Our will-to-order into thermal waste;
How much lies smashed that cannot be replaced.

O let none say I Love until aware
What huge resources it will take to nurse
    One ruining speck, one tiny hair
That casts a shadow through the universe:
We are the deaf immured within a loud
And foreign language of revolt, a crowd
Of poaching hands and mouths who out of fear
Have learned a safer life than we can bear.

Nature by nature in unnature ends:
Echoing each other like two waterfalls,
    Tristan, Isolde, the great friends,
Make passion out of passion's obstacles;
Deliciously postponing their delight,
Prolong frustration till it lasts all night,
Then perish lest Brangaene's worldly cry
Should sober their cerebral ecstasy.

But, dying, conjure up their opposite,
Don Juan, so terrified of death he hears

Each moment recommending it,
And knows no argument to counter theirs;
Trapped in their vile affections, he must find
Angels to keep him chaste; a helpless, blind,
Unhappy spook, he haunts the urinals,
Existing solely by their miracles.

That syllogistic nightmare must reject
The disobedient phallus for the sword;
    The lovers of themselves collect,
And Eros is politically adored:
New Machiavellis flying through the air
Express a metaphysical despair,
Murder their last voluptuous sensation,
All passion in one passionate negation.

Beloved, we are always in the wrong,
Handling so clumsily our stupid lives,
    Suffering too little or too long,
Too careful even in our selfish loves:
The decorative manias we obey
Die in grimaces round us every day,
Yet through their tohu-bohu comes a voice
Which utters an absurd command—Rejoice.

Rejoice. What talent for the makeshift thought
A living corpus out of odds and ends?
    What pedagogic patience taught
Pre-occupied and savage elements
To dance into a segregated charm?
Who showed the whirlwind how to be an arm,
And gardened from the wilderness of space
The sensual properties of one dear face?

Rejoice, dear love, in Love's peremptory word;
All chance, all love, all logic, you and I,
   Exist by grace of the Absurd,
And without conscious artifice we die:
O, lest we manufacture in our flesh
The lie of our divinity afresh,
Describe round our chaotic malice now,
The arbitrary circle of a vow.

The scarves, consoles, and fauteuils of the mind
May be composed into a picture still,
   The matter of corrupt mankind
Resistant to the dream that makes it ill,
Not by our choice but our consent: beloved, pray
That Love, to Whom necessity is play,
Do what we must yet cannot do alone
And lay your solitude beside my own.

That reason may not force us to commit
That sin of the high-minded, sublimation,
   Which damns the soul by praising it,
Force our desire, O Essence of creation,
To seek Thee always in Thy substances,
Till the performance of those offices
Our bodies, Thine opaque enigmas, do,
Configure Thy transparent justice too.

Lest animal bias should decline our wish
For Thy perfection to identify
   Thee with Thy things, to worship fish,
Or solid apples, or the wavering sky,
Our intellectual motions with Thy light
To such intense vibration, Love, excite,
That we give forth a quiet none can tell
From that in which the lichens live so well.

That this round O of faithfulness we swear
May never wither to an empty nought
   Nor petrify into a square,
Mere habits of affection freeze our thought
In their inert society, lest we
Mock virtue with its pious parody
And take our love for granted, Love, permit
Temptations always to endanger it.

Lest, blurring with old moonlight of romance
The landscape of our blemishes, we try
   To set up shop on Goodwin Sands,
That we, though lovers, may love soberly,
O Fate, O *Felix Osculum,* to us
Remain nocturnal and mysterious:
Preserve us from presumption and delay;
O hold us to the voluntary way.

The Sphinx

Did it once issue from the carver's hand
Healthy? Even the earliest conquerors saw
The face of a sick ape, a bandaged paw,
A Presence in the hot invaded land.

The lion of a tortured stubborn star,
It does not like the young, nor love, nor learning:
Time hurt it like a person; it lies, turning
A vast behind on shrill America,

And witnesses. The huge hurt face accuses,
And pardons nothing, least of all success.
The answers that it utters have no uses

33

To those who face akimbo its distress:
"Do people like me?" No. The slave amuses
The lion: "Am I to suffer always?" Yes.

Something Is Bound to Happen

Doom is dark and deeper than any sea-dingle.
Upon what man it fall
In spring, day-wishing flowers appearing,
Avalanche sliding, white snow from rock-face,
That he should leave his house,
No cloud-soft hand can hold him, restraint by women;
But ever that man goes
Through place-keepers, through forest trees,
A stranger to strangers over undried sea,
Houses for fishes, suffocating water,
Or lonely on fell as chat,
By pot-holed becks
A bird stone-haunting, an unquiet bird.

There head falls forward, fatigued at evening,
And dreams of home,
Waving from window, spread of welcome,
Kissing of wife under single sheet;
But waking sees
Bird-flocks nameless to him, through doorway voices
Of new men making another love.

Save him from hostile capture,
From sudden tiger's spring at corner;
Protect his house,
His anxious house where days are counted
From thunderbolt protect,

From gradual ruin spreading like a stain;
Converting number from vague to certain,
Bring joy, bring day of his returning,
Lucky with day approaching, with leaning dawn.

Are You There? *

Each lover has some theory of his own
About the difference between the ache
Of being with his love, and being alone:

Why what, when dreaming, is dear flesh and bone
That really stirs the senses, when awake,
Appears a simulacrum of his own.

Narcissus disbelieves in the unknown;
He cannot join his image in the lake
So long as he assumes he is alone.

The child, the waterfall, the fire, the stone,
Are always up to mischief, though, and take
The universe for granted as their own.

The elderly, like Proust, are always prone
To think of love as a subjective fake;
The more they love, the more they feel alone.

Whatever view we hold, it must be shown
Why every lover has a wish to make
Some kind of otherness his own:
Perhaps, in fact, we never are alone.

A Bride in the 30's

Easily, my dear, you move, easily your head,
And easily as through leaves of a photograph album I'm led
Through the night's delights and the day's impressions,   2
Past the tall tenements and the trees in the wood,
Though sombre the sixteen skies of Europe
          And the Danube flood.

Looking and loving our behaviours pass
The stones, the steels, and the polished glass;
Lucky to love the strategic railway,
The sterile farms where his looks are fed,
And in the policed unlucky city
          Lucky his bed.

He from these lands of terrifying mottoes
Makes worlds as innocent as Beatrix Potter's;
Through bankrupt countries where they mend the roads
Along the endless plains his will is,
Intent as a collector, to pursue
          His greens and lilies

Easy for him to find in your face
The pool of silence and the tower of grace,
To conjure a camera into a wishing rose;
Simple to excite in the air from a glance
The horses, the fountains, the side-drum, the trombone,
          And the dance, the dance.

Summoned by such a music from our time
Such images to audience come
As vanity cannnot dispel nor bless;
Hunger and love in their variations,

Grouped invalids watching the flight of the birds,
        And single assassins,

Ten million of the desperate marching by,
Five feet, six feet, seven feet high,
Hitler and Mussolini in their wooing poses,
Churchill acknowledging the voters' greeting,
Roosevelt at the microphone, Van der Lubbe laughing,
        And our first meeting

But love except at our proposal
Will do no trick at his disposal,
Without opinions of his own performs
The programme that we think of merit,
And through our private stuff must work
        His public spirit.

Certain it became while we were still incomplete
There were certain prizes for which we would
        never compete;
A choice was killed by every childish illness,
The boiling tears amid the hot-house plants,
The rigid promise fractured in the garden
        And the long aunts

And every day there bolted from the field
Desires to which we could not yield;
Fewer and clearer grew the plans,
Schemes for a life and sketches for a hatred,
And early among my interesting scrawls
        Appeared your portrait.

You stand now before me, flesh and bone
These ghosts would like to make their own.

Are they your choices? O be deaf
When hatred would proffer her immediate pleasure,
And glory swap her fascinating rubbish
       For your one treasure.

Be deaf, too, standing uncertain now,
A pine-tree shadow across your brow,
To what I hear and wish I did not,
The voice of love saying lightly, brightly—
"Be Lubbe, be Hitler, but be my good
       Daily, nightly."

The power that corrupts, that power to excess
The beautiful quite naturally possess;
To them the fathers and the children turn,
And all who long for their destruction,
The arrogant and self-insulted, wait
       The looked instruction.

Shall idleness ring then your eyes like the pest,
O will you, unnoticed and mildly like the rest,
Will you join the lost in their sneering circles,
Forfeit the beautiful interest and fall
Where the engaging face is the face of the betrayer
       And the pang is all?

Wind shakes the tree; the mountains darken;
But the heart repeats though we would not hearken:
"Yours is the choice to whom the gods awarded
The language of learning and the language of love,
Crooked to move as a moneybag or a cancer,
       Or straight as a dove."

The Novelist

Encased in talent like a uniform,
The rank of every poet is well known;
They can amaze us like a thunderstorm,
Or die so young, or live for years alone.

They can dash forward like hussars: but he
Must struggle out of his boyish gift and learn
How to be plain and awkward, how to be
One after whom none think it worth to turn.

For, to achieve his lightest wish, he must
Become the whole of boredom, subject to
Vulgar complaints like love, among the Just

Be just, among the Filthy filthy too,
And in his own weak person, if he can,
Must suffer dully all the wrongs of Man.

I Shall Be Enchanted

Enter with him
These legends, Love;
For him assume
Each diverse form
To legend native,
As legend queer;
That he may do
What these require,
Be, Love, like him
To legend true.

When he to ease
His heart's disease

Must cross in sorrow
Corrosive seas,
As dolphin go;
As cunning fox
Guide through the rocks,
Tell in his ear
The common phrase
Required to please
The guardians there;
And when across
The livid marsh
Big birds pursue,
Again be true,
Between his thighs
As pony rise,
And swift as wind
Bear him away
Till cries and they
Are left behind.

But when at last,
These dangers passed,
His grown desire
Of legend tire,
O then, Love, standing
At legends' ending,
Claim your reward;
Submit your neck
To the ungrateful stroke
Of his reluctant sword,
That, starting back,
His eyes may look
Amazed on you,
Find what he wanted

Is faithful too
But disenchanted,
Your finite love.

The Climbers

Fleeing the short-haired mad executives,
The sad and useless faces round my home,
Upon the mountains of my fear I climb;
Above, the breakneck scorching rock, the caves,
No col, no water; with excuse concocted,
Soon on a lower alp I fall and pant,
Cooling my face there in the faults that flaunt
The life which they have stolen and perfected.

Climbing with you was easy as a vow:
We reached the top not hungry in the least,
But it was eyes we looked at, not the view,
Saw nothing but ourselves, left-handed, lost;
Returned to shore, the rich interior still
Unknown. Love gave the power, but took the will.

Another Time

For us like any other fugitive,
Like the numberless flowers that cannot number
And all the beasts that need not remember,
It is today in which we live.

So many try to say Not Now,
So many have forgotten how
To say I Am, and would be
Lost, if they could, in history.

Bowing, for instance, with such old-world grace
To a proper flag in a proper place,
Muttering like ancients as they stump upstairs
Of Mine and His or Ours and Theirs.

Just as if time were what they used to will
When it was gifted with possession still,
Just as if they were wrong
In no more wishing to belong.

No wonder then so many die of grief,
So many are so lonely as they die;
No one has yet believed or liked a lie,
Another time has other lives to live.

To You Simply *

For what as easy,
For what though small,
For what is well
Because between,
To you simply
From me I mean

Who goes with who
The bedclothes say
As I and you
Go kissed away,
The data given,
The senses even

Fate is not late,
Nor the speech rewritten,
Nor one word forgotten,

Said at the start
About heart,
By heart, for heart.

Missing

From scars where kestrels hover,
The leader looking over
Into the happy valley,
Orchard and curving river,
May turn away to see
The slow fastidious line
That disciplines the fell,
Hear curlew's creaking call
From angles unforseen,
The drumming of a snipe
Surprise where driven sleet
Had scalded to the bone
And streams are acrid yet
To an unaccustomed lip;
The tall unwounded leader
Of doomed companions, all
Whose voices in the rock
Are now perpetual,
Fighters for no one's sake,
Who died beyond the border.

Heroes are buried who
Did not believe in death
And bravery is now
Not in the dying breath
But resisting the temptations
To skyline operations.

Yet glory is not new;
The summer visitors
Still come from far and wide,
Choosing their spots to view
The prize competitors,
Each thinking that he will
Find heroes in the wood,
Far from the capital

Where lights and wine are set
For supper by the lake,
But leaders must migrate:
"Leave for Cape Wrath tonight,"
And the host after waiting
Must quench the lamps and pass
Alive into the house.

The Love Letter

From the very first coming down
Into a new valley with a frown
Because of the sun and a lost way,
You certainly remained: today
I, crouching behind a sheep-pen, heard
Travel across a sudden bird,
Cry out against the storm, and found
The year's arc a completed round
And love's worn circuit re-begun,
Endless with no dissenting turn.
Shall see, shall pass, as we have seen
The swallow on the tile, spring's green
Preliminary shiver, passed
A solitary truck, the last
Of shunting in the Autumn. But now

To interrupt the homely brow,
Thought warmed to evening through and through
Your letter comes, speaking as you,
Speaking of much but not to come.

Nor speech is close nor fingers numb,
If love not seldom has received
An unjust answer, was deceived.
I, decent with the seasons, move
Different or with a different love,
Nor question overmuch the nod,
The stone smile of this country god
That never was more reticent,
Always afraid to say more than it meant.

The Model *

Generally, reading palms or handwriting or faces
  Is a job of translation, since the kind
    Gentleman often is
  A seducer, the frowning schoolgirl may
    Be dying to be asked to stay;
But the body of this old lady exactly indicates her mind;

Rorschach or Binet could not add to what a fool can see
  From the plain fact that she is alive and well;
    For when one is eighty
  Even a teeny-weeny bit of greed
    Makes one very ill indeed,
And a touch of despair is instantaneously fatal:

Whether the town once drank bubbly out of her shoes
      or whether

She was a governess with a good name
    In Church circles, if her
Husband spoiled her or if she lost her son,
    Is by this time all one.
She survived her true condition; she forgave;
    she became.

So the painter may please himself; give her an
    English park,
    Rice-fields in China, or a slum tenement;
    Make the sky light or dark;
Put green plush behind her or a red brick wall.
    She will compose them all,
Centring the eye on their essential human element.

The Cultural Presupposition

Happy the hare at morning, for she cannot read
The Hunter's waking thoughts, lucky the leaf
Unable to predict the fall, lucky indeed
The rampant suffering suffocating jelly
Burgeoning in pools, lapping the grits of the desert,
But what shall man do, who can whistle tunes by heart,
Knows to the bar when death shall cut him short like the cry of
    the shearwater,
What can he do but defend himself from his knowledge?

How comely are his places of refuge and the tabernacles of
    his peace,
The new books upon the morning table, the lawns and the
    afternoon terraces!
Here are the playing-fields where he may forget his ignorance
To operate within a gentleman's agreement: twenty-two sins
    have here a certain licence.

Here are the thickets where accosted lovers combatant
May warm each other with their wicked hands,
Here are the avenues for incantation and workshops for the
    cunning engravers.
The galleries are full of music, the pianist is storming the keys,
    the great cellist is crucified over his instrument,
That none may hear the ejaculations of the sentinels
Nor the sigh of the most numerous and the most poor; the thud
    of their falling bodies
Who with their lives have banished hence the serpent and the
    faceless insect.

Paysage Moralisé

Hearing of harvests rotting in the valleys,
Seeing at end of street the barren mountains,
Round corners coming suddenly on water,
Knowing them shipwrecked who were launched for islands,
We honour founders of these starving cities
Whose honour is the image of our sorrow,

Which cannot see its likeness in their sorrow
That brought them desperate to the brink of valleys;
Dreaming of evening walks through learned cities
They reined their violent horses on the mountains,
Those fields like ships to castaways on islands,
Visions of green to them who craved for water.

They built by rivers and at night the water
Running past windows comforted their sorrow;
Each in his little bed conceived of islands
Where every day was dancing in the valleys
And all the green trees blossomed on the mountains
Where love was innocent, being far from cities.

47

But dawn came back and they were still in cities;
No marvellous creature rose up from the water;
There was still gold and silver in the mountains
But hunger was a more immediate sorrow,
Although to moping villagers in valleys
Some waving pilgrims were describing islands . . .

"The gods," they promised, "visit us from islands,
Are stalking, head-up, lovely, through our cities;
Now is the time to leave your wretched valleys
And sail with them across the lime-green water,
Sitting at their white sides, forget your sorrow,
The shadow cast across your lives by mountains"

So many, doubtful, perished in the mountains,
Climbing up crags to get a view of islands,
So many, fearful, took with them their sorrow
Which stayed them when they reached unhappy cities,
So many, careless, dived and drowned in water,
So many, wretched, would not leave their valleys.

It is our sorrow. Shall it melt? Ah, water
Would gush, flush, green these mountains and
        these valleys,
And we rebuild our cities, not dream of islands.

In Memory of W. B. Yeats
(d. Jan. 1939)

I

He disappeared in the dead of winter:
The brooks were frozen, the airports almost deserted,
And snow disfigured the public statues;

48

The mercury sank in the mouth of the dying day.
O all the instruments agree
The day of his death was a dark cold day.

Far from his illness
The wolves ran on through the evergreen forests,
The peasant river was untempted by the fashionable quays;
By mourning tongues
The death of the poet was kept from his poems.

But for him it was his last afternoon as himself,
An afternoon of nurses and rumours;
The provinces of his body revolted,
The squares of his mind were empty,
Silence invaded the suburbs,
The current of his feeling failed: he became his admirers.

Now he is scattered among a hundred cities
And wholly given over to unfamiliar affections;
To find his happiness in another kind of wood
And be punished under a foreign code of conscience.
The words of a dead man
Are modified in the guts of the living.

But in the importance and noise of tomorrow
When the brokers are roaring like beasts on the floor of
    the Bourse,
And the poor have the sufferings to which they are
    fairly accustomed,
And each in the cell of himself is almost convinced of
    his freedom;
A few thousand will think of this day
As one thinks of a day when one did something slightly unusual.

O all the instruments agree
The day of his death was a dark cold day.

2

You were silly like us: your gift survived it all;
The parish of rich women, physical decay,
Yourself; mad Ireland hurt you into poetry.
Now Ireland has her madness and her weather still,
For poetry makes nothing happen: it survives
In the valley of its saying where executives
Would never want to tamper; it flows south
From ranches of isolation and the busy griefs,
Raw towns that we believe and die in; it survives,
A way of happening, a mouth.

3

Earth, receive an honoured guest;
William Yeats is laid to rest:
Let the Irish vessel lie
Emptied of its poetry.

Time that is intolerant
Of the brave and innocent,
And indifferent in a week
To a beautiful physique,

Worships language and forgives
Everyone by whom it lives;
Pardons cowardice, conceit,
Lays its honours at their feet.

Time that with this strange excuse
Pardoned Kipling and his views,
And will pardon Paul Claudel,
Pardons him for writing well.

In the nightmare of the dark
All the dogs of Europe bark,
And the living nations wait,
Each sequestered in its hate;

Intellectual disgrace
Stares from every human face,
And the seas of pity lie
Locked and frozen in each eye.

Follow, poet, follow right
To the bottom of the night,
With your unconstraining voice
Still persuade us to rejoice;

With the farming of a verse
Make a vineyard of the curse,
Sing of human unsuccess
In a rapture of distress;

In the deserts of the heart
Let the healing fountain start,
In the prison of his days
Teach the free man how to praise.

Hell

Hell is neither here nor there
Hell is not anywhere
Hell is hard to bear.

It is so hard to dream posterity
Or haunt a ruined century
And so much easier to be.

Only the challenge to our will,
Our pride in learning any skill,
Sustains our effort to be ill.

To talk the dictionary through
Without a chance word coming true
Is more than Darwin's apes could do.

Yet pride alone could not insist
Did we not hope, if we persist,
That one day Hell might actually exist.

In time, pretending to be blind
And universally unkind
Might really send us out of our mind.

If we were really wretched and asleep
It would be easy then to weep,
It would be natural to lie,
There'd be no living left to die.

Schoolchildren

Here are all the captivities; the cells are as real:
But these are unlike the prisoners we know
Who are outraged or pining or wittily resigned
            Or just wish all away.

For they dissent so little, so nearly content
With the dumb play of the dog, the licking and rushing;
The bars of love are so strong, their conspiracies
            Weak like the vows of drunkards.

Indeed their strangeness is difficult to watch:
The condemned see only the fallacious angels of a vision;
So little effort lies behind their smiling,
       The beast of vocation is afraid.

But watch them, O, set against our size and timing
The almost neuter, the slightly awkward perfection;
For the sex is there, the broken bootlace is broken,
       The professor's dream is not true.

Yet the tyranny is so easy. The improper word
Scribbled upon the fountain, is that all the rebellion?
The storm of tears shed in the corner, are these
       The seeds of the new life?

To E. M. Forster

Here, though the bombs are real and dangerous,
And Italy and King's are far away,
And we're afraid that you will speak to us,
You promise still the inner life shall pay.

As we run down the slope of Hate with gladness
You trip us up like an unnoticed stone,
And just as we are closeted with Madness
You interrupt us like the telephone.

For we are Lucy, Turton, Philip, we
Wish international evil, are excited
To join the jolly ranks of the benighted

Where Reason is denied and Love ignored:
But, as we swear our lie, Miss Avery
Comes out into the garden with the sword.

True Enough

His aging nature is the same
As when childhood wore his name
In an atmosphere of love
And to itself appeared enough:
Only now when he has come
In walking distance of his tomb,
He at last discovers who
He had always been to whom
He so often was untrue.

Matthew Arnold

His gift knew what he was—a dark disordered city;
Doubt hid it from the father's fond chastising sky;
Where once the mother-farms had glowed protectively,
Stood the haphazard alleys of the neighbour's pity.

—Yet would have gladly lived in him and learned his ways,
And grown observant like a beggar, and become
Familiar with each square and boulevard and slum,
And found in the disorder a whole world to praise.

But all his homeless reverence, revolted, cried:
"I am my father's forum and he shall be heard,
Nothing shall contradict his holy final word,
Nothing." And thrust his gift in prison till it died,

And left him nothing but a jailor's voice and face,
And all rang hollow but the clear denunciation
Of a gregarious optimistic generation
That saw itself already in a father's place.

The Traveller

Holding the distance up before his face
And standing under the peculiar tree,
He seeks the hostile unfamiliar place,
It is the strangeness that he tries to see

Of lands where he will not be asked to stay;
And fights with all his powers to be the same,
The One who loves Another far away,
And has a home, and wears his father's name.

Yet he and his are always the Expected:
The harbours touch him as he leaves the steamer,
The Soft, the Sweet, the Easily-Accepted;

The cities hold his feeling like a fan;
And crowds make room for him without a murmur,
As the earth has patience with the life of man.

The Diaspora

How he survived them they could never understand:
Had they not beggared him themselves to prove
They could not live without their dogmas or their land?

No worlds they drove him from were ever big enough:
How *could* it be the earth the Unconfined
Meant when It bade them set no limits to their love?

And he fulfilled the rôle for which he was designed:
On heat with fear, he drew their terrors to him,
And was a godsend to the lowest of mankind.

Till there was no place left where they could still pursue him
Except that exile which he called his Race.
But, envying him even that, they plunged right through him

Into a land of mirrors without time or space,
And all they had to strike now was the human face.

For the Last Time

In gorgeous robes befitting the occasion
For weeks their spiritual and temporal lordships met
To reconcile eternity with time and set
The earth of marriage on a sure foundation:
The little town was full of spies; corrupt mankind
Chatted or wagered on its expectation.

The doors swung back at last: success had been complete.
The formulae essential to salvation
Were found for ever, and the true relation
Of Agape to Eros finally defined:
The burghers hung out flags in celebration,
The peasants danced and roasted oxen in the street.

As they dispersed, four heralds galloped up with news:

"The tribes are moving on the Western Marches.
Out East a virgin has conceived a son again.
The Southern harbours are infested with the Jews.
The Northern provinces are much deluded
By one who claims there are not seven stars, but ten."

Who wrote upon the council-chamber arches
That sad exasperated cry of tired old men:
—*Postremum Sanctus Spiritus effudit?*

September 1, 1939

I sit in one of the dives
On Fifty-second Street
Uncertain and afraid
As the clever hopes expire
Of a low dishonest decade:
Waves of anger and fear
Circulate over the bright
And darkened lands of the earth,
Obsessing our private lives;
The unmentionable odour of death
Offends the September night.

Accurate scholarship can
Unearth the whole offence
From Luther until now
That has driven a culture mad,
Find what occurred at Linz,
What huge imago made
A psychopathic god:
I and the public know
What all schoolchildren learn,
Those to whom evil is done
Do evil in return.

Exiled Thucydides knew
All that a speech can say
About Democracy,
And what dictators do,
The elderly rubbish they talk
To an apathetic grave;
Analysed all in his book,
The enlightenment driven away,

57

The habit-forming pain,
Mismanagement and grief:
We must suffer them all again.

Into this neutral air
Where blind skyscrapers use
Their full height to proclaim
The strength of Collective Man,
Each language pours its vain
Competitive excuse:
But who can live for long
In an euphoric dream;
Out of the mirror they stare,
Imperialism's face
And the international wrong.

Faces along the bar
Cling to their average day:
The lights must never go out,
The music must always play,
All the conventions conspire
To make this fort assume
The furniture of home;
Lest we should see where we are,
Lost in a haunted wood,
Children afraid of the night
Who have never been happy or good.

The windiest militant trash
Important Persons shout
Is not so crude as our wish:
What mad Nijinsky wrote
About Diaghilev
Is true of the normal heart;
For the error bred in the bone

Of each woman and each man
Craves what it cannot have,
Not universal love
But to be loved alone.

From the conservative dark
Into the ethical life
The dense commuters come,
Repeating their morning vow;
"I *will* be true to the wife,
I'll concentrate more on my work,"
And helpless governors wake
To resume their compulsory game:
Who can release them now,
Who can reach the deaf,
Who can speak for the dumb?

Defenceless under the night
Our world in stupor lies;
Yet, dotted everywhere,
Ironic points of light
Flash out wherever the Just
Exchange their messages:
May I, composed like them
Or Eros and of dust,
Beleaguered by the same
Negation and despair,
Show an affirming flame.

Danse Macabre

It's farewell to the drawing-room's civilised cry,
The professor's sensible whereto and why,
The frock-coated diplomat's social aplomb,
Now matters are settled with gas and with bomb.

The works for two pianos, the brilliant stories
Of reasonable giants and remarkable fairies,
The pictures, the ointments, the frangible wares
And the branches of olive are stored upstairs.

For the Devil has broken parole and arisen,
He has dynamited his way out of prison,
Out of the well where his Papa throws
The rebel angel, the outcast rose.

Like influenza he walks abroad,
He stands by the bridge, he waits by the ford,
As a goose or a gull he flies overhead,
He hides in the cupboard and under the bed.

O were he to triumph, dear heart, you know
To what depths of shame he would drag you low;
He would steal you away from me, yes, my dear,
He would steal you and cut off your beautiful hair.

Millions already have come to their harm,
Succumbing like doves to his adder's charm;
Hundreds of trees in the wood are unsound:
I'm the axe that must cut them down to the ground.

For I, after all, am the Fortunate One,
The Happy-Go-Lucky, the spoilt Third Son;
For me it is written the Devil to chase
And to rid the earth of the human race.

The behaving of man is a world of horror,
A sedentary Sodom and slick Gomorrah;
I must take charge of the liquid fire
And storm the cities of human desire.

The buying and selling, the eating and drinking,
The disloyal machines and irreverent thinking,
The lovely dullards again and again
Inspiring their bitter ambitious men.

I shall come, I shall punish, the Devil be dead,
I shall have caviar thick on my bread,
I shall build myself a cathedral for home
With a vacuum cleaner in every room.

I shall ride the parade in a platinum car,
My features shall shine, my name shall be Star,
Day-long and night-long the bells I shall peal,
And down the long street I shall turn the cartwheel.

So Little John, Long John, Peter and Paul,
And poor little Horace with only one ball,
You shall leave your breakfast, your desk and your play
On a fine summer morning the Devil to slay.

For it's order and trumpet and anger and drum
And power and glory command you to come;
The graves shall fly open and let you all in,
And the earth shall be emptied of mortal sin.

The fishes are silent deep in the sea,
The skies are lit up like a Christmas tree,
The star in the West shoots its warning cry:
"Mankind is alive, but Mankind must die."

So good-bye to the house with its wallpaper red,
Good-bye to the sheets on the warm double bed,
Good-bye to the beautiful birds on the wall,
It's good-bye, dear heart, good-bye to you all.

Hongkong 1938

Its leading characters are wise and witty;
Substantial men of birth and education
With wide experience of administration,
They know the manners of a modern city.

Only the servants enter unexpected;
Their silence has a fresh dramatic use:
Here in the East the bankers have erected
A worthy temple to the Comic Muse.

Ten thousand miles from home and What's-her-name,
The bugle on the Late Victorian hill
Puts out the soldier's light; off-stage, a war

Thuds like the slamming of a distant door:
We cannot postulate a General Will;
For what we are, we have ourselves to blame.

1929

I

It was Easter as I walked in the public gardens
Hearing the frogs exhaling from the pond,
Watching traffic of magnificent cloud
Moving without anxiety on open sky—
Season when lovers and writers find
An altering speech for altering things,
An emphasis on new names, on the arm
A fresh hand with fresh power.
But thinking so I came at once
Where solitary man sat weeping on a bench,

Hanging his head down, with his mouth distorted
Helpless and ugly as an embryo chicken.

So I remember all of those whose death
Is necessary condition of the season's setting forth,
Who sorry in this time look only back
To Christmas intimacy, a winter dialogue
Fading in silence, leaving them in tears.
And recent particulars come to mind;
The death by cancer of a once hated master,
A friend's analysis of his own failure,
Listened to at intervals throughout the winter
At different hours and in different rooms.
But always with success of others for comparison,
The happiness, for instance, of my friend Kurt Groote,
Absence of fear in Gerhart Meyer
From the sea, the truly strong man.

A 'bus ran home then, on the public ground
Lay fallen bicycles like huddled corpses:
No chattering valves of laughter emphasised
Nor the swept gown ends of a gesture stirred
The sessile hush; until a sudden shower
Fell willing into grass and closed the day,
Making choice seem a necessary error.

2

Coming out of me living is always thinking,
Thinking changing and changing living,
Am feeling as it was seeing—
In city leaning on harbour parapet
To watch a colony of duck below
Sit, preen, and doze on buttresses
Or upright paddle on flickering stream,

63

Casually fishing at a passing straw.
Those find sun's luxury enough,
Shadow know not of homesick foreigner
Nor restlessness of intercepted growth.

All this time was anxiety at night,
Shooting and barricade in street.
Walking home late I listened to a friend
Talking excitedly of final war
Of proletariat against police—
That one shot girl of nineteen through the knees
They threw that one down concrete stair—
Till I was angry, said I was pleased.

Time passes in Hessen, in Gutensberg,
With hill-top and evening holds me up,
Tiny observer of enormous world.
Smoke rises from factory in field,
Memory of fire: On all sides heard
Vanishing music of isolated larks:
From village square voices in hymn,
Men's voices, an old use.
And I above standing, saying in thinking:

"Is first baby, warm in mother,
Before born and is still mother,
Time passes and now is other,
Is knowledge in him now of other,
Cries in cold air, himself no friend.
In grown man also, may see in face
In his day-thinking and in his night-thinking
Is wareness and is fear of other,
Alone in flesh, himself no friend."

He says, "We must forgive and forget,"
Forgetting saying but is unforgiving
And unforgiving is in his living;
Body reminds in him to loving,
Reminds but takes no further part,
Perfunctorily affectionate in hired room
But takes no part and is unloving
But loving death. May see in dead,
In face of dead that loving wish,
As one returns from Africa to wife
And his ancestral property in Wales.

Yet sometimes men look and say good
At strict beauty of locomotive,
Completeness of gesture or unclouded eye;
In me so absolute unity of evening
And field and distance was in me for peace,
Was over me in feeling without forgetting
Those ducks' indifference, that friend's hysteria,
Without wishing and with forgiving,
To love my life, not as other,
Not as bird's life, not as child's,
"Cannot," I said, "being no child now nor a bird."

3

Order to stewards and the study of time,
Correct in books, was earlier than this
But joined this by the wires I watched from train,
Slackening of wire and posts' sharp reprimand,
In month of August to a cottage coming.

Being alone, the frightened soul
Returns to this life of sheep and hay
No longer his: he every hour

Moves further from this and must so move,
As child is weaned from his mother and leaves home
But taking the first steps falters, is vexed,
Happy only to find home, a place
Where no tax is levied for being there.

So, insecure, he loves and love
Is insecure, gives less than he expects.
He knows not if it be seed in time to display
Luxuriantly in a wonderful fructification
Or whether it be but a degenerate remnant
Of something immense in the past but now
Surviving only as the infectiousness of disease
Or in the malicious caricature of drunkenness;
Its end glossed over by the careless but known long
To finer perception of the mad and ill.

Moving along the track which is himself,
He loves what he hopes will last, which gone,
Begins the difficult work of mourning,
And as foreign settlers to strange country come,
By mispronunciation of native words
And by intermarriage create a new race
And a new language, so may the soul
Be weaned at last to independent delight.

Startled by the violent laugh of a jay
I went from wood, from crunch underfoot,
Air between stems as under water;
As I shall leave the summer, see autumn come
Focussing stars more sharply in the sky,
See frozen buzzard flipped down the weir
And carried out to sea, leave autumn,
See winter, winter for earth and us,

A forethought of death that we may find ourselves at death
Not helplessly strange to the new conditions.

4

It is time for the destruction of error.
The chairs are being brought in from the garden,
The summer talk stopped on that savage coast
Before the storms, after the guests and birds:
In sanatoriums they laugh less and less,
Less certain of cure; and the loud madman
Sinks now into a more terrible calm.

The falling leaves know it, the children,
At play on the fuming alkali-tip
Or by the flooded football ground, know it—
This is the dragon's day, the devourer's:
Orders are given to the enemy for a time
With underground proliferation of mould,
With constant whisper and the casual question,
To haunt the poisoned in his shunned house,
To destroy the efflorescence of the flesh,
The intricate play of the mind, to enforce
Conformity with the orthodox bone,
With organized fear, the articulated skeleton.

You whom I gladly walk with, touch,
Or wait for as one certain of good,
We know it, we know that love
Needs more than the admiring excitement of union,
More than the abrupt self-confident farewell,
The heel on the finishing blade of grass,
The self-confidence of the falling root,
Needs death, death of the grain, our death,
Death of the old gang; would leave them

67

In sullen valley where is made no friend,
The old gang to be forgotten in the spring,
The hard bitch and the riding-master,
Stiff underground; deep in clear lake
The lolling bridegroom, beautiful, there.

Many Happy Returns *
(For John Rettger)

Johnny, since today is
February the twelfth when
Neighbours and relations
   Think of you and wish,
Though a staunch Aquarian,
Graciously accept the
Verbal celebrations
   Of a doubtful Fish.

Seven years ago you
Warmed your mother's heart by
Making a successful
   Début on our stage;
Naiveté's an act that
You already know you
Cannot get away with
   Even at your age.

So I wish you first a
Sense of theatre; only
Those who love illusion
   And know it will go far:
Otherwise we spend our
Lives in a confusion

Of what we say and do with
   Who we really are.

You will any day now
Have this revelation;
"Why, we're all like people
   Acting in a play."
And will suffer, Johnny,
Man's unique temptation
Precisely at the moment
   You utter this cliché.

Remember if you can then,
Only the All-Father
Can change the cast or give them
   Easier lines to say;
Deliberate interference
With others for their own good
Is not allowed the author
   Of the play within The Play.

Just because our pride's an
Evil there's no end to,
Birthdays and the arts are
   Justified, for when
We consciously pretend to
Own the earth or play at
Being gods, thereby we
   Own that we are men.

As a human creature
You will all too often
Forget your proper station,
   Johnny, like us all;

Therefore let your birthday
Be a wild occasion
Like a Saturnalia
   Or a Servants' Ball.

What else shall I wish you?
Following convention
Shall I wish you Beauty
   Money, Happiness?
Or anything you mention?
No, for I recall an
Ancient proverb;—Nothing
   Fails like a success.

What limping devil sets our
Head and heart at variance,
That each time the Younger
   Generation sails,
The old and weather-beaten
Deny their own experience
And pray the gods to send them
   Calm seas, auspicious gales?

I'm not such an idiot
As to claim the power
To peer into the vistas
   Of your future, still
I'm prepared to guess you
Have not found your life as
Easy as your sister's
   And you never will.

If I'm right about this,
May you in your troubles,

Neither (like so many
　　In the U. S. A.)
Be ashamed of any
Suffering as vulgar,
Nor bear them like a hero
　　In the biggest way.

All the possibilities
It had to reject are
What give life and warmth to
　　An actual character;
The roots of wit and charm tap
Secret springs of sorrow,
Every brilliant doctor
　　Hides a murderer.

Then, since all self-knowledge
Tempts man into envy,
May you, by acquiring
　　Proficiency in what
Whitehead calls the art of
Negative Prehension,
Love without desiring
　　All that you are not.

Tao is a tightrope,
So to keep your balance,
May you always, Johnny,
　　Manage to combine
Intellectual talents
With a sensual gusto,
The Socratic Doubt with
　　The Socratic Sign.

That is all that I can
Think of at this moment
And it's time I brought these
    Verses to a close:
Happy Birthday, Johnny,
Live beyond your income,
Travel for enjoyment,
    Follow your own nose.

Nobody Understands Me

Just as his dream foretold, he met them all:
The smiling grimy boy at the garage
Ran out before he blew his horn; the tall
Professor in the mountains with his large
Tweed pockets full of plants addressed him hours
Before he would have dared; the deaf girl too
Seemed to expect him at the green chateau;
The meal was laid, the guest room full of flowers.

More, the talk always took the wished-for turn,
Dwelt on the need for stroking and advice;
Yet, at each meeting, he was forced to learn,
The same misunderstanding would arise.
Which was in need of help? Were they or he
The physician, bridegroom, and incendiary?

Mundus et Infans *
(For Arthur and Angelyn Stevens)

Kicking his mother until she let go of his soul
Has given him a healthy appetite: clearly, her rôle
    In the New Order must be
To supply and deliver his raw materials free;
    Should there be any shortage,

72

She will be held responsible; she also promises
To show him all such attentions as befit his age.
    Having dictated peace,

With one fist clenched behind his head, heel drawn up to thigh,
The cocky little ogre dozes off, ready,
    Though, to take on the rest
Of the world at the drop of a hat or the mildest
    Nudge of the impossible,
Resolved, cost what it may, to seize supreme power and
Sworn to resist tyranny to the death with all
    Forces at his command.

A pantheist not a solipsist, he co-operates
With a universe of large and noisy feeling-states
    Without troubling to place
Them anywhere special, for, to his eyes, Funnyface
    Or Elephant as yet
Mean nothing. His distinction between Me and Us
Is a matter of taste; his seasons are Dry and Wet;
    He thinks as his mouth does.

Still his loud iniquity is still what only the
Greatest of saints become—someone who does not lie:
    He because he cannot
Stop the vivid present to think, they by having got
    Past reflection into
A passionate obedience in time. We have our Boy-
Meets-Girl era of mirrors and muddle to work through,
    Without rest, without joy.

Therefore we love him because his judgments are so
Frankly subjective that his abuse carries no
    Personal sting. We should

Never dare offer our helplessness as a good
    Bargain; without at least
Promising to overcome a misfortune we blame
History or Banks or the Weather for: but this beast
    Dares to exist without shame.

Let him praise our Creator with the top of his voice,
Then, and the motions of his bowels; let us rejoice
    That he lets us hope, for
He may never become a fashionable or
    Important personage:
However bad he may be, he has not yet gone mad;
Whoever we are now, we were no worse at his age;
    So of course we ought to be glad

When he bawls the house down. Has he not a perfect right
To remind us at every moment how we quite
    Rightly expect each other
To go upstairs or for a walk if we must cry over
    Spilt milk, such as our wish
That, since, apparently, we shall never be above
Either or both, we had never learned to distinguish
    Between hunger and love?

Law Like Love

    Law, say the gardeners, is the sun,
    Law is the one
    All gardeners obey
    Tomorrow, yesterday, today.

    Law is the wisdom of the old
    The impotent grandfathers shrilly scold;

74

The grandchildren put out a treble tongue,
Law is the senses of the young.

Law, says the priest with a priestly look,
Expounding to an unpriestly people,
Law is the words in my priestly book,
Law is my pulpit and my steeple.

Law, says the judge as he looks down his nose,
Speaking clearly and most severely,
Law is as I've told you before,
Law is as you know I suppose,
Law is but let me explain it once more,
Law is The Law.

Yet law-abiding scholars write;
Law is neither wrong nor right,
Law is only crimes
Punished by places and by times,
Law is the clothes men wear
Anytime, anywhere,
Law is Good-morning and Good-night.

Others say, Law is our Fate;
Others say, Law is our State;
Others say, others say
Law is no more
Law has gone away.

And always the loud angry crowd
Very angry and very loud
Law is We,
And always the soft idiot softly Me.

If we, dear, know we know no more
Than they about the law,
If I no more than you
Know what we should and should not do
Except that all agree
Gladly or miserably
That the law is
And that all know this,
If therefore thinking it absurd
To identify Law with some other word,
Unlike so many men
I cannot say Law is again,
No more than they can we suppress
The universal wish to guess
Or slip out of our own position
Into an unconcerned condition.
Although I can at least confine
Your vanity and mine
To stating timidly
A timid similarity,
We shall boast anyway:
Like love I say.

Like love we don't know where or why
Like love we can't compel or fly
Like love we often weep
Like love we seldom keep.

Edward Lear

Left by his friend to breakfast alone on the white
Italian shore, his Terrible Demon arose
Over his shoulder; he wept to himself in the night,
A dirty landscape-painter who hated his nose.

76

The legions of cruel inquisitive They
Were so many and big like dogs: he was upset
By Germans and boats; affection was miles away:
But guided by tears he successfully reached his Regret.

How prodigious the welcome was. Flowers took his hat
And bore him off to introduce him to the tongs;
The demon's false nose made the table laugh; a cat
Soon had him waltzing madly, let him squeeze her hand;
Words pushed him to the piano to sing comic songs;

And children swarmed to him like settlers. He became a land.

The Bonfires

Look there! The sunk road winding
To the fortified farm.
Listen! The cock's alarm
In the strange valley.

Are we the stubborn athletes;
Are we then to begin
The run between the gin
And bloody falcon?

The horns of the dark squadron
Converging to attack;
The sound behind our back
Of glaciers calving.

In legend all were simple,
And held the straitened spot;
But we in legend not,
Are not simple.

In weakness how much further;
Along what crooked route
By hedgehog's gradual foot,
Or fish's fathom.

Bitter the blue smoke rises
From garden bonfires lit,
To where we burning sit:
Good, if it's thorough,

Leaving no double traitor
In days of luck and heat,
To time the double beat,
At last together.

Too Dear, Too Vague

Love by ambition
Of definition
Suffers partition
And cannot go
From yes to no
For no is not love; no is no
The shutting of a door
The tightening jaw
A conscious sorrow;
And saying yes
Turns love into success,
Views from the rail
Of land and happiness,
Assured of all
The sofas creak
And were this all, love were

But cheek to cheek
And dear to dear.

Voices explain
Love's pleasure and love's pain,
Still tap the knee
And cannot disagree,
Hushed for aggression
Of full confession,
Likeness to likeness
Of each old weakness;
Love is not there
Love has moved to another chair.
Aware already
Of who stands next
And is not vexed
And is not giddy,
Leaves the North in place
With a good grace
And would not gather
Another to another,
Designs his own unhappiness
Foretells his own death and is faithless.

Meiosis

Love had him fast but though he fought for breath
He struggled only to possess Another,
The snare forgotten in the little death,
Till you, the seed to which he was a mother,
That never heard of love, through love was free,
While he within his arms a world was holding,
To take the all-night journey under sea,
Work west and northward, set up building.

Cities and years constricted to your scope,
All sorrow simplified though almost all
Shall be as subtle when you are as tall:
Yet clearly in that "almost" all his hope
That hopeful falsehood cannot stem with love
The flood on which all move and wish to move.

Oxford

Nature is so near: the rooks in the college garden
Like agile babies still speak the language of feeling;
By the tower the river still runs to the sea and will run,
   And the stones in that tower are utterly
   Satisfied still with their weight.

And the minerals and creatures, so deeply in love with
    their lives
Their sin of accidie excludes all others,
Challenge the nervous students with a careless beauty,
   Setting a single error
   Against their countless faults.

O in these quadrangles where Wisdom honours herself
Does the original stone merely echo that praise
Shallowly, or utter a bland hymn of comfort,
   The founder's equivocal blessing
   On all who worship Success?

Promising to the sharp sword all the glittering prizes,
The cars, the hotels, the service, the boisterous bed,
Then power to silence outrage with a testament,
   The widow's tears forgotten,
   The fatherless unheard.

Whispering to chauffeurs and little girls, to tourists
     and dons,
That Knowledge is conceived in the hot womb of Violence
Who in a late hour of apprehension and exhaustion
     Strains to her weeping breast
     That blue-eyed darling head.

And is that child happy with his box of lucky books
And all the jokes of learning? Birds cannot grieve:
Wisdom is a beautiful bird; but to the wise
     Often, often is it denied
     To be beautiful or good.

Without are the shops, the works, the whole green county
Where a cigarette comforts the guilty and a kiss the weak;
There thousands fidget and poke and spend their money:
     Eros Paidagogos
     Weeps on his virginal bed.

Ah, if that thoughtless almost natural world
Would snatch his sorrow to her loving sensual heart!
But he is Eros and must hate what most he loves;
     And she is of Nature; Nature
     Can only love herself.

And over the talkative city like any other
Weep the non-attached angels. Here too the knowledge
     of death
Is a consuming love: And the natural heart refuses
     The low unflattering voice
     That rests not till it find a hearing.

Please Make Yourself at Home

Not as that dream Napoleon, rumour's dread and centre,
Before whose riding all the crowds divide,
Who dedicates a column and withdraws,
Not as that general favourite and breezy visitor
To whom the weather and the ruins mean so much,
Nor as any of those who always will be welcome,
As luck or history or fun,
Do not enter like that: all these depart.

Claim, certainly, the stranger's right to pleasure:
Ambassadors will surely entertain you
With knowledge of operas and men,
Bankers will ask for your opinion
And the heiress' cheek lean ever so slightly towards you,
The mountains and the shopkeepers accept you
And all your walks be free.

But politeness and freedom are never enough,
Not for a life. They lead
Up to a bed that only looks like marriage;
Even the disciplined and distant admiration
For thousands who obviously want nothing
Becomes just a dowdy illness. These have their moderate success;
They exist in the vanishing hour.

But somewhere always, nowhere particularly unusual,
Almost anywhere in the landscape of water and houses,
His crying competing unsuccessfully with the cry
Of the traffic or the birds, is always standing
The one who needs you, that terrified
Imaginative child who only knows you
As what the uncles call a lie,

But knows he has to be the future and that only
The meek inherit the earth, and is neither
Charming, successful, nor a crowd;
Alone among the noise and policies of summer
His weeping climbs towards your life like a vocation.

All Over Again

Not from this life, not from this life is any
To keep; sleep, day and play would not help there
Dangerous to new ghost; new ghost learns from many
Learns from old timers what death is, where.

Who's jealous of his latest company
From one day to the next final to us,
A changed one, would use sorrow to deny
Sorrow, to replace death? Sorrow is sleeping thus.

Unforgetting is not today's forgetting
For yesterday, not bedrid scorning,
But a new begetting
An unforgiving morning.

Not All the Candidates Pass

Now from my window-sill I watch the night,
The church clock's yellow face, the green pier light
Burn for a new imprudent year;
The silence buzzes in my ear;
The jets in both the dormitories are out.

Under the darkness nothing seems to stir;
The lilac bush like a conspirator
Shams dead upon the lawn, and there

Above the flagstaff the Great Bear
Hangs as a portent over Helensburgh.

But deaf to prophecy or China's drum
The blood moves strangely in its moving home,
Diverges, loops, to travel further
Than the long still shadow of the father,
Though to the valley of regret it come.

Now in this season when the ice is loosened,
In scrubbed laboratories research is hastened
And cameras at the growing wood
Are pointed; for the long-lost good
Desire like a police-dog is unfastened.

O Lords of Limit, training dark and light
And setting a tabu 'twixt left and right,
The influential quiet twins
From whom all property begins,
Look leniently upon us all tonight.

Oldest of masters whom the schoolboy fears,
Failing to find his pen or keep back tears,
Collecting stamps or butterflies,
Hoping in some way to appease
The malice of the erratic examiners,

No one has seen you: none can say;—"Of late—
Here. You can see the marks—They lay in wait."
But in my thoughts tonight you seem
Forms which I saw once in a dream,
The stocky keepers of a wild estate.

With guns beneath your arms, in sun and wet,
At doorways posted or on ridges set,

By copse or bridge we know you there
Whose sleepless presences endear
Our peace to us with a perpetual threat.

We know you moody, silent, sensitive,
Quick to be offended, slow to forgive,
But to your discipline the heart
Submits when we have fallen apart
Into the isolated dishonest life.

Look not too closely, be not over-quick;
We have no invitation, but we are sick,
Using the mole's device, the carriage
Of peacock or rat's desperate courage,
And we shall only pass you by a trick.

At the end of my corridor are boys who dream
Of a new bicycle or winning team;
On their behalf guard all the more
This late-maturing Northern shore,
Who to their serious season must shortly come.

Deeper towards the summer the year moves on.
What if the starving visionary have seen
The carnival within our gates,
Your bodies kicked about the streets,
We need your power still: use it, that none,

O, from their tables break uncontrollably away,
Lunging, insensible to injury,
Dangerous in the room, or out wildly
Spinning like a top in the field,
Mopping and mowing through the sleepless day.

Pascal

O had his mother, near her time, been praying
Up to her crucifix and prayed too long?
Until exhausted she grew stiff like wood;
The future of herself hung dangerous and heavy
From her uprightness like a malefactor,
And in a trance she re-negotiated
The martyrdom that even in Auvergne
Would be demanded as the price for life

Knowledge was lifted up on Love but faced
Away from her towards the lives in refuge,
Directed always to the moon-struck jeering neighbours
Who'd grown aware of being watched and come
Uneasily, against their native judgment,
And still were coming up the local paths
From every gate of the protective town
And every crevice of the noon-hot landscape.

None who conceivably could hate him were excluded;
His back was turned on no one but herself
Who had to go on holding him and bear
The terror in their faces as they screamed "Be Angry,"
The stolid munching of their puzzled animals
Who'd raised their heads from grazing; even ploughs
They'd left behind to see him hurt were noticed;
Nothing in France was disregarded but her worship.

Did then the patient tugging of his will
Not to turn round for comfort shake her faith,
O when she saw the magistrate-in-charge,
The husband who had given him to her look up
Into that fascinating sorrow, and was certain

86

That even *he* forgot her, did she then deny
The only bond they shared, the right to suffer,
And join the others in a wish to murder?

Whatever happened, he was born deserted
And lonelier than any adult: they at least
Had dwelt in childhoods once where dogs were hopeful
And chairs could fly and doors remove a tyrant;
Even the ablest could recall a day
Of diagnosis when the first stab of his talent
Ran through the beardless boy and spoilt the sadness
Of the closed life the stupid never leave.

However primitive, all others had their ferry
Over the dreadful water to those woods from which,
Irrelevant like flies that win a coward's battle,
The flutes and laughter of the happily diverted
Broke in effectively across his will
To build a life upon original disorder:
How could he doubt the evidence he had
Of Paris and the earth? His misery was real.

All dreams led back into the nightmare garden
Where the great families who should have loved him slept
Loving each other, not a single rose
Dared leave its self-regard, and he alone was kneeling,
Submitting to a night that promised nothing,
Not even punishment, but let him pray;
Prayer bled to death in its abyssal spaces,
Mocked by the silence of their unbelief.

Yet like a lucky orphan he had been discovered
And instantly adopted by a Gift;
And she became the sensible protector
Who found a passage through the caves of accusation,

And even in the canyon of distress was able
To use the echo of his weakness as a proof
That joy was probable and took the place
Of the poor lust and hunger he had never known.

And never told him he was different from the others,
Too weak to face their innocently brutal questions,
Assured him he was stronger than Descartes,
And let him think it was his own finesse
That promised him a miracle, and doubt by doubt
Restored the ruined chateau of his faith;
Until at last, one Autumn, all was ready:
And in the night the Unexpected came.

The empty was transformed into possession,
The cold burst into flames; creation was on fire
And his weak moment blazing like a bush,
A symptom of the order and the praise;
And he had place like Abraham and Jacob,
And was incapable of evil like a star,
For isolation had been utterly consumed,
And everything that could exist was holy.

All that was really willed would be accomplished:
The crooked custom take its final turning
Into the truth it always meant to reach;
The barrack's filthy oath could not arrest
Its move towards the just, nor flesh annihilate
The love that somewhere every day persuades it,
Brought to a sensual incandescence in the dark,
To do the deed that has made all the saints.

Then it was over. By the morning he was cool,
His faculties for sin restored completely,
And eight years to himself. But round his neck

Now hung a louder cry than the familiar tune
Libido Excellendi whistled as he wrote
The lucid and unfair. And still it rings
Wherever there are children doubt and deserts,
Or cities that exist for mercy and for judgment.

Perhaps

O Love, the interest itself in thoughtless Heaven,
Make simpler daily the beating of man's heart; within,
There in the ring where name and image meet,

Inspire them with such a longing as will make his thought
Alive like patterns a murmuration of starlings,
Rising in joy over wolds, unwittingly weave.

Here too on our little reef display your power,
This fortress perched on the edge of the Atlantic scarp,
The mote between all Europe and the exile-crowded sea;

And make us as *Newton* was who, in his garden watching
The apple falling towards *England,* became aware
Between himself and her of an eternal tie.

For now that dream which so long had contented our will,
I mean, of uniting the dead into a splendid empire,
Under whose fertilising flood the *Lancashire* moss

Sprouted up chimneys, and *Glamorgan* hid a life
Grim as a tidal rock-pool's in its glove-shaped valleys,
Is already retreating into her maternal shadow;

Leaving the furnaces gasping in the impossible air,
That flotsam at which *Dumbarton* gapes and hungers;
While upon wind-loved *Rowley* no hammer shakes

The cluster of mounds like a midget golf-course, graves
Of some who created these intelligible dangerous marvels,
Affectionate people, but crude their sense of glory.

Far-sighted as falcons, they looked down another future;
For the seed in their loins were hostile though afraid of
        their pride,
And, tall with a shadow now, inertly wait.

In bar, in netted chicken-farm, in lighthouse,
Standing on these impoverished constricted acres,
The ladies and gentlemen apart, too much alone,

Consider the years of the measured world begun,
The barren virtuous marriage of stone and water.
Yet, O, at this very moment of a hopeless sigh,

When, inland, they are thinking their thoughts but
        watching these islands
As children in *Chester* look to *Moel Fammau* to decide
On picnics by the clearness or withdrawal of her
        treeless crown.

Some possible dream, long coiled in the ammonite's slumber
Is uncurling, prepared to lay on our talk and reflection
Its military silence, its surgeon's idea of pain;

And out of the future into actual history,
As when *Merlin*, tamer of horses, and his lords to whom
Stonehenge was still a thought, the *Pillars* passed

And into the undared ocean swung north their prow,
Drives through the night and star-concealing dawn
For the virgin roadsteads of our hearts an unwavering keel.

Casino

Only the hands are living; to the wheel attracted,
Are moved as deer trek desperately towards a creek
   Through the dust and scrub of the desert, or gently
   As sunflowers turn to the light.

And, as the night takes up the cries of feverish children,
The cravings of lions in dens, the loves of dons,
   Gathers them all and remains the night, the
   Great room is full of their prayers

To the last feast of isolation self-invited
They flock, and in the rite of disbelief are joined;
   From numbers all their stars are recreated,
   The enchanted, the world, the sad.

Without, the rivers flow among the wholly living,
Quite near their trysts; and the mountains part them; and
    the bird
   Deep in the greens and moistures of summer
   Sings towards their work.

But here no nymph comes naked to the youngest shepherd;
The fountain is deserted; the laurel will not grow;
   The labyrinth is safe but endless, and broken
   Is Ariadne's thread.

As deeper in these hands is grooved their fortune: "Lucky
Were few, and it is possible that none was loved;
   And what was godlike in this generation
   Was never to be born."

Such Nice People

On Sunday walks
Past the shut gates of works
The conquerors come
And are handsome.

Sitting all day
By the open window
Say what they say
Know what to know
Who brought and taught
Unusual images
And new tunes to old cottages,
With so much done
Without a thought
Of the anonymous lampoon
The cellar counterplot,
Though in the night
Pursued by eaters
They clutch at gaiters
That straddle and deny
Escape that way,
Though in the night
Is waking fright.

Father by son
Lives on and on
Though over date
And motto on the gate
The lichen grows
From year to year,
Still here and there
That Roman nose

Is noticed in the villages
And father's son
Knows what they said
And what they did.

Not meaning to deceive,
Wish to give suck
Enforces make-believe
And what was fear
Of fever and bad-luck
Is now a scare
At certain names
A need for charms
For certain words
At certain fords,
And what was livelihood
Is tallness, strongness,
Words and longness,
All glory and all story,
Solemn and not so good.

Spring 1940

O season of repetition and return,
Of light, and the primitive visions of light
    Opened in little ponds disturbing
    The blind water that conducts excitement,

How lucid the image in your shining well
Of a limpid day, how eloquent your streams
    Of lives without language, the cell ma-
    -noeuvres and the molecular bustle.

O hour of images when we sniff the herb
Of childhood and forget who we are and dream
    Like whistling boys of the vast spaces
    Of the Inconsistent racing towards us

With all its appealing private detail. But
Our ways are revealing; crossing the legs
    Or resting the cheek in the hand, we
    Hide the mouths through which the Disregarded

Will always enter. For we know we're not boys
And never will be: part of us all hates life,
    And some are completely against it.
    Spring leads the truculent sailors into

The park, and the plump little girls, but none
Are determined like the tiny brains who found
    The great communities of summer:
    Only on battlefields, where the dying

With low voices and not very much to say
Repair the antique silence the insects broke
    In an architectural passion,
    Can night return to our cooling fibres.

O not even war can frighten us enough,
That last attempt to eliminate the Strange
    By uniting us all in a terror
    Of something known, even that's a failure

Which cannot stop us taking our walks alone,
Scared by the unknown unconditional dark,
    Down the avenues of our longing:
    For however they dream they are scattered,

Our bones cannot help reassembling themselves
Into the philosophic city where dwells
    The knowledge they cannot get out of;
    And neither a Spring nor a war can ever

So condition his ears as to keep the song
That is not a sorrow from the Double Man.
    O what weeps is the love that hears, an
    Accident occurring in his substance.

In Father's Footsteps

Our hunting fathers told the story
    Of the sadness of the creatures,
Pitied the limits and the lack
    Set in their finished features;
Saw in the lion's intolerant look,
Behind the quarry's dying glare,
Love raging for the personal glory
    That reason's gift would add,
The liberal appetite and power,
    The rightness of a god.

Who, nurtured in that fine tradition,
    Predicted the result,
Guessed Love by nature suited to
    The intricate ways of guilt,
That human ligaments could so
His southern gestures modify
And make it his mature ambition
    To think no thought but ours,
To hunger, work illegally,
    And be anonymous?

A Summer Night 1933

(*To Geoffrey Hoyland*)

Out on the lawn I lie in bed,
Vega conspicuous overhead
   In the windless nights of June,
As congregated leaves complete
Their day's activity; my feet
   Point to the rising moon.

Lucky, this point in time and space
Is chosen as my working-place,
   Where the sexy airs of summer,
The bathing hours and the bare arms,
The leisured drives through a land of farms
   Are good to the newcomer.

Equal with colleagues in a ring
I sit on each calm evening
   Enchanted as the flowers
The opening light draws out of hiding
With all its gradual dove-like pleading,
   Its logic and its powers

That later we, though parted then,
May still recall these evenings when
   Fear gave his watch no look;
The lion griefs loped from the shade
And on our knees their muzzles laid,
   And Death put down his book

Now north and south and east and west
Those I love lie down to rest;
   The moon looks on them all,

The healers and the brilliant talkers
The eccentrics and the silent walkers,
   The dumpy and the tall.

She climbs the European sky,
Churches and power-station lie
   Alike among earth's fixtures:
Into the galleries she peers
And blankly as a butcher stares
   Upon the marvellous pictures

To gravity attentive, she
Can notice nothing here, though we
   Whom hunger does not move,
From gardens where we feel secure
Look up and with a sigh endure
   The tyrannies of love:

And, gentle, do not care to know,
Where Poland draws her eastern bow,
   What violence is done,
Nor ask what doubtful act allows
Our freedom in this English house,
   Our picnics in the sun.

Soon, soon, through dykes of our content
The crumpling flood will force a rent
   And, taller than a tree,
Hold sudden death before our eyes
Whose river dreams long hid the size
   And vigours of the sea.

But when the waters make retreat
And through the black mud first the wheat

In shy green stalks appears,
When stranded monsters gasping lie,
And sounds of riveting terrify
　　Their whorled unsubtle ears,

May these delights we dread to lose,
This privacy, need no excuse
　　But to that strength belong,
As through a child's rash happy cries
The drowned parental voices rise
　　In unlamenting song.

After discharges of alarm
All unpredicted let them calm
　　The pulse of nervous nations,
Forgive the murderer in his glass,
Tough in their patience to surpass
　　The tigress her swift motions.

Montaigne

Outside his library window he could see
A gentle landscape terrified of grammar,
Cities where lisping was compulsory
And provinces where it was death to stammer.

The hefty lay exhausted. O it took
This donnish undersexed conservative
To start a revolution, and to give
The Flesh its weapons to defeat the Book.

When devils drive the reasonable wild,
They strip their adult century so bare,
Love must be regrown from the sensual child:

To doubt becomes a way of definition,
Even belles lettres legitimate as prayer,
And laziness an act of pure contrition.

Epitaph on a Tyrant

Perfection, of a kind, was what he was after,
And the poetry he invented was easy to understand;
He knew human folly like the back of his hand,
And was greatly interested in armies and fleets;
When he laughed, respectable senators burst with laughter,
And when he cried the little children died in the streets.

The Prophets

Perhaps I always knew what they were saying:
Even the early messengers who walked
Into my life from books where they were staying,
Those beautiful machines that never talked
But let the small boy worship them and learn
All their long names whose hardness made him proud;
Love was the word they never said aloud
As something that a picture can't return.

And later when I hunted the Good Place,
Abandoned lead-mines let themselves be caught;
There was no pity in the adit's face,
The rusty winding-engine never taught
One obviously too apt, to say Too Late:
Their lack of shyness was a way of praising
Just what I didn't know, why I was gazing,
While all their lack of answer whispered "Wait,"
And taught me gradually without coercion,

And all the landscape round them pointed to
The calm with which they took complete desertion
As proof that you existed.

                    It was true.
For now I have the answer from the face
That never will go back into a book
But asks for all my life, and is the Place
Where all I touch is moved to an embrace,
And there is no such thing as a vain look.

The Capital

Quarter of pleasures where the rich are always waiting,
Waiting expensively for miracles to happen,
O little restaurant where the lovers eat each other,
Café where exiles have established a malicious village;

You with your charm and your apparatus have abolished
The strictness of winter and the spring's compulsion;
Far from your lights the outraged punitive father,
The dullness of mere obedience here is apparent.

Yet with orchestras and glances, O, you betray us
To belief in our infinite powers; and the innocent
Unobservant offender falls in a moment
Victim to the heart's invisible furies.

In unlighted streets you hide away the appalling;
Factories where lives are made for a temporary use
Like collars or chairs, rooms where the lonely are battered
Slowly like pebbles into fortuitous shapes.

But the sky you illumine, your glow is visible far
Into the dark countryside, the enormous, the frozen,

Where, hinting at the forbidden like a wicked uncle,
Night after night to the farmer's children you beckon.

Autumn 1940

Returning each morning from a timeless world,
The senses open upon a world of time;
    After so many years the light is
    Novel still and immensely ambitious.

But, translated from her own informal world,
The ego is bewildered and does not want
    A shining novelty this morning,
    And does not like the noise or the people.

For behind the doors of this ambitious day
Stand shadows with enormous grudges, outside
    Its chartered ocean of perception
    Misshapen coastguards drunk with foreboding;

And whispering websters stealing through this world
Discredit so much literature and praise:
    Summer was worse than we expected,
    And now cold autumn comes on the water.

The lesser lives retire on their savings, their
Small deposits of starches and nuts, and soon
    Will be asleep or travelling or
    Dead; but this year the towns of our childhood

Are changing complexion along with the woods,
And many who have shared our conduct will add
    Their pinches of detritus to the
    Nutritive chain of determined being,

And even the uneliminated decline
To a vita minima, huddling for warmth
    The hard- and the soft-mouthed together
    In a coma of waiting, just breathing

In a darkness of tribulation and death,
While blizzards havoc the gardens, and the old
    Folly becomes unsafe, the mill-wheels
    Rust and the weirs fall slowly to pieces.

Will the inflamed ego attempt as before
To migrate again to her family place,
    To the hanging gardens of Eros
    And the moons of his magical summer?

But the local train does not run any more,
The heretical roses have lost their scent,
    And her Cornish Hollow of tryst is
    Swarming now with discourteous villains

Whom father's battered hat cannot wish away,
And the fancy-governed sequence leads us all
    Back to that labyrinth where either
    We are found or lose ourselves for ever.

Oh what sign can we make to be found? How can
We will the knowledge that we must know to will?
    The waste is a suburb of prophets,
    But few have seen Jesus and so many

Judas the Abyss. The rocks are big and bad,
And death so substantial in the thinning air;
    Learning screams in the narrow gate where
    Events are traded with time, but who can

Tell what logic must and must not leave to fate,
Or what laws we are permitted to obey?
    There are no birds; the predatory
    Glaciers glitter in the chilly evening;

And death is probable. Nevertheless,
Whatever the situation and the blame,
    Let the lips do formal contrition
    For whatever is going to happen;

Time remembered bear witness to time required,
The positive and negative ways through time
    Embrace and encourage each other
    In a brief moment of intersection;

That the orgulous spirit may while it can
Conform to its temporal focus with praise,
    Acknowledging the attributes of
    One immortal one infinite Substance,

And the shabby structure of indolent flesh
Give a resonant echo to the Word which was
    From the beginning, and the shining
    Light be comprehended by the darkness.

Blessed Event

Round the three actors in any Blessed Event
Is always standing an invisible audience of four;
The double twins, the fallen natures of Man.

On the Left they remember difficult childhoods,
On the Right they have forgotten why they were so happy,
Above sit the Best Decisive People,
Below they must kneel all day, so as not to be governed.

Four voices just audible in the hush of any Christmas,
Expressing their kinds of hopeful attention:
—"Accept my friendship or die"—
—"I shall keep order and not very much will happen"—
—"Bring me luck and of course I'll support you"—
—"I smell blood and an era of prominent madmen."

But the Three hear nothing, and are blind to even the landscape
With its rivers and towns and pretty pieces of nonsense:
For He, all father, repenting their animal nights,
Cries—"Why did she have to be tortured? It was all my fault";
Once more a virgin, she whispers—"The future shall
    never suffer";
And the New Life awkwardly touches its home, beginning
    to fumble
About in the Truth for the straight successful Way
That must always appear to end in some dreadful defeat.

Shut Your Eyes and Open Your Mouth

Sentries against inner and outer,
At stated interval is feature;
And how shall enemy on these
Make sudden raid or lasting peace?
For bribery were vain to try
Against the incorruptible eye
Too amply paid with tears, the chin
Has hairs to hide its weakness in,
And proud bridge and indignant nostril
Nothing to do but to look noble.
But in between these lies the mouth;
Watch that, that you may parley with:
There strategy comes easiest,

Though it seem stern, was seen compressed
Over a lathe, refusing answer,
It will release the ill-fed prisoner
It will do murder or betray
For either party equally,
Yielding at last to a close kiss
It will admit tongue's soft advance,
So longed for, given in abandon,
Given long since, had it but known.

Heavy Date

Sharp and silent in the
Clear October lighting
Of a Sunday morning
    The great city lies;
And I at a window
Looking over water
At the world of Business
    With a lover's eyes.

All mankind, I fancy,
When anticipating
Anything exciting
    Like a rendezvous,
Occupy the time in
Purely random thinking,
For when love is waiting
    Logic will not do.

Much as he would like to
Concentrate completely
On the precious Object,
    Love has not the power:

Goethe put it neatly;
No one cares to watch the
Loveliest sunset after
    Quarter of an hour.

Malinowski, Rivers,
Benedict and others
Show how common culture
    Shapes the separate lives:
Matrilineal races
Kill their mothers' brothers
In their dreams and turn their
    Sisters into wives.

Who when looking over
Faces in the subway,
Each with its uniqueness,
    Would not, did he dare,
Ask what forms exactly
Suited to their weakness
Love and desperation
    Take to govern there.

Would not like to know what
Influence occupation
Has on human vision
    Of the human fate:
Do all clerks for instance
Pigeon-hole creation,
Brokers see the Ding-an-
    -sich as Real Estate?

When a politician
Dreams about his sweetheart,

Does he multiply her
　　Face into a crowd,
Are her fond responses
All-or-none reactions,
Does he try to buy her,
　　Is the kissing loud?

Strange are love's mutations:
Thus, the early poem
Of the flesh sub rosa
　　Has been known to grow
Now and then into the
Amor intellectu-
-alis of Spinoza;
　　How we do not know.

Slowly we are learning,
We at least know this much,
That we have to unlearn
　　Much that we were taught,
And are growing chary
Of emphatic dogmas;
Love like Matter is much
　　Odder than we thought.

Love requires an Object,
But this varies so much,
Almost, I imagine,
　　Anything will do:
When I was a child, I
Loved a pumping-engine,
Thought it every bit as
　　Beautiful as you.

Love has no position,
Love's a way of living,
One kind of relation
    Possible between
Any things or persons
Given one condition,
The one sine qua non
    Being mutual need.

Through it we discover
An essential secret
Called by some Salvation
    And by some Success;
Crying for the moon is
Naughtiness and envy,
We can only love what-
    -ever we possess.

I believed for years that
Love was the conjunction
Of two oppositions;
    That was all untrue;
Every young man fears that
He is not worth loving:
Bless you, darling, I have
    Found myself in you.

When two lovers meet, then
There's an end of writing
Thought and Analytics:
    Lovers, like the dead,
In their loves are equal;
Sophomores and peasants,
Poets and their critics
    Are the same in bed.

Venus Will Now Say a Few Words

Since you are going to begin today
Let us consider what it is you do.
You are the one whose part it is to lean,
For whom it is not good to be alone.
Laugh warmly turning shyly in the hall
Or climb with bare knees the volcanic hill,
Acquire that flick of wrist and after strain
Relax in your darling's arms like a stone
Remembering everything you can confess,
Making the most of firelight, of hours of fuss;
But joy is mine not yours—to have come so far,
Whose cleverest invention was lately fur;
Lizards my best once who took years to breed,
Could not control the temperature of blood.
To reach that shape for your face to assume,
Pleasure to many and despair to some,
I shifted ranges, lived epochs handicapped
By climate, wars, or what the young men kept,
Modified theories on the types of dross,
Altered desire and history of dress.

You in the town now call the exile fool
That writes home once a year as last leaves fall,
Think—Romans had a language in their day
And ordered roads with it, but it had to die:
Your culture can but leave—forgot as sure
As place-name origins in favourite shire—
Jottings for stories, some often-mentioned Jack,
And references in letters to a private joke,
Equipment rusting in unweeded lanes,
Virtues still advertised on local lines;

And your conviction shall help none to fly,
Cause rather a perversion on next floor.

Nor even is despair your own, when swiftly
Comes general assault on your ideas of safety:
That sense of famine, central anguish felt
For goodness wasted at peripheral fault,
Your shutting up the house and taking prow
To go into the wilderness to pray,
Means that I wish to leave and to pass on,
Select another form, perhaps your son;
Though he reject you, join opposing team
Be late or early at another time,
My treatment will not differ—he will be tipped,
Found weeping, signed for, made to answer, topped.
Do not imagine you can abdicate;
Before you reach the frontier you are caught;
Others have tried it and will try again
To finish that which they did not begin:
Their fate must always be the same as yours,
To suffer the loss they were afraid of, yes,
Holders of one position, wrong for years.

Petition

Sir, no man's enemy, forgiving all
But will its negative inversion, be prodigal:
Send to us power and light, a sovereign touch
Curing the intolerable neural itch,
The exhaustion of weaning, the liar's quinsy,
And the distortions of ingrown virginity.
Prohibit sharply the rehearsed response
And gradually correct the coward's stance;
Cover in time with beams those in retreat

That, spotted, they turn though the reverse were great;
Publish each healer that in city lives
Or country houses at the end of drives;
Harrow the house of the dead; look shining at
New styles of architecture, a change of heart.

Dover 1937

Steep roads, a tunnel through the downs are the approaches;
A ruined pharos overlooks a constructed bay;
The sea-front is almost elegant; all this show
Has, somewhere inland, a vague and dirty root:
            Nothing is made in this town.

But the dominant Norman castle floodlit at night
And the trains that fume in the station built on the sea
Testify to the interests of its regular life:
Here live the experts on what the soldiers want
            And who the travellers are,

Whom the ships carry in and out between the lighthouses
That guard for ever the made privacy of this bay
Like twin stone dogs opposed on a gentleman's gate:
Within these breakwaters English is spoken; without
            Is the immense improbable atlas.

The eyes of the departing migrants are fixed on the sea,
To conjure their special fates from the impersonal water:
"I see an important decision made on a lake,
An illness, a beard, Arabia found in a bed,
            Nanny defeated, Money."

And filled with the tears of the beaten or calm with fame,
The eyes of the returning thank the historical cliffs:

III

"The heart has at last ceased to lie, and the clock to accuse;
In the shadow under the yew, at the children's party
                    Everything will be explained."

And the old town with its keep and its Georgian houses
Has built its routine upon these unusual moments;
The vows, the tears, the slight emotional signals
Are here eternal and unremarkable gestures
                    Like ploughing or soldiers' songs:

Soldiers who swarm in the pubs in their pretty clothes,
As fresh and silly as girls from a high-class academy:
The Lion, the Rose or the Crown will not ask them to die,
Not here, not now. All they are killing is time,
                    Their pauper civilian future.

Above them, expensive and lovely as a rich child's toy,
The aeroplanes fly in the new European air,
On the edge of that air that makes England of
        minor importance;
And the tides warn bronzing bathers of a cooling star,
                    With half its history done.

High over France the full moon, cold and exciting
Like one of those dangerous flatterers one meets and loves
When one is very unhappy, returns the human stare:
The night has many recruits; for thousands of pilgrims
                    The Mecca is coldness of heart.

And the cry of the gulls at dawn is sad like work:
The soldier guards the traveller who pays for the soldier;
Each one prays in the dusk for himself and neither
Controls the years. Some are temporary heroes:
                    Some of these people are happy.

As Well as Can Be Expected

Taller today, we remember similar evenings,
Walking together in the windless orchard
Where the brook runs over the gravel, far from the glacier.

Again in the room with the sofa hiding the grate,
Look down to the river when the rain is over,
See him turn to the window, hearing our last
Of Captain Ferguson.

It is seen how excellent hands have turned to commonness.
One staring too long, went blind in a tower,
One sold all his manors to fight, broke through, and faltered.

Nights come bringing the snow, and the dead howl
Under the headlands in their windy dwelling
Because the Adversary put too easy questions
On lonely roads.

But happy now, though no nearer each other,
We see the farms lighted all along the valley;
Down at the mill-shed the hammering stops
And men go home.

Noises at dawn will bring
Freedom for some, but not this peace
No bird can contradict: passing, but is sufficient now
For something fulfilled this hour, loved or endured.

Through the Looking-Glass

The earth turns over; our side feels the cold;
And life sinks choking in the wells of trees:
The ticking heart comes to a standstill, killed;

The icing on the pond waits for the boys.
Among the holly and the gifts I move,
The carols on the piano, the glowing hearth,
All on traditional sympathy with birth,
Put by your challenge to the shifts of Love.

Your portrait hangs before me on the wall,
And there what view I wish for I shall find,
The wooded or the stony, though not all
The painter's gifts can make its flatness round;
Though each blue iris see the heaven of failures,
That mirror world where Logic is reversed,
Where age becomes the handsome child at last,
The glass sea parted for the country sailors

There move the enormous comics, drawn from life—
My father as an Airedale and a gardener,
My mother chasing letters with a knife.
You are not present as a character;
(Only the family have speaking parts).
You are a valley or a river-bend,
The one an aunt refers to as a friend,
The tree from which the weasel racing starts.

Behind me roars the other world it matches,
Love's daytime kingdom which I say you rule,
His total state where all must wear your badges
Keep order perfect as a naval school.
Noble emotions, organized and massed,
Line the straight flood-lit tracks of memory
To cheer your image as it flashes by,
All lust at once informed on and suppressed.

Yours is the only name expressive there,
And family affection speaks in cypher.

Lay-out of hospital and street and square
That comfort to its homesick children offer,
As I, their author, stand between these dreams,
Unable to choose either for a home,
Your would-be lover who has never come
In the great bed at midnight to your arms

Such dreams are amorous; they are indeed:
But no one but myself is loved in these,
While time flies on above the dreamer's head,
Flies on, flies on, and with your beauty flies,
And pride succeeds to each succeeding state,
Still able to buy up the life within,
License no liberty except his own,
Order the fireworks after the defeat.

Language of moderation cannot hide: —
My sea is empty and its waves are rough;
Gone from the map the shore where childhood played,
Tight-fisted as a peasant, eating love;
Lost in my wake the archipelago,
Islands of self through which I sailed all day
Planting a pirate's flag, a generous boy;
And lost the way to action and to you.

Lost if I steer. Tempest and tide may blow
Sailor and ship past the illusive reef,
And I yet land to celebrate with you
The birth of natural order and true love:
With you enjoy the untransfigured scene,
My father down the garden in his gaiters,
My mother at her bureau writing letters,
Free to our favours, all our titles gone.

115

The Lesson *

The first time that I dreamed, we were in flight,
And fagged with running; there was civil war,
A valley full of thieves and wounded bears.

Farms blazed behind us; turning to the right,
We came at once to a tall house, its door
Wide open, waiting for its long-lost heirs.

An elderly clerk sat on the bedroom stairs
Writing; but we had tiptoed past him when
He raised his head and stuttered—"Go away."
We wept and begged to stay:
He wiped his pince-nez, hesitated, then
Said no, he had no power to give us leave;
Our lives were not in order; we must leave.

* * *

The second dream began in a May wood;
We had been laughing; your blue eyes were kind,
Your excellent nakedness without disdain.

Our lips met, wishing universal good;
But on their impact sudden flame and wind
Fetched you away and turned me loose again

To make a focus for a wide wild plain,
Dead level and dead silent and bone dry,
Where nothing could have suffered, sinned, or grown.
On a high chair alone
I sat, my little master, asking why
The cold and solid object in my hands
Should be a human hand, one of your hands.

* * *

And the last dream was this: we were to go
To a great banquet and a Victory Ball
After some tournament or dangerous test.

Only our seats had velvet cushions, so
We must have won; though there were crowns for all,
Ours were of gold, of paper all the rest.

O fair or funny was each famous guest.
Love smiled at Courage over priceless glass,
And rockets died in hundreds to express
Our learned carelessness.
A band struck up; all over the green grass
A sea of paper crowns rose up to dance:
Ours were too heavy; we did not dance.

        *   *   *

I woke. You were not there. But as I dressed
Anxiety turned to shame, feeling all three
Intended one rebuke. For had not each
In its own way tried to teach
My will to love you that it cannot be,
As I think, of such consequence to want
What anyone is given, if they want?

Aera sub Lege

The Hidden Law does not deny
Our laws of probability,
But takes the atom and the star
And human beings as they are,
And answers nothing when we lie.

It is the only reason why
No government can codify,

And verbal definitions mar
              The Hidden Law.

Its utter patience will not try
To stop us if we want to die;
When we escape It in a car,
When we forget It in a bar,
These are the ways we're punished by
              The Hidden Law.

Our Bias

The hour-glass whispers to the lion's paw,
The clock-towers tell the gardens day and night,
How many errors Time has patience for,
How wrong they are in being always right.

Yet Time, however loud its chimes or deep,
However fast its falling torrent flows,
Has never put the lion off his leap
Nor shaken the assurance of the rose.

For they, it seems, care only for success:
While we choose words according to their sound
And judge a problem by its awkwardness;

And Time with us was always popular.
When have we not preferred some going round
To going straight to where we are?

Christmas 1940 *

The journals give the quantities of wrong,
Where the impatient massacre took place,

118

How many and what sort it caused to die,
But, O, what finite integers express
The realm of malice where these facts belong?
How can the mind make sense, bombarded by
A stream of incompatible mishaps,
The bloom and buzz of a confessed collapse?

What properties define our person since
This massive vagueness moved in on our lives,
What laws require our substance to exist?
Our strands of private order are dissolved
And lost our routes to self-inheritance,
Position and Relation are dismissed,
An epoch's Providence is quite worn out,
The lion of Nothing chases us about.

"Beware! Beware! The Great Boyg has you down,"
Some deeper instinct in revulsion cries,
"The Void desires to have you for its creature,
A doll through whom It may ventriloquise
Its vast resentment as your very own,
Because Negation has nor form nor feature,
And all Its lust to power is impotent
Unless the actual It hates consent.

The universe of pure extension where
Nothing except the universe was lonely,
For Promise was occluded in its womb
Where the immortal families had only
To fall to pieces and accept repair,
Their nursery, their commonplace, their tomb,
All acts accessory to their position,
Died when the first plant made its apparition.

Through a long adolescence, then, the One
Slept in the sadness of its disconnected
Aggressive creatures—as a latent wish
The local genius of the rose protected,
Or an unconscious irony within
The independent structure of the fish;
But Flesh grew weaker, stronger grew the Word,
Until on earth the Great Exchange occurred.

Now to maturity must crawl that child
In whom the old equations are reversed
For that is cause which was effect before,
Now he must learn for what he has been nursed
That through his self-annulment the real world
Of self-enduring instants may endure
Its final metamorphosis and pass
Into invisibility at last."

The sacred auras fade from well and wood,
The great geometries enclose our lives
In fields of normal enmity no more,
The definitions and the narratives
Are insufficient for our solitude,
Venus cannot predict our passion, nor
The Dioscuri plant their olive trees
To guide us through the ambiguities.

And winds of terror force us to confess
The settled world of past events has not
A faiblesse any longer for the dull
To swim in like an aqueous habitat;
We are reduced to our true nakedness:
Either we serve the Unconditional,
Or some Hitlerian monster will supply
An iron convention to do evil by.

O beggar, bigwig, mugwump, none but have
Some vision of that holy centre where
All time's occasions are refreshed; the lost
Are met by all the other places there,
The rival errors recognise their love,
Fall weeping on each other's neck at last;
The rich need not confound the Persons, nor
The Substance be divided by the poor.

It is the vision that objectifies:
Only its Roman rigour can bestow
On earth and sea "la douceur angevine,"
Only its prayer can make the children grow,
Only its trembling can externalise
The bland Horatian life of friends and wine;
It is the tension of its inner dread
That moulds the beautiful patrician head.

Our way remains, our world, our day, our sin;
We may, as always, by our own consent
Be cast away: but neither depth nor height
Nor any other creature can prevent
Our reasonable and lively motions in
This modern void where only Love has weight,
And Fate by Faith is freely understood,
And he who works shall find our Fatherhood.

Rimbaud

The nights, the railway-arches, the bad sky,
His horrible companions did not know it;
But in that child the rhetorician's lie
Burst like a pipe: the cold had made a poet.

Drinks bought him by his weak and lyric friend
His senses systematically deranged,
To all accustomed nonsense put an end;
Till he from lyre and weakness was estranged.

Verse was a special illness of the ear;
Integrity was not enough; that seemed
The hell of childhood: he must try again.

Now, galloping through Africa, he dreamed
Of a new self, the son, the engineer,
His truth acceptable to lying men.

The Decoys

There are some birds in these valleys
Who flutter round the careless
With intimate appeal,
By seeming kindness trained to snaring,
They feel no falseness.

Under the spell completely
They circle can serenely,
And in the tricky light
The masked hill has a purer greenness.
Their flight looks fleeter.

But fowlers, O, like foxes,
Lie ambushed in the rushes.
Along the harmless tracks
The madman keeper crawls through brushwood,
Axe under oxter.

Alas, the signal given,
Fingers on trigger tighten.

The real unlucky dove
Must smarting fall away from brightness
Its love from living.

Like Us

These had stopped seeking
But went on speaking,
Have not contributed,
But have diluted.

These ordered light
But had no right,
And handed on
War and a son

Wishing no harm.
But to be warm
These went to sleep
On the burning heap.

Leap Before You Look *

The sense of danger must not disappear:
The way is certainly both short and steep,
However gradual it looks from here;
Look if you like, but you will have to leap.

Tough-minded men get mushy in their sleep
And break the by-laws any fool can keep;
It is not the convention but the fear
That has a tendency to disappear.

The worried efforts of the busy heap,
The dirt, the imprecision, and the beer
Produce a few smart wisecracks every year;
Laugh if you can, but you will have to leap.

The clothes that are considered right to wear
Will not be either sensible or cheap,
So long as we consent to live like sheep
And never mention those who disappear.

Much can be said for social savoir-faire,
But to rejoice when no one else is there
Is even harder than it is to weep;
No one is watching, but you have to leap.

A solitude ten thousand fathoms deep
Sustains the bed on which we lie, my dear:
Although I love you, you will have to leap;
Our dream of safety has to disappear.

In Memory of Ernst Toller

(d. May 1939)

The shining neutral summer has no voice
To judge America, or ask how a man dies;
And the friends who are sad and the enemies who rejoice

Are chased by their shadows lightly away from the grave
Of one who was egotistical and brave,
Lest they should learn without suffering how to forgive.

What was it, Ernst, that your shadow unwittingly said?
O did the child see something horrid in the woodshed
Long ago? Or had the Europe which took refuge in your head

Already been too injured to get well?
O for how long, like the swallows in that other cell,
Had the bright little longings been flying in to tell

About the big and friendly death outside,
Where people do not occupy or hide;
No towns like Munich; no need to write?

Dear Ernst, lie shadowless at last among
The other war-horses who existed till they'd done
Something that was an example to the young.

We are lived by powers we pretend to understand:
They arrange our loves; it is they who direct at the end
The enemy bullet, the sickness, or even our hand.

It is their tomorrow hangs over the earth of the living
And all that we wish for our friends: but existence is believing
We know for whom we mourn and who is grieving.

Happy Ending

The silly fool, the silly fool
Was sillier in school
But beat the bully as a rule.

The youngest son, the youngest son
Was certainly no wise one
Yet could surprise one.

Or rather, or rather
To be posh, we gather,
One should have no father.

Simple to prove
That deeds indeed
In life succeed
But love in love
And tales in tales
Where no one fails.

At the Grave of Henry James *

The snow, less intransigeant than their marble,
Has left the defence of whiteness to these tombs;
   For all the pools at my feet
Accommodate blue now, and echo such clouds as occur
To the sky, and whatever bird or mourner the passing
   Moment remarks they repeat

While the rocks, named after singular spaces
Within which images wandered once that caused
   All to tremble and offend,
Stand here in an innocent stillness, each marking the spot
Where one more series of errors lost its uniqueness
   And novelty came to an end.

To whose real advantage were such transactions
When words of reflection were exchanged for trees?
   What living occasion can
Be just to the absent? O noon but reflects on itself,
And the small taciturn stone that is the only witness
   To a great and talkative man

Has no more judgment than my ignorant shadow
Of odious comparisons or distant clocks
   Which challenge and interfere
With the heart's instantaneous reading of time, time that is

A warm enigma no longer in you for whom I
    Surrender my private cheer

Startling the awkward footsteps of my apprehension,
The flushed assault of your recognition is
    The *donnée* of this doubtful hour:
O stern proconsul of intractable provinces,
O poet of the difficult, dear addicted artist,
    Assent to my soil and flower.

As I stand awake on our solar fabric,
That primary machine, the earth, which gendarmes, banks,
    And aspirin pre-suppose.
On which the clumsy and sad may all sit down, and any
        who will
Say their a-ha to the beautiful, the common locus
    Of the master and the rose.

Our theatre, scaffold, and erotic city
Where all the infirm species are partners in the act
    Of encroachment bodies crave,
Though solitude in death is *de rigueur* for their flesh
And the self-denying hermit flies as it approaches
    Like the carnivore to a cave.

That its plural numbers may unite in meaning,
Its vulgar tongues unravel the knotted mass
    Of the improperly conjunct,
Open my eyes now to all its hinted significant forms,
Sharpen my ears to detect amid its brilliant uproar
    The low thud of the defunct.

O dwell, ironic at my living centre,
Half ancestor, half child; because the actual self
    Round whom time revolves so fast

Is so afraid of what its motions might possibly do
That the actor is never there when his really important
    Acts happen. Only the past

Is present, no one about but the dead as,
Equipped with a few inherited odds and ends,
    One after another we are
Fired into life to seek that unseen target where all
Our equivocal judgments are judged and resolved in
    One whole Alas or Hurrah.

And only the unborn remark the disaster
When, though it makes no difference to the pretty airs
    The bird of Appetite sings,
And Amour Propre is his usual amusing self,
Out from the jungle of an undistinguished moment
    The flexible shadow springs.

Now more than ever, when torches and snare-drum
Excite the squat women of the saurian brain
    Till a milling mob of fears
Breaks in insultingly on anywhere, when in our dreams
Pigs play on the organs and the blue sky runs shrieking
    As the Crack of Doom appears,

Are the good ghosts needed with the white magic
Of their subtle loves. War has no ambiguities
    Like a marriage; the result
Required of its *affaire fatale* is simple and sad,
The physical removal of all human objects
    That conceal the Difficult.

Then remember me that I may remember
The test we have to learn to shudder for is not
    An historical event,

That neither the low democracy of a nightmare nor
An army's primitive tidiness may deceive me
   About our predicament.

That catastrophic situation which neither
Victory nor defeat can annul; to be
   Deaf yet determined to sing,
To be lame and blind yet burning for the Great Good Place,
To be radically corrupt yet mournfully attracted
   By the Real Distinguished Thing.

And shall I not specially bless you as, vexed with
My little inferior questions, today I stand
   Beside the bed where you rest
Who opened such passionate arms to your *Bon* when It ran
Towards you with its overwhelming reasons pleading
   All beautifully in Its breast?

O with what innocence your hand submitted
To these formal rules that help a child to play,
   While your heart, fastidious as
A delicate nun, remained true to the rare noblesse
Of your lucid gift and, for its own sake, ignored the
   Resentful muttering Mass.

Whose ruminant hatred of all which cannot
Be simplified or stolen is still at large;
   No death can assuage its lust
To vilify the landscape of Distinction and see
The heart of the Personal brought to a systolic standstill,
   The Tall to diminished dust.

Preserve me, Master, from its vague incitement;
Yours be the disciplinary image that holds
   Me back from agreeable wrong

And the clutch of eddying muddle, lest Proportion shed
The alpine chill of her shrugging editorial shoulder
    On my loose impromptu song.

Suggest; so may I segregate my disorder
Into districts of prospective value: approve;
    Lightly, lightly, then, may I dance
Over the frontier of the obvious and fumble no more
In the old limp pocket of the minor exhibition,
    Nor riot with irrelevance.

And no longer shoe geese or water stakes, but
Bolt in my day my grain of truth to the barn
    Where tribulations may leap
With their long-lost brothers at last in the festival
Of which not one had a dissenting image, and the
    Flushed immediacy sleep.

Into this city from the shining lowlands
Blows a wind that whispers of uncovered skulls
    And fresh ruins under the moon,
Of hopes that will not survive the *secousse* of this spring
Of blood and flames, of the terror that walks by night and
    The sickness that strikes at noon.

All will be judged. Master of nuance and scruple,
Pray for me and for all writers living or dead;
    Because there are many whose works
Are in better taste than their lives; because there is no end
To the vanity of our calling: make intercession
    For the treason of all clerks.

Because the darkness is never so distant,
And there is never much time for the arrogant
    Spirit to flutter its wings,

Or the broken bone to rejoice, or the cruel to cry
For Him whose property is always to have mercy, the author
  And giver of all good things.

It's Too Much

The Spring unsettles sleeping partnerships,
Foundries improve their casting process, shops
Open a further wing on credit till
The winter. In summer boys grow tall
With running races on the froth-wet sand,
War is declared there, here a treaty signed;
Here a scrum breaks up like a bomb, there troops
Deploy like birds. But proudest into traps
Have fallen. These gears which ran in oil for week
By week, needing no look, now will not work;
Those manors mortgaged twice to pay for love
Go to another.

                O how shall man live
Whose thought is born, child of one farcical night,
To find him old? The body warm but not
By choice, he dreams of folk in dancing bunches,
Of tart wine spilt on home-made benches,
Where learns, one drawn apart, a secret will
Restore the dead; but comes thence to a wall.
Outside on frozen soil lie armies killed
Who seem familiar but they are cold.
Now the most solid wish he tries to keep
His hands show through; he never will look up,
Say "I am good." On him misfortune falls
More than enough. Better where no one feels,
The out-of-sight, buried too deep for shafts.

The Ship

The streets are brightly lit; our city is kept clean:
The third class have the greasiest cards, the first play high;
The beggars sleeping in the bows have never seen
What can be done in staterooms; no one asks why.

Lovers are writing letters, sportsmen playing ball;
One doubts the honour, one the beauty, of his wife;
A boy's ambitious; perhaps the captain hates us all;
Someone perhaps is leading the civilized life.

It is our culture that with such calm progresses
Over the barren plains of a sea; somewhere ahead
The septic East, a war, new flowers and new dresses.

Somewhere a strange and shrewd Tomorrow goes to bed
Planning the test for men from Europe; no one guesses
Who will be most ashamed, who richer, and who dead.

Family Ghosts

The strings' excitement, the applauding drum
Are but the initiating ceremony
That out of cloud the ancestral face may come.

And never hear their subaltern mockery,
Graphiti-writers, moss-grown with whimsies,
Loquacious when the watercourse is dry.

It is your face I see, and morning's praise
Of you is ghost's approval of the choice,
Filtered through roots of the effacing grass.

Fear, taking me aside, would give advice
"To conquer her, the visible enemy,
It is enough to turn away the eyes."

Yet there's no peace in this assaulted city
But speeches at the corners, hope for news,
Outside the watchfires of a stronger army.

And all emotions to expression came,
Recovering the archaic imagery:
This longing for assurance takes the form

Of a hawk's vertical stooping from the sky;
These tears, salt for a disobedient dream,
The lunatic agitation of the sea;

While this despair with hardened eyeballs cries
"A Golden Age, a Silver . . . rather this,
Massive and taciturn years, the Age of Ice."

The Creatures

They are our past and our future: the poles between which our
desire unceasingly is discharged.

A desire in which love and hatred so perfectly oppose themselves
that we cannot voluntarily move; but await the extraordinary
compulsion of the deluge and the earthquake.

Their affections and indifferences have been a guide to all
reformers and tyrants.

Their appearances amid our dreams of machinery have brought
a vision of nude and fabulous epochs.

O Pride so hostile to our Charity.

But what their pride has retained, we may by charity more
generously recover.

A Healthy Spot *

They're nice—one would never dream of going over
Any contract of theirs with a magnifying
Glass, or of locking up one's letters—also
Kind and efficient—one gets what one asks for.
Just what is wrong, then, that, living among them,
One is constantly struck by the number of
Happy marriages and unhappy people?
They attend all the lectures on Post-War Problems,
For they do mind, they honestly want to help; yet,
As they notice the earth in their morning papers,
What sense do they make of its folly and horror
Who have never, one is convinced, felt a sudden
Desire to torture the cat or do a strip-tease
In a public place? Have they ever, one wonders,
Wanted so much to see a unicorn, even
A dead one? Probably. But they won't say so,
Ignoring by tacit consent our hunger
For eternal life, that caged rebuked question
Occasionally let out at clambakes or
College reunions, and which the smoke-room story
Alone, ironically enough, stands up for.

Pur

This lunar beauty
Has no history,
Is complete and early;

134

If beauty later
Bear any feature,
It had a lover
And is another.

This like a dream
Keeps other time,
And daytime is
The loss of this;
For time is inches
And the heart's changes,
Where ghost has haunted,
Lost and wanted.

But this was never
A ghost's endeavour
Nor, finished this,
Was ghost at ease;
And till it pass
Love shall not near
The sweetness here,
Nor sorrow take
His endless look.

But I Can't *

Time will say nothing but I told you so,
Time only knows the price we have to pay;
If I could tell you I would let you know.

If we should weep when clowns put on their show,
If we should stumble when musicians play,
Time will say nothing but I told you so.

There are no fortunes to be told, although,
Because I love you more than I can say,
If I could tell you I would let you know.

The winds must come from somewhere when they blow,
There must be reasons why the leaves decay;
Time will say nothing but I told you so.

Perhaps the roses really want to grow,
The vision seriously intends to stay;
If I could tell you I would let you know.

Suppose the lions all get up and go,
And all the brooks and soldiers run away;
Will Time say nothing but I told you so?
If I could tell you I would let you know.

Which Side Am I Supposed to Be On?

Though aware of our rank and alert to obey orders,
Watching with binoculars the movement of the grass for
    an ambush,
The pistol cocked, the code-word committed to memory;
              The youngest drummer
Knows all the peace-time stories like the oldest soldier,
              Though frontier-conscious.

About the tall white gods who landed from their open boat,
Skilled in the working of copper, appointing our feast-days,
Before the islands were submerged, when the weather was calm,
              The maned lion common,
An open wishing-well in every garden;
              When love came easy.

136

Perfectly certain, all of us, but not from the records,
Not from the unshaven agent who returned to the camp;
The pillar dug from the desert recorded only
                    The sack of a city,
The agent clutching his side collapsed at our feet,
                    "Sorry! They got me!"

Yes, they were living here once but do not now,
Yes, they are living still but do not here;
Lying awake after Lights Out a recruit may speak up:
                    "Who told you all this?"
The tent-talk pauses a little till a veteran answers
                    "Go to sleep, Sonny!"

Turning over he closes his eyes, and then in a moment
Sees the sun at midnight bright over cornfield and pasture,
Our hope. . . . Someone jostles him, fumbling for boots,
                    Time to change guard:
Boy, the quarrel was before your time, the aggressor
                    No one you know.

Your childish moments of awareness were all of our world,
At five you sprang, already a tiger in the garden,
At night your mother taught you to pray for our Daddy
                    Far away fighting,
One morning you fell off a horse and your brother mocked you:
                    "Just like a girl!"

You've got their names to live up to and questions won't help,
You've a very full programme, first aid, gunnery, tactics,
The technique to master of raids and hand-to-hand fighting;
                    Are you in training?
Are you taking care of yourself? are you sure of passing
                    The endurance test?

137

Now we're due to parade on the square in front of the Cathedral,
When the bishop has blessed us, to file in after the choirboys,
To stand with the wine-dark conquerors in the roped-off pews,
            Shout ourselves hoarse:
"They ran like hares; we have broken them up like firewood;
            They fought against God."

While in a great rift in the limestone miles away
At the same hour they gather, tethering their horses beside them;
A scarecrow prophet from a boulder foresees our judgment,
            Their oppressors howling;
And the bitter psalm is caught by the gale from the rocks:
            "How long shall they flourish?"

What have we all been doing to have made from Fear
That laconic war-bitten captain addressing them now?
"Heart and head shall be keener, mood the more
            As our might lessens":
To have caused their shout "We will fight till we lie down beside
            The Lord we have loved."

There's Wrath who has learnt every trick of guerrilla warfare,
The shamming dead, the night-raid, the feinted retreat;
Envy their brilliant pamphleteer, to lying
            As husband true,
Expert impersonator and linguist, proud of his power
            To hoodwink sentries.

Gluttony living alone, austerer than us,
Big simple Greed, Acedia famed with them all
For her stamina, keeping the outposts, and somewhere Lust
            With his sapper's skill,
Muttering to his fuses in a tunnel "Could I meet here with Love,
            I would hug her to death."

138

There are faces there for which for a very long time
We've been on the look-out, though often at home we imagined,
Catching sight of a back or hearing a voice through a doorway.
            We had found them at last;
Put our arms round their necks and looked in their eyes
        and discovered
                We were unlucky.

And some of them, surely, we seem to have seen before:
Why, that girl who rode off on her bicycle one fine
        summer evening
And never returned, she's there; and the banker we'd noticed
                Worried for weeks;
Till he failed to arrive one morning and his room was empty,
                Gone with a suitcase.

They speak of things done on the frontier we were never told,
The hidden path to their squat Pictish tower
They will never reveal though kept without sleep, for their
        code is
                "Death to the squealer":
They are brave, yes, though our newspapers mention
        their bravery
                In inverted commas.

But careful; back to our lines; it is unsafe there,
Passports are issued no longer; that area is closed;
There's no fire in the waiting-room now at the climbers' Junction,
                And all this year
Work has been stopped on the power-house; the wind
        whistles under
                The half-built culverts.

Do you think that because you have heard that on Christmas Eve
In a quiet sector they walked about on the skyline,

Exchanged cigarettes, both learning the words for "I love you"
            In either language:
You can stroll across for a smoke and a chat any evening?
            Try it and see.

That rifle-sight you're designing; is it ready yet?
You're holding us up; the office is getting impatient;
The square munition works out on the old allotments
            Needs stricter watching;
If you see any loiterers there you may shoot without warning,
            We must stop that leakage.

All leave is cancelled tonight; we must say good-bye.
We entrain at once for the North; we shall see in the morning
The headlands we're doomed to attack; snow down to
      the tide-line:
            Though the bunting signals
"Indoors before it's too late; cut peat for your fires,"
            We shall lie out there.

Year After Year

      Though he believe it, no man is strong.
      He thinks to be called the fortunate,
      To bring home a wife, to live long.

      But he is defeated; let the son
      Sell the farm lest the mountain fall;
      His mother and her mother won.

      His fields are used up where the moles visit,
      The contours worn flat; if there show
      Passage for water he will miss it:

140

Give up his breath, his woman, his team;
No life to touch, though later there be
Big fruit, eagles above the stream.

What Do You Think?

To ask the hard question is simple;
Asking at meeting
With the simple glance of acquaintance
To what these go
And how these do:
To ask the hard question is simple,
The simple act of the confused will.
But the answer

Is hard and hard to remember:
On steps or on shore
The ears listening
To words at meeting,
The eyes looking
At the hands helping,
Are never sure
Of what they learn
From how these things are done.
And forgetting to listen or see
Makes forgetting easy;
Only remembering the method of remembering,
Remembering only in another way,
Only the strangely exciting lie,
Afraid
To remember what the fish ignored,
How the bird escaped, or if the sheep obeyed.

Till, losing memory,
Bird, fish, and sheep are ghostly,
And ghosts must do again
What gives them pain.
Cowardice cries
For windy skies,
Coldness for water,
Obedience for a master.

Shall memory restore
The steps and the shore,
The face and the meeting place;
Shall the bird live,
Shall the fish dive,
And sheep obey
In a sheep's way;
Can love remember
The question and the answer,
For love recover
What has been dark and rich and warm all over?

The Unknown Citizen

(To JS/o7/M/378
This Marble Monument
Is Erected by the State)

He was found by the Bureau of Statistics to be
One against whom there was no official complaint,
And all the reports on his conduct agree
That, in the modern sense of an old-fashioned word, he
    was a saint,
For in everything he did he served the Greater Community.
Except for the War till the day he retired
He worked in a factory and never got fired,

But satisfied his employers, Fudge Motors Inc.
Yet he wasn't a scab or odd in his views,
For his Union reports that he paid his dues,
(Our report on his Union shows it was sound)
And our Social Psychology workers found
That he was popular with his mates and liked a drink.
The Press are convinced that he bought a paper every day
And that his reactions to advertisements were normal in
      every way.
Policies taken out in his name prove that he was fully insured,
And his Health-card shows he was once in hospital but left
      it cured.
Both Producers Research and High-Grade Living declare
He was fully sensible to the advantages of the Instalment Plan
And had everything necessary to the Modern Man,
A phonograph, a radio, a car and a frigidaire.
Our researchers into Public Opinion are content
That he held the proper opinions for the time of year;
When there was peace, he was for peace; when there was war,
      he went.
He was married and added five children to the population,
Which our Eugenist says was the right number for a parent of
      his generation,
And our teachers report that he never interfered with
      their education.
Was he free? Was he happy? The question is absurd:
Had anything been wrong, we should certainly have heard.

What's the Matter?

To lie flat on the back with the knees flexed
And sunshine on the soft receptive belly,
Or face down, the insolent spine relaxed,
No more compelled to cower or to bully,

Is good; and good to see them passing by
Below on the white side-walk in the heat,
The dog, the lady with parcels, and the boy:
There is the casual life outside the heart.

Yes, we are out of sight and earshot here.
Are you aware what weapon you are loading,
To what this teasing talk is quietly leading?
Our pulses count but do not judge the hour.
Who are you with from whom you turn away,
At whom you dare not look? Do you know why?

Remember

Tonight the many come to mind
Sent forward in the thaw with anxious marrow;
For such might now return with a bleak face,
An image, pause half-lighted in the door,
A greater but not fortunate in all,
Come home deprived of an astonishing end—
Morgan's who took a clean death in the north
Shouting against the wind, or Cousin Dodd's,
Passed out in her chair, the snow falling—
The too-loved clays, born over by diverse drifts,
Fallen upon the far side of all enjoyment,
Unable to move closer, shall not speak
Out of that grave, stern to no capital fault;
Enough to have lightly touched the unworthy thing.

It's So Dull Here

To settle in this village of the heart,
My darling, can you bear it? True, the Hall
With its yews and famous dovecote is still there

Just as in childhood, but the grand old couple
Who loved us all so equally are dead,
And now it is a licensed house for tourists,
None too particular: one of the new
Trunk roads passes the very door already,
And the thin cafés spring up overnight.
The sham ornamentation, the strident swimming pool,
The identical and townee smartness,
Will you really see these as home and not depend
For comfort on the chance, the shy encounter
With the irresponsible beauty of a stranger?
O can you see precisely in our gaucheness
The neighbours' strongest wish, to serve and love?

The Walking Tour

To throw away the key and walk away,
Not abrupt exile, the neighbours asking why,
But following a line with left and right
An altered gradient at another rate
Learns more than maps upon the whitewashed wall
The hand put up to ask; and makes us well
Without confession of the ill. All pasts
Are single old past now, although some posts
Are forwarded, held looking on a new view;
The future shall fulfil a surer vow
Not smiling at queen over the glass rim
Nor making gunpowder in the top room,
Not swooping at the surface still like gulls
But with prolonged drowning shall develop gills.

But there are still to tempt; areas not seen
Because of blizzards or an erring sign

Whose guessed-at wonders would be worth alleging,
And lies about the cost of a night's lodging.
Travellers may sleep at inns but not attach,
They sleep one night together, not asked to touch;
Receive no normal welcome, not the pressed lip,
Children to lift, not the assuaging lap.
Crossing the pass descend the growing stream
Too tired to hear except the pulses' strum,
Reach villages to ask for a bed in
Rock shutting out the sky, the old life done.

Herman Melville
(For Lincoln Kirstein)

Towards the end he sailed into an extraordinary mildness,
And anchored in his home and reached his wife
And rode within the harbour of her hand,
And went across each morning to an office
As though his occupation were another island.

Goodness existed: that was the new knowledge
His terror had to blow itself quite out
To let him see it; but it was the gale had blown him
Past the Cape Horn of sensible success
Which cries: "This rock is Eden. Shipwreck here."

But deafened him with thunder and confused with lightning:
—The maniac hero hunting like a jewel
The rare ambiguous monster that had maimed his sex,
Hatred for hatred ending in a scream,
The unexplained survivor breaking off the nightmare—
All that was intricate and false; the truth was simple.

146

Evil is unspectacular and always human,
And shares our bed and eats at our own table,
And we are introduced to Goodness every day,
Even in drawing-rooms among a crowd of faults;
He has a name like Billy and is almost perfect
But wears a stammer like a decoration:
And every time they meet the same thing has to happen;
It is the Evil that is helpless like a lover
And has to pick a quarrel and succeeds,
And both are openly destroyed before our eyes.

For now he was awake and knew
No one is ever spared except in dreams;
But there was something else the nightmare had distorted—
Even the punishment was human and a form of love:
The howling storm had been his father's presence
And all the time he had been carried on his father's breast.

Who now had set him gently down and left him.
He stood upon the narrow balcony and listened:
And all the stars above him sang as in his childhood
"All, all is vanity," but it was not the same;
For now the words descended like the calm of mountains—
—Nathaniel had been shy because his love was selfish—
But now he cried in exultation and surrender
"The Godhead is broken like bread. We are the pieces."

And sat down at his desk and wrote a story.

When the Devil Drives

Under boughs between our tentative endearments how should
    we hear

But with flushing pleasure drums distant over difficult country,
        Events not actual
        In time's unlenient will?

Which we shall not avoid, though at a station's chance delay
Lines branch to peace, iron up valleys to a hidden village;
        For we have friends to catch
        And none leave coach.

Sharers of our own day, thought smiling of, but nothing known,
What industries decline, what chances are of revolution,
        What murders flash
        Under composed flesh.

Knowledge no need to us whose wrists enjoy the chafing leash,
Can plunder high nests; who sheer off from old like gull
    from granite,
        From their mind's constant sniffling,
        Their blood's dulled shuffling.

Who feebling, still have time to wonder at the well-shaped heads
Conforming every day more closely to the best in albums:
        Fathers in sons may track
        Their voices trick.

But their ancestral curse, jumbled perhaps and put away,
Baffled for years, at last in one repeats its potent pattern
        And blows fall more than once,
        Although he wince:

Who was to moorland market town retired for work or love,
May creep to sumps, pile up against the door, crouching in cases,
        This anger falling
        Opens, empties that filling.

Let each one share our pity, hard to withhold and hard to bear.
None knows of the next day if it be less or more, the sorrow:
     Escaping cannot try;
     Must wait though it destroy.

The Riddle

Underneath the leaves of life,
Green on the prodigious tree,
     In a trance of grief
Stand the fallen man and wife:
Far away the single stag
Banished to a lonely crag
Gazes placid out to sea,
And from thickets round about
Breeding animals look in
     On Duality,
And the birds fly in and out
     Of the world of man.

Down in order from the ridge,
Bayonets glittering in the sun,
     Soldiers who will judge
Wind towards the little bridge:
Even politicians speak
Truths of value to the weak,
Necessary acts are done
By the ill and the unjust;
But the Judgment and the Smile,
     Though these two-in-one
See creation as they must,
     None shall reconcile.

Bordering our middle earth
Kingdoms of the Short and Tall,
    Rivals for our faith,
Stir up envy from our birth:
So the giant who storms the sky
In an angry wish to die
Wakes the hero in us all,
While the tiny with their power
To divide and hide and flee,
    When our fortunes fall
Tempt to a belief in our
    Immortality.

Lovers running each to each
Feel such timid dreams catch fire
    Blazing as they touch,
Learn what love alone can teach:
Happy on a tousled bed
Praise Blake's acumen who said:
"One thing only we require
Of each other; we must see
In another's lineaments
    Gratified desire";
That is our humanity;
    Nothing else contents.

Nowhere else could I have known
Than, beloved, in your eyes
    What we have to learn,
That we love ourselves alone:
All our terrors burned away
We can learn at last to say:
"All our knowledge comes to this,
That existence is enough,

That in savage solitude
   Or the play of love
Every living creature is
   Woman, Man, and Child."

Do Be Careful

Upon this line between adventure
Prolong the meeting out of good nature
Obvious in each agreeable feature.

Calling of each other by name
Smiling, taking a willing arm
Has the companionship of a game.

But should the walk do more than this
Out of bravado or drunkenness
Forward or back are menaces.

On neither side let foot slip over
Invading Always, exploring Never,
For this is hate and this is fear.

On narrowness stand, for sunlight is
Brightest only on surfaces;
No anger, no traitor, but peace.

Brussels in Winter

Wandering the cold streets tangled like old string,
Coming on fountains silent in the frost,
The city still escapes you; it has lost
The qualities that say "I am a Thing."

Only the homeless and the really humbled
Seem to be sure exactly where they are,
And in their misery are all assembled;
The winter holds them like the Opera.

Ridges of rich apartments rise tonight
Where isolated windows glow like farms:
A phrase goes packed with meaning like a van,

A look contains the history of man,
And fifty francs will earn the stranger right
To warm the heartless city in his arms.

We All Make Mistakes

Watch any day his nonchalant pauses, see
His dextrous handling of a wrap as he
Steps after into cars, the beggar's envy.

"There is a free one," many say, but err.
He is not that returning conqueror,
Nor ever the poles' circumnavigator.

But poised between shocking falls on razor-edge
Has taught himself this balancing subterfuge
Of the accosting profile, the erect carriage.

The song, the varied action of the blood
Would drown the warning from the iron wood
Would cancel the inertia of the buried:

Travelling by daylight on from house to house
The longest way to the intrinsic peace,
With love's fidelity and with love's weakness.

January 1, 1931

Watching in three planes from a room overlooking the courtyard
                    That year decaying,
Stub-end of year that smoulders to ash of winter,
                    The last day dropping;
Lo, a dream met me in middle night, I saw in a vision
Life pass as a gull, as a spy, as a dog-hated dustman:
And heard a voice saying—"Subjects, Objects, all of you,
                    Read of your losses."

Shaped me a Lent scene first, a bed, hard, surgical,
                    And a wound hurting;
The hour in the night when Lawrence died and I came
                    Round from the morphia.
A train went clanking over the bridges leaving the city;
A sleep-walker pushed on groaning down the velvet passage;
The night-nurse visited—"We shall not all sleep, dearie,"
                    She said, and left me.

Felt sap collecting anon in unlighted cylinders
                    For birdward facing;
The flat snake moving again in the pit, the schoolboy
                    From home migrating.
After a night of storm was a lawn in sunlight,
A colleague bending for measurements there at the rain-gauge,
Gritting his teeth after breakfast, the Headmaster muttered
                    "Call no man happy."

Came summer like a flood, did never greediest gardener
                    Make blossoms flusher:
Sunday meant lakes for many, a browner body
                    Beauty from burning:
Far out in the water two heads discussed the position,

153

Out of the reeds like a fowl jumped the undressed German,
And Pretzel signalled from the sand dunes like a
     wooden madman
               "Destroy this temple."

It did fall. The quick hare died to the hound's hot breathing,
               The Jewess fled Southwards;
The drunken Scotsman, regarding the moons hedge-rising,
               Shook and saluted:
And in cold Europe, in the middle of Autumn destruction,
Maverick stood, his face grown lined with wincing
In front of ignorance—"Tell the English," he shivered,
               "Man is a spirit."

What I saw further was general but in sorrow,
               Many together
Forgiving each other in the dark of the picture palaces
               But past forgiveness;
The pair walking out on the mole, getting ready to quarrel,
The exile from superb Africa, employed in a laundry;
Deserters, mechanics, conjurers, delicate martyrs,
               All self-regarders.

I saw the brain-track perfected, laid for conveying
               The fatal error,
Sending the body to islands or after its father,
               Cold with a razor:
One sniffed at a root to make him dream of a woman,
One laid his hands on the heads of dear little pages;
Neither in the bed nor on the *arrête* was there shown me
               One with power.

"Save me!" the voice commanded, but as I paused hesitant
               A troop rushed forward.

Granny in mittens, the Judge, the bucolic doctor,
           And the suave archdeacon.
The captains grouped round the flagstaff shut up their glasses,
Broke yelping over the gravel—as I stood a spectator,
One tapped my shoulder and asked me "How did you fall, sir?"
           Whereat I awakened.

Roof-line sharpens, intense in the New Year morning;
           Far down in courtyard
Beggar addresses the earth on the state of East Europe:
           "Won't you speak louder?
Have you heard of someone swifter than Syrian horses?
Has he thrown the bully of Corinth in the sanded circle?
Has he crossed the Isthmus already? is he seeking brilliant
           Athens and us?"

Have a Good Time

"We have brought you," they said, "a map of the country;
Here is the line that runs to the vats,
This patch of green on the left is the wood,
We've pencilled an arrow to point out the bay.
No thank you, no tea; why look at the clock.
Keep it? Of course. It goes with our love.

We shall watch your future and send our love.
We lived for years, you know, in the country.
Remember at week-ends to wind up the clock.
We've wired to our manager at the vats.
The tides are perfectly safe in the bay,
But whatever you do don't go to the wood.

There's a flying trickster in that wood,
And we shan't be there to help with our love.

Keep fit by bathing in the bay,
You'll never catch fever then in the country.
You're sure of a settled job at the vats
If you keep their hours and live by the clock."

He arrived at last; it was time by the clock.
He crossed himself as he passed the wood;
Black against evening sky the vats
Brought tears to his eyes as he thought of their love;
Looking out over the darkening country
He saw the pier in the little bay.

At the week-ends the divers in the bay
Distracted his eyes from the bandstand clock;
When down with fever and in the country
A skein of swans above the wood
Caused him no terror; he came to love
The moss that grew on the derelict vats.

And he has met sketching at the vats
Guests from the new hotel in the bay;
Now curious following his love,
His pulses differing from the clock,
Finds consummation in the wood
And sees for the first time the country.

Sees water in the wood and trees by the bay,
Hears a clock striking near the vats;
"This is your country and the home of love."

Let History Be My Judge

We made all possible preparations,
Drew up a list of firms,

Constantly revised our calculations
And allotted the farms,

Issued all the orders expedient
In this kind of case:
Most, as was expected, were obedient,
Though there were murmurs, of course;

Chiefly against our exercising
Our old right to abuse:
Even some sort of attempt at rising
But these were mere boys.

For never serious misgiving
Occurred to anyone,
Since there could be no question of living
If we did not win.

The generally accepted view teaches
That there was no excuse,
Though in the light of recent researches
Many would find the cause.

In a not uncommon form of terror;
Others, still more astute,
Point to possibilities of error
At the very start.

As for ourselves there is left remaining
Our honour at least,
And a reasonable chance of retaining
Our faculties to the last.

Orpheus

What does the song hope for? And the moved hands
A little way from the birds, the shy, the delightful?
        To be bewildered and happy,
        Or most of all the knowledge of life?

But the beautiful are content with the sharp notes of the air;
The warmth is enough. O if winter really
        Oppose, if the weak snowflake,
        What will the wish, what will the dance do?

The Exiles

What siren zooming is sounding our coming
Up frozen fjord forging from freedom
        What shepherd's call
        When stranded on hill,
        With broken axle
        On track to exile?

With labelled luggage we alight at last
Joining joking at the junction on the moor
        With practised smile
        And harmless tale
        Advance to meet
        Each new recruit.

Expert from uplands, always in oilskins,
Recliner from library, laying down law,
        Owner from shire,
        All meet on this shore
        Facing each prick
        With ginger pluck.

Our rooms are ready, the register signed,
There is time to take a turn before dark,
   See the blistering paint
   On the scorching front,
   Or icicles sombre
   On pierhead timber.

To climb the cliff path to the coastguard's point
Past the derelict dock deserted by rats,
   Look from concrete sill
   Of fort for sale
   To the bathers' rocks,
   The lovers' ricks.

Our boots will be brushed, our bolsters pummelled,
Cupboards are cleared for keeping our clothes.
   Here we shall live
   And somehow love
   Though we only master
   The sad posture.

Picnics are promised and planned for July
To the wood with the waterfall, walks to find,
   Traces of birds,
   A mole, a rivet,
   In factory yards
   Marked strictly private.

There will be skating and curling at Christmas—indoors
Charades and ragging; then riders pass
   Some afternoons
   In snowy lanes
   Shut in by wires,
   Surplus from wars.

In Spring we shall spade the soil on the border
For blooming of bulbs; we shall bow in Autumn
        When trees make passes,
        As high gale pushes,
        And bewildered leaves
        Fall on our lives.

Watching through windows the wastes of evening,
The flare of foundries at fall of the year,
        The slight despair
        At what we are,
        The marginal grief
        Is source of life.

In groups forgetting the gun in the drawer
Need pray for no pardon, are proud till recalled
        By music on water
        To lack of stature,
        Saying Alas
        To less and less.

Till holding our hats in our hands for talking,
Or striding down streets for something to see,
        Gas-light in shops,
        The fate of ships
        And the tide-wind
        Touch the old wound.

Till the town is ten and the time is London
And nerves grow numb between north and south
        Hear last in corner
        The pffwungg of burner
        Accepting dearth,
        The shadow of death.

Few and Simple *

Whenever you are thought, the mind
Amazes me with all the kind
Old such-and-such it says about you
As if I were the one that you
Attach unique importance to,
Not one who would but didn't get you.

Startling us both at certain hours,
The flesh that mind insists is ours,
Though I, for one, by now know better,
Gets ready for no-matter-what
As if it had forgotten that
What happens is another matter.

Few as they are, these facts are all
The richest moment can recall,
However it may choose to group them,
And, simple as they look, enough
To make the most ingenious love
Think twice of trying to escape them.

Canzone *

When shall we learn, what should be clear as day,
We cannot choose what we are free to love?
Although the mouse we banished yesterday
Is an enraged rhinoceros today,
Our value is more threatened than we know:
Shabby objections to our present day
Go snooping round its outskirts; night and day
Faces, orations, battles, bait our will
As questionable forms and noises will;

Whole phyla of resentments every day
Give status to the wild men of the world
Who rule the absent-minded and this world.

We are created from and with the world
To suffer with and from it day by day:
Whether we meet in a majestic world
Of solid measurements or a dream world
Of swans and gold, we are required to love
All homeless objects that require a world.
Our claim to own our bodies and our world
Is our catastrophe. What can we know
But panic and caprice until we know
Our dreadful appetite demands a world
Whose order, origin, and purpose will
Be fluent satisfaction of our will?

Drift, Autumn, drift; fall, colours, where you will:
Bald melancholia minces through the world.
Regret, cold oceans, the lymphatic will
Caught in reflection on the right to will:
While violent dogs excite their dying day
To bacchic fury; snarl, though, as they will,
Their teeth are not a triumph for the will
But utter hesitation. What we love
Ourselves for is our power not to love,
To shrink to nothing or explode at will,
To ruin and remember that we know
What ruins and hyaenas cannot know.

If in this dark now I less often know
That spiral staircase where the haunted will
Hunts for its stolen luggage, who should know
Better than you, beloved, how I know

What gives security to any world,
Or in whose mirror I begin to know
The chaos of the heart as merchants know
Their coins and cities, genius its own day?
For through our lively traffic all the day,
In my own person I am forced to know
How much must be forgotten out of love,
How much must be forgiven, even love.

Dear flesh, dear mind, dear spirit, O dear love,
In the depths of myself blind monsters know
Your presence and are angry, dreading Love
That asks its images for more than love;
The hot rampageous horses of my will,
Catching the scent of Heaven, whinny: Love
Gives no excuse to evil done for love,
Neither in you, nor me, nor armies, nor the world
Of words and wheels, nor any other world.
Dear fellow-creature, praise our God of Love
That we are so admonished, that no day
Of conscious trial be a wasted day.

Or else we make a scarecrow of the day,
Loose ends and jumble of our common world,
And stuff and nonsense of our own free will;
Or else our changing flesh may never know
There must be sorrow if there can be love.

In Memory of Sigmund Freud
(d. Sept. 1939)

When there are so many we shall have to mourn,
When grief has been made so public, and exposed

To the critique of a whole epoch
The frailty of our conscience and anguish,

Of whom shall we speak? For every day they die
Among us, those who were doing us some good,
                And knew it was never enough but
                Hoped to improve a little by living.

Such was this doctor: still at eighty he wished
To think of our life, from whose unruliness
                So many plausible young futures
                With threats or flattery ask obedience.

But his wish was denied him; he closed his eyes
Upon that last picture common to us all,
                Of problems like relatives standing
                Puzzled and jealous about our dying.

For about him at the very end were still
Those he had studied, the nervous and the nights,
                And shades that still waited to enter
                The bright circle of his recognition

Turned elsewhere with their disappointment as he
Was taken away from his old interest
                To go back to the earth in London,
                An important Jew who died in exile.

Only Hate was happy, hoping to augment
His practice now, and his shabby clientèle
                Who think they can be cured by killing
                And covering the gardens with ashes.

They are still alive but in a world he changed
Simply by looking back with no false regrets;
                    All that he did was to remember
                    Like the old and be honest like children.

He wasn't clever at all: he merely told
The unhappy Present to recite the Past
                    Like a poetry lesson till sooner
                    Or later it faltered at the line where

Long ago the accusations had begun,
And suddenly knew by whom it had been judged,
                    How rich life had been and how silly,
                    And was life-forgiven and more humble.

Able to approach the Future as a friend
Without a wardrobe of excuses, without
                    A set mask of rectitude or an
                    Embarrassing over-familiar gesture.

No wonder the ancient cultures of conceit
In his technique of unsettlement foresaw
                    The fall of princes, the collapse of
                    Their lucrative patterns of frustration.

If he succeeded, why, the Generalised Life
Would become impossible, the monolith
                    Of State be broken and prevented
                    The co-operation of avengers.

Of course they called on God: but he went his way,
Down among the Lost People like Dante, down
                    To the stinking fosse where the injured
                    Lead the ugly life of the rejected.

And showed us what evil is: not as we thought
Deeds that must be punished, but our lack of faith,
        Our dishonest mood of denial,
        The concupiscence of the oppressor.

And if something of the autocratic pose,
The paternal strictness he distrusted, still
        Clung to his utterance and features,
        It was a protective imitation

For one who lived among enemies so long;
If often he was wrong and at times absurd,
        To us he is no more a person
        Now but a whole climate of opinion.

Under whom we conduct our differing lives:
Like weather he can only hinder or help,
        The proud can still be proud but find it
        A little harder, and the tyrant tries

To make him do but doesn't care for him much.
He quietly surrounds all our habits of growth;
        He extends, till the tired in even
        The remotest most miserable duchy

Have felt the change in their bones and are cheered,
And the child unlucky in his little State,
        Some hearth where freedom is excluded,
        A hive whose honey is fear and worry,

Feels calmer now and somehow assured of escape;
While as they lie in the grass of our neglect,
        So many long-forgotten objects
        Revealed by his undiscouraged shining

Are returned to us and made precious again;
Games we had thought we must drop as we grew up,
>> Little noises we dared not laugh at,
>> Faces we made when no one was looking.

But he wishes us more than this: to be free
Is often to be lonely; he would unite
>> The unequal moieties fractured
>> By our own well-meaning sense of justice.

Would restore to the larger the wit and will
The smaller possesses but can only use
>> For arid disputes, would give back to
>> The son the mother's richness of feeling.

But he would have us remember most of all
To be enthusiastic over the night
>> Not only for the sense of wonder
>> It alone has to offer, but also

Because it needs our love: for with sad eyes
Its delectable creatures look up and beg
>> Us dumbly to ask them to follow;
>> They are exiles who long for the future

That lies in our power. They too would rejoice
If allowed to serve enlightenment like him,
>> Even to bear our cry of "Judas,"
>> As he did and all must bear who serve it.

One rational voice is dumb: over a grave
The household of Impulse mourns one dearly loved.
>> Sad is Eros, builder of cities,
>> And weeping anarchic Aphrodite.

167

The Voyage

Where does the journey look which the watcher upon
    the quay,
Standing under his evil star, so bitterly envies?
When the mountains swim away with slow calm strokes,
    and the gulls
Abandon their vow? Does it still promise the Juster Life?

And, alone with his heart at last, does the traveller find
In the vaguer touch of the wind and the fickle flash of
    the sea
Proofs that somewhere there exists, really, the Good Place,
As certain as those the children find in stones and holes?

No, he discovers nothing: he does not want to arrive.
The journey is false; the false journey really an illness
On the false island where the heart cannot act and will
    not suffer:
He condones the fever; he is weaker than he thought; his
    weakness is real.

But at moments, as when the real dolphins with leap
    and abandon
Cajole for recognition, or, far away, a real island
Gets up to catch his eye, the trance is broken: he remembers
The hours, the places where he was well; he believes in joy.

And maybe the fever shall have a cure, the true journey
    an end
Where hearts meet and are really true: and away this sea
    that parts
The hearts that alter, but is the same, always; and goes
Everywhere, joining the false and the true, but cannot suffer.

Crisis

Where do They come from? Those whom we so much dread
As on our dearest location falls the chill
        Of their crooked wing and endangers
        The melting friend, the aqueduct, the flower.

Terrible Presences that the ponds reflect
Back at the famous, and when the blond boy
        Bites eagerly into the shining
        Apple, emerge in their shocking fury.

And we realise the woods are deaf and the sky
Nurses no one, and we are awake and these
        Like farmers have purpose and knowledge,
        And towards us their hate is directed.

We are the barren pastures to which they bring
The resentment of outcasts; on us they work
        Out their despair; they wear our weeping
        As the disgraceful badge of their exile.

O we conjured them here like a lying map;
Desiring the extravagant joy of life
        We lured with a mirage of orchards
        Fat in the lazy climate of refuge.

Our money sang like streams on the aloof peaks
Of our thinking that beckoned them on like girls;
        Our culture like a West of wonder
        Shone a solemn promise in their faces.

We expected the beautiful or the wise
Ready to see a charm in our childish fib,
        Pleased to find nothing but stones and
        Able at once to create a garden.

But those who come are not even children with
The big indiscriminate eyes we had lost,
        Occupying our narrow spaces
        With their anarchist vivid abandon.

They arrive, already adroit, having learned
Restraint at the table of a father's rage;
        In a mother's distorting mirror
        They discovered the Meaning of Knowing.

These pioneers have long adapted themselves
To the night and the nightmare; they come equipped
        To reply to terror with terror,
        With lies to unmask the least deception.

For a future of marriage nevertheless
The bed is prepared; though all our whiteness shrinks
        From the hairy and clumsy bridegroom,
        We conceive in the shuddering instant.

For the barren must wish to bear though the Spring
Punish; and the crooked that dreads to be straight
        Cannot alter its prayer but summons
        Out of the dark a horrible rector.

O the striped and vigorous tiger can move
With style through the borough of murder; the ape
        Is really at home in the parish
        Of grimacing and licking: but we have

Failed as their pupils. Our tears well from a love
We have never outgrown; our cities predict
        More than we hope; even our armies
        Have to express our need of forgiveness.

Epithalamion

(For Giuseppe Antonio Borgese and
Elizabeth Mann, Nov. 23, 1939)

While explosives blow to dust
Friends and hopes, we cannot pray,
Absolute conviction must
Seem the whole of life to youth,
Battle's stupid gross event
Keep all learning occupied:
Yet the seed becomes the tree;
Happier savants may decide
That this quiet wedding of
A Borgese and a Mann
Planted human unity;
Hostile kingdoms of the truth,
Fighting fragments of content,
Here were reconciled by love,
Modern policy begun
　　On this day.

A priori dogmas brought
Into one collective will
All the European thought:
Eagle theologians swept
With an autocratic eye
Hungry for potential foes
The whole territory of truth
Where the great cathedrals rose;
Gentle to instinctive crimes,
With a sharp indulgence heard
Paradox-debating youth,
Listened where the injured wept
For the first rebellious sigh,

171

And unerringly at times
On some small progressive bird
        Swooped to kill.

But beneath them as they flew
Merchants with more prudent gaze
Broke eternity in two:
Unconcerned at the controls
Sat an ascetic engineer
In whose intellectual hand
Worlds of dull material lay,
All that bankers understand;
While elected by the heart
Out of sentiment, a lamb
With haemorrhages night and day
Saved enthusiastic souls;
Sorrow apt to interfere,
Wit that spoils romantic art,
In the social diagram
        Knew their place.

Yet no lie has only friends
Too polite to ask for proof:
Patriots, peering through the lens
Of their special discipline
At the map of knowledge, see
Superstition overcome
As all national frontiers melt
In a true imperium;
Fearing foreign skills no more,
Feel in each conative act
Such a joy as Dante felt
When, a total failure in
An inferior city, he,

Dreaming out his anger, saw
All the scattered leaves of fact
     Bound by love.

May this bed of marriage be
Symbol now of the rebirth
Asked of old humanity:
Let creative limbs explore
All creation's pleasure then;
Laughing horses, rocks that scream,
All the flowers that ever flew
Through the banquet of a dream,
Find in you a common love
Of extravagant sanity;
Till like Leonardo who,
Jostled by the sights of war
And unpleasant greedy men,
At Urbino watched a dove,
Your experience justify
     Life on earth.

Grateful in your happiness,
Let your Ariels fly away
To a gay unconsciousness
And a freely chosen task:
Shame at our shortcomings makes
Lame magicians of us all,
Forcing our invention to
An illegal miracle
And a theatre of disguise;
Brilliantly your angels took
Every lover's rôle for you,
Wore seduction like a mask
Or were frigid for your sakes;

Set these shadows, now your eyes
On the whole of substance look,
        Free today.

Kindly to each other turn,
Every timid vice forgive
With a quaker's quiet concern
For the uncoercive law,
Till your double wish be one,
Till, as you successful lie,
Begotten possibility,
Censoring the nostalgic sigh
To be nothing or be right,
Form its ethical resolve
Now to suffer and to be:
Though the kingdoms are at war,
All the peoples see the sun,
All the dwellings stand in light,
All the unconquered worlds revolve,
        Life must live.

Vowing to redeem the State,
Now let every girl and boy
To the heaven of the Great
All their prayers and praises lift:
Mozart with ironic breath
Turning poverty to song,
Goethe ignorant of sin
Placing every human wrong,
Blake the industrious visionary,
Tolstoi the great animal,
Hellas-loving Hoelderlin,
Wagner who obeyed his gift
Organised his wish for death

Into a tremendous cry,
Looking down upon us, all
Wish us joy.

The Watershed

Who stands, the crux left of the watershed,
On the wet road between the chafing grass
Below him sees dismantled washing-floors,
Snatches of tramline running to the wood,
An industry already comatose,
Yet sparsely living. A ramshackle engine
At Cashwell raises water; for ten years
It lay in flooded workings until this,
Its latter office, grudgingly performed,
And further here and there, though many dead
Lie under the poor soil, some acts are chosen
Taken from recent winters; two there were
Cleaned out a damaged shaft by hand, clutching
The winch the gale would tear them from; one died
During a storm, the fells impassable,
Not at his village, but in wooden shape
Through long abandoned levels nosed his way
And in his final valley went to ground.

Go home, now, stranger, proud of your young stock,
Stranger, turn back again, frustrate and vexed:
This land, cut off, will not communicate,
Be no accessory content to one
Aimless for faces rather there than here.
Beams from your car may cross a bedroom wall,
They wake no sleeper; you may hear the wind
Arriving driven from the ignorant sea
To hurt itself on pane, on bark of elm

Where sap unbaffled rises, being spring;
But seldom this. Near you, taller than grass,
Ears poise before decision, scenting danger.

Better Not

Who will endure
Heat of day and winter danger,
Journey from one place to another?
Nor be content to lie
Till evening upon headland over bay,
Between the land and sea;
Or smoking wait till hour of food,
Leaning on chained-up gate
At edge of wood?

Metals run
Burnished or rusty in the sun
From town to town,
And signals all along are down;
Yet nothing passes
But envelopes between these places,
Snatched at the gate and panting read indoors,
And first spring flowers arriving smashed,
Disaster stammered over wires,
And pity flashed.
For should professional traveller come,
Asked at the fireside he is dumb,
Declining with a small mad smile,
And all the while
Conjectures on the maps that lie
About in ships long high and dry
Grow stranger and stranger.

There is no change of place
But shifting of the head
To keep off glare of lamp from face,
Or climbing over to wall-side of bed;
No one will ever know
For what conversion brilliant capital is waiting,
What ugly feast may village band be celebrating;
For no one goes
Further than railhead or the ends of piers,
Will neither go nor send his son
Further through foothills than the rotting stack
Where gaitered gamekeeper with dog and gun
Will shout "Turn back."

The Questioner Who Sits So Sly

Will you turn a deaf ear
To what they said on the shore,
Interrogate their poises
In their rich houses;

Of stork-legged heaven-reachers
Of the compulsory touchers
The sensitive amusers
And masked amazers?

Yet wear no ruffian badge
Nor lie behind the hedge
Waiting with bombs of conspiracy
In arm-pit secrecy;

Carry no talisman
For germ or the abrupt pain
Needing no concrete shelter
Nor porcelain filter?

Will you wheel death anywhere
In his invalid chair,
With no affectionate instant
But his attendant?

For to be held for friend
By an undeveloped mind
To be joke for children is
Death's happiness:

Whose anecdotes betray
His favourite colour as blue
Colour of distant bells
And boys' overalls.

His tales of the bad lands
Disturb the sewing hands;
Hard to be superior
On parting nausea;

To accept the cushions from
Women against martyrdom.
Yet applauding the circuits
Of racing cyclists.

Never to make signs
Fear neither maelstrom nor zones
Salute with soldiers' wives
When the flag waves;

Remembering there is
No recognized gift for this;
No income, no bounty,
No promised country.

178

But to see brave sent home
Hermetically sealed with shame
And cold's victorious wrestle
With molten metal.

A neutralizing peace
And an average disgrace
Are honour to discover
For later other.

Luther

With conscience cocked to listen for the thunder
He saw the Devil busy in the wind,
Over the chiming steeples and then under
The doors of nuns and doctors who had sinned.

What apparatus could stave off disaster
Or cut the brambles of man's error down?
Flesh was a silent dog that bites its master,
World a still pond in which its children drown.

The fuse of Judgment spluttered in his head:
"Lord, smoke these honeyed insects from their hives;
All Works, Great Men, Societies, are bad;
The Just shall live by Faith . . ." he cried in dread.

And men and women of the world were glad
Who never trembled in their useful lives.

As He Is

Wrapped in a yielding air, beside
The flower's soundless hunger,

Close to the tree's clandestine tide,
  Close to the bird's high fever,
  Loud in his hope and anger,
Erect about his skeleton,
  Stands the expressive lover,
  Stands the deliberate man.

Beneath the hot incurious sun,
  Past stronger beasts and fairer
He picks his way, a living gun,
  With gun and lens and bible,
  A militant enquirer,
The friend, the rash, the enemy,
  The essayist, the able,
  Able at times to cry.

The friendless and unhated stone
  Lies everywhere about him,
The Brothered-One, the Not-Alone,
  The brothered and the hated
  Whose family have taught him
To set against the large and dumb,
  The timeless and the rooted,
  His money and his time.

For mother's fading hopes become
  Dull wives to his dull spirits
Soon dulled by nurse's moral thumb,
  That dullard fond betrayer,
  And, childish, he inherits,
So soon by legal father tricked,
  The tall and gorgeous tower,
  Gorgeous but locked, but locked.

And ruled by dead men never met,
   By pious guess deluded,
Upon the stool of madness set
   Or stool of desolation,
   Sits murderous and clear-headed;
Enormous beauties round him move,
   For grandiose is his vision
   And grandiose his love.

Determined on Time's honest shield
   The lamb must face the tigress,
Their faithful quarrel never healed
   Though, faithless, he consider
   His dream of vaguer ages,
Hunter and victim reconciled,
   The lion and the adder,
   The adder and the child.

Fresh loves betray him, every day
   Over his green horizon
A fresh deserter rides away,
   And miles away birds mutter
   Of ambush and of treason;
To fresh defeats he still must move,
   To further griefs and greater,
   And the defeat of grief.

Spain 1937

Yesterday all the past. The language of size
Spreading to China along the trade-routes; the diffusion
         Of the counting-frame and the cromlech;
Yesterday the shadow-reckoning in the sunny climates.

Yesterday the assessment of insurance by cards,
The divination of water; yesterday the invention
                Of cart-wheels and clocks, the taming of
Horses; yesterday the bustling world of the navigators.

Yesterday the abolition of fairies and giants;
The fortress like a motionless eagle eyeing the valley,
                The chapel built in the forest;
Yesterday the carving of angels and of frightening gargoyles.

The trial of heretics among the columns of stone;
Yesterday the theological feuds in the taverns
                And the miraculous cure at the fountain;
Yesterday the Sabbath of Witches. But today the struggle.

Yesterday the installation of dynamos and turbines;
The construction of railways in the colonial desert;
                Yesterday the classic lecture
On the origin of Mankind. But today the struggle.

Yesterday the belief in the absolute value of Greek;
The fall of the curtain upon the death of a hero;
                Yesterday the prayer to the sunset,
And the adoration of madmen. But today the struggle.

As the poet whispers, startled among the pines
Or, where the loose waterfall sings, compact, or upright
                On the crag by the leaning tower:
"O my vision. O send me the luck of the sailor."

And the investigator peers through his instruments
At the inhuman provinces, the virile bacillus
                Or enormous Jupiter finished:
"But the lives of my friends. I inquire, I inquire."

And the poor in their fireless lodgings dropping the sheets
Of the evening paper: "Our day is our loss. O show us
                    History the operator, the
Organiser, Time the refreshing river."

And the nations combine each cry, invoking the life
That shapes the individual belly and orders
                    The private nocturnal terror:
"Did you not found once the city state of the sponge,

"Raise the vast military empires of the shark
And the tiger, establish the robin's plucky canton?
                    Intervene. O descend as a dove or
A furious papa or a mild engineer: but descend."

And the life, if it answers at all, replies from the heart
And the eyes and the lungs, from the shops and squares of
        the city:
                    "O no, I am not the Mover,
Not today, not to you. To you I'm the

"Yes-man, the bar-companion, the easily-duped:
I am whatever you do; I am your vow to be
                    Good, your humorous story;
I am your business voice; I am your marriage.

"What's your proposal? To build the Just City? I will.
I agree. Or is it the suicide pact, the romantic
                    Death? Very well, I accept, for
I am your choice, your decision: yes, I am Spain."

Many have heard it on remote peninsulas,
On sleepy plains, in the aberrant fishermen's islands,
                    In the corrupt heart of the city;
Have heard and migrated like gulls or the seeds of a flower.

They clung like burrs to the long expresses that lurch
Through the unjust lands, through the night, through the
    alpine tunnel;
            They floated over the oceans;
They walked the passes: they came to present their lives.

On that arid square, that fragment nipped off from hot
Africa, soldered so crudely to inventive Europe,
            On that tableland scored by rivers,
Our fever's menacing shapes are precise and alive.

Tomorrow, perhaps, the future: the research on fatigue
And the movements of packers; the gradual exploring of
    all the
            Octaves of radiation;
Tomorrow the enlarging of consciousness by diet
    and breathing.

Tomorrow the rediscovery of romantic love;
The photographing of ravens; all the fun under
            Liberty's masterful shadow;
Tomorrow the hour of the pageant-master and the musician.

Tomorrow, for the young, the poets exploding like bombs,
The walks by the lake, the winter of perfect communion;
            Tomorrow the bicycle races
Through the suburbs on summer evenings: but today
    the struggle.

Today the inevitable increase in the chances of death;
The conscious acceptance of guilt in the fact of murder;
            Today the expending of powers
On the flat ephemeral pamphlet and the boring meeting.

Today the makeshift consolations; the shared cigarette;
The cards in the candle-lit barn and the scraping concert,
            The masculine jokes; today the
Fumbled and unsatisfactory embrace before hurting.

The stars are dead; the animals will not look:
We are left alone with our day, and the time is short and
            History to the defeated
May say Alas but cannot help or pardon.

The Witnesses

Young men late in the night
    Toss on their beds
Their pillows do not comfort
    Their uneasy heads,
The lot that decides their fate
    Is cast tomorrow,
One must depart and face
    Danger and sorrow.

Is it me? Is it me?

Look in your heart and see:
    There lies the answer.
Though the heart like a clever
    Conjuror or dancer
Deceive you often into many
    A curious sleight
And motives like stowaways
    Are found too late.

*What shall he do, whose heart
    Chooses to depart?*

185

He shall against his peace
   Feel his heart harden,
Envy the heavy birds
   At home in a garden.
For walk he must the empty
   Selfish journey
Between the needless risk
   And the endless safety.

Will he safe and sound
   Return to his own ground?

Clouds and lions stand
   Before him dangerous
And the hostility of dreams.
   Oh let him honour Us
Lest he should he ashamed
   In the hour of crisis,
In the valleys of corrosion
   Tarnish his brightness.

Who are You, whose speech
   Sounds far out of reach?

You are the town and We are the clock.
We are the guardians of the gate in the rock.
   The Two.
On your left and on your right
In the day and in the night,
   We are watching you.

Wiser not to ask just what has occurred
To them who disobeyed our word;
   To those

We were the whirlpool, we were the reef,
We were the formal nightmare, grief
   And the unlucky rose.

Climb up the crane, learn the sailor's words
When the ships from the islands laden with birds
   Come in;
Tell you stories of fishing and other men's wives,
The expansive dreams of constricted lives,
   In the lighted inn.

But do not imagine We do not know,
Or that what you hide with such care won't show
   At a glance:
Nothing is done, nothing is said,
But don't make the mistake of believing us dead;
   I shouldn't dance.

We're afraid in that case you'll have a fall;
We've been watching you over the garden wall
   For hours:
The sky is darkening like a stain;
Something is going to fall like rain,
   And it won't be flowers.

When the green field comes off like a lid,
Revealing what was much better hid—
   Unpleasant:
And look, behind you without a sound
The woods have come up and are standing round
   In deadly crescent.

The bolt is sliding in its groove;
Outside the window is the black remov-
   -er's van:

And now with sudden swift emergence
Come the hooded women, the hump-backed surgeons,
    And the Scissor Man.

This might happen any day;
So be careful what you say
    And do:
Be clean, be tidy, oil the lock,
Weed the garden, wind the clock;
    Remember the Two.

Part II

LETTER TO A WOUND

Letter to a Wound

The maid has just cleared away tea and I shall not be disturbed until supper. I shall be quite alone in this room, free to think of you if I choose, and believe me, my dear, I do choose. For a long time now I have been aware that you are taking up more of my life every day, but I am always being surprised to find how far this has gone. Why, it was only yesterday, I took down all those photographs from my mantelpiece—Gabriel, Olive, Mrs. Marshall, Molim, and the others. How could I have left them there like that so long, memorials to my days of boasting? As it is, I've still far too many letters. (Vow. To have a grand clearance this week—hotel bills—bus tickets from Damascus, presentation pocket-mirrors, foreign envelopes, etc.)

Looking back now to that time before I lost my "health" (Was that really only last February?) I can't recognize myself. The discontinuity seems absolute. But of course the change was really gradual. Over and over again in the early days when I was in the middle of writing a newsy letter to M., or doing tricks in the garden to startle R. and C., you showed your resentment by a sudden bout of pain. I had outbursts, wept even, at what seemed to me then your insane jealousy, your bad manners, your passion for spoiling things. What a little idiot I was not to trust your more exquisite judgment, which declined absolutely to let me go on behaving like a child. People would have tried to explain it all. You would not insult me with pity. I think I've learned my lesson now. Thank you, my dear. I'll try my hardest not to let you down again.

Do you realize we have been together now for almost a year? Eighteen months ago, if anyone had foretold this to me I should have asked him to leave the house. Haven't I ever told you about my first interview with the surgeon?

He kept me waiting three-quarters of an hour. It was raining outside. Cars passed or drew up squeaking by the curb. I sat in my overcoat, restlessly turning over the pages of back numbers of illustrated papers, accounts of the Battle of Jutland, jokes about special constables and conscientious objectors. A lady came down with a little girl. They put on their hats, speaking in whispers, tight-lipped. Mr. Gangle would see me. A nurse was just coming out as I entered, carrying a white-enamelled bowl containing a pair of scissors, some instruments, soiled swabs of cotton wool. Mr. Gangle was washing his hands. The examination on the hard leather couch under the brilliant light was soon over. Washing again as I dressed he said nothing. Then reaching for a towel turned, "I'm afraid," he said. . . .

Outside I saw nothing, walked, not daring to think. I've lost everything, I've failed. I wish I was dead. And now, here we are, together, intimate, mature.

Later. At dinner Mrs. T. announced that she'd accepted an invitation for me to a whist-drive at the Stewarts' on Wednesday. "It's so good for you to get out in the evenings sometimes. You're as bad as Mr. Bedder." She babbled on, secretly disappointed, I think, that I did not make more protest. Certainly six months ago she couldn't have brought it off, which makes me think what a great change has come over us recently. In what I might call our honeymoon stage, when we had both realized what we meant to each other (how slow I was, wasn't I?) and that this would always be so, I was obsessed (You too a little? No?) by what seemed my extraordinary fortune. I pitied everybody. Little do you know, I said to myself, looking at my neighbour on the bus, what has happened to the little man in the black hat sitting next to you. I was always smiling. I mortally offended Mrs. Hunter, I remember, when she was describing her son's career at Cambridge. She thought I was laughing at her. In restaurants I found myself drawing pictures of you on the bottom of the table mats. "Who'll ever guess what that is?" Once, when a whore accosted me, I bowed, "I deeply regret it, Madam, but I have a friend." Once I carved on a seat in the park "We have sat here. You'd better not."

Now I see that all that sort of thing is juvenile and silly, merely a reaction against insecurity and shame. You as usual of course were the first to realize this, making yourself felt whenever I had been particularly rude or insincere.

Thanks to you, I have come to see a profound significance in relations I never dreamt of considering before, an old lady's affection for a small boy, the Waterhouses and their retriever, the curious bond between Offal and Snig, the partners in the hardware shop on the front. Even the close-ups on the films no longer disgust nor amuse me. On the contrary they sometimes make me cry; knowing you has made me understand.

It's getting late and I have to be up betimes in the morning. You are so quiet these days that I get quite nervous, remove the dressing. No I am safe, you are still there. The wireless says that the frost is coming. When it does, we know what to expect, don't we? But I am calm. I can wait. The surgeon was dead right. Nothing will ever part us. Good-night and God bless you, my dear.

Better burn this.

Part III

SONGS AND OTHER MUSICAL PIECES

I

As I walked out one evening,
   Walking down Bristol Street,
The crowds upon the pavement
   Were fields of harvest wheat.

And down by the brimming river
   I heard a lover sing
Under an arch of the railway:
   "Love has no ending.

I'll love you, dear, I'll love you
   Till China and Africa meet,
And the river jumps over the mountain
   And the salmon sing in the street.

I'll love you till the ocean
   Is folded and hung up to dry,
And the seven stars go squawking
   Like geese about the sky.

The years shall run like rabbits,
   For in my arms I hold
The Flower of the Ages,
   And the first love of the world."

But all the clocks in the city
   Began to whirr and chime:
"O let not Time deceive you,
   You cannot conquer Time.

In the burrows of the Nightmare
   Where Justice naked is,
Time watches from the shadow
   And coughs when you would kiss.

In headaches and in worry
  Vaguely life leaks away,
And Time will have his fancy
  Tomorrow or today.

Into many a green valley
  Drifts the appalling snow;
Time breaks the threaded dances
  And the diver's brilliant bow.

O plunge your hands in water,
  Plunge them in up to the wrist;
Stare, stare in the basin
  And wonder what you've missed.

The glacier knocks in the cupboard,
  The desert sighs in the bed,
And the crack in the tea-cup opens
  A lane to the land of the dead.

Where the beggars raffle the banknotes
  And the Giant is enchanting to Jack,
And the Lily-white Boy is a Roarer,
  And Jill goes down on her back.

O look, look in the mirror,
  O look in your distress;
Life remains a blessing
  Although you cannot bless.

O stand, stand at the window
  As the tears scald and start;
You shall love your crooked neighbor
  With your crooked heart."

It was late, late in the evening,
    The lovers they were gone;
The clocks had ceased their chiming,
    And the deep river ran on.

II

At last the secret is out, as it always must come in the end,
The delicious story is ripe to tell to the intimate friend;
Over the tea-cups and in the square the tongue has its desire;
Still waters run deep, my dear, there's never smoke
        without fire.

Behind the corpse in the reservoir, behind the ghost on
        the links,
Behind the lady who dances and the man who madly drinks,
Under the look of fatigue, the attack of migraine and
        the sigh
There is always another story, there is more than meets
        the eye.

For the clear voice suddenly singing, high up in the
        convent wall,
The scent of the elder bushes, the sporting prints in the hall,
The croquet matches in summer, the handshake, the cough,
        the kiss,
There is always a wicked secret, a private reason for this.

III *

    Carry her over the water,
    And set her down under the tree,

Where the culvers white all day and all night,
    And the winds from every quarter
Sing agreeably, agreeably, agreeably of love.

Put a gold ring on her finger,
    And press her close to your heart,
While the fish in the lake their snapshots take,
    And the frog, that sanguine singer,
Sings agreeably, agreeably, agreeably of love.

The streets shall all flock to your marriage,
    The houses turn round to look,
The tables and chairs say suitable prayers,
    And the horses drawing your carriage
Sing agreeably, agreeably, agreeably of love.

IV

Dear, though the night is gone,
Its dream still haunts today,
That brought us to a room
Cavernous, lofty as
A railway terminus,
And crowded in that gloom
Were beds, and we in one
In a far corner lay.

Our whisper woke no clocks,
We kissed and I was glad
At everything you did,
Indifferent to those
Who sat with hostile eyes
In pairs on every bed,

Arms round each other's neck,
Inert and vaguely sad.

O but what worm of guilt
Or what malignant doubt
Am I the victim of,
That you then, unabashed,
Did what I never wished,
Confessed another love;
And I, submissive, felt
Unwanted and went out?

V *

Eyes look into the well,
Tears run down from the eye;
The tower cracked and fell
From the quiet winter sky.

Under the midnight stone
Love was buried by thieves;
The robbed heart begs for a bone,
The damned rustle like leaves.

Face down in the flooded brook
With nothing more to say,
Lies One the soldiers took,
And spoiled and threw away.

VI

Fish in the unruffled lakes
The swarming colours wear,
Swans in the winter air

A white perfection have,
And the great lion walks
Through his innocent grove;
Lion, fish, and swan
Act, and are gone
Upon Time's toppling wave.

We till shadowed days are done,
We must weep and sing
Duty's conscious wrong,
The Devil in the clock,
The Goodness carefully worn
For atonement or for luck;
We must lose our loves,
On each beast and bird that moves
Turn an envious look.

Sighs for folly said and done
Twist our narrow days;
But I must bless, I must praise
That you, my swan, who have
All gifts that to the swan
Impulsive Nature gave,
The majesty and pride,
Last night should add
Your voluntary love.

VII *

"Gold in the North," came the blizzard to say,
I left my sweetheart at the break of day,
The gold ran out and my love turned grey.
You don't know all, sir, you don't know all.

"The West," said the sun, "for enterprise,"
A bullet in Frisco put me wise,
My last words were "God damn your eyes."
You don't know all, sir, you don't know all.

In the streets of New York I was young and swell,
I rode the market, the market fell,
One morning I woke and found myself in hell,
You don't know all, sir, you don't know all.

In Alabama my heart was full,
Down by the river bank I stole,
The waters of grief went over my soul,
You don't know all, ma'am, you don't know all.

In the saloons I heaved a sigh,
Lost in deserts of alkali I lay down to die;
There's always a sorrow can get you down,
All the world's whiskey won't ever drown.

Some think they're strong, some think they're smart,
Like butterflies they're pulled apart,
America can break your heart.
You don't know all, sir, you don't know all.

VIII *

Song for St. Cecilia's Day

I

In a garden shady this holy lady
With reverent cadence and subtle psalm,
Like a black swan as death came on
Poured forth her song in perfect calm:

203

And by ocean's margin this innocent virgin
Constructed an organ to enlarge her prayer,
And notes tremendous from her great engine
Thundered out on the Roman air.

Blonde Aphrodite rose up excited,
Moved to delight by the melody,
White as an orchid she rode quite naked
In an oyster shell on top of the sea;
At sounds so entrancing the angels dancing
Came out of their trance into time again,
And around the wicked in Hell's abysses
The huge flame flickered and eased their pain.

Blessed Cecilia, appear in visions
To all musicians, appear and inspire:
Translated Daughter, come down and startle
Composing mortals with immortal fire.

II

I cannot grow;
I have no shadow
To run away from,
I only play.

I cannot err;
There is no creature
Whom I belong to,
Whom I could wrong.

I am defeat
When it knows it
Can now do nothing
By suffering.

All you lived through,
Dancing because you
No longer need it
For any deed.

I shall never be
Different. Love me.

III

O ear whose creatures cannot wish to fall,
O calm of spaces unafraid of weight,
Where Sorrow is herself, forgetting all
The gaucheness of her adolescent state,
Where Hope within the altogether strange
From every outworn image is released,
And Dread born whole and normal like a beast
Into a world of truths that never change:
Restore our fallen day; O re-arrange.

O dear white children casual as birds,
Playing among the ruined languages,
So small beside their large confusing words,
So gay against the greater silences
Of dreadful things you did: O hang the head,
Impetuous child with the tremendous brain,
O weep, child, weep, O weep away the stain,
Lost innocence who wished your lover dead,
Weep for the lives your wishes never led.

O cry created as the bow of sin
Is drawn across our trembling violin.
O weep, child, weep, O weep away the stain.
O law drummed out by hearts against the still
Long winter of our intellectual will.

That what has been may never be again.
O flute that throbs with the thanksgiving breath
Of convalescents on the shores of death.
O bless the freedom that you never chose.
O trumpets that unguarded children blow
About the fortress of their inner foe.
O wear your tribulation like a rose.

IX *

Jumbled in the common box
Of their dark stupidity,
Orchid, swan, and Caesar lie;
Time that tires of everyone
Has corroded all the locks
Thrown away the key for fun.

In its cleft the torrent mocks
Prophets who in days gone by
Made a profit on each cry,
Persona grata now with none;
And a jackass language shocks
Poets who can only pun.

Silence settles on the clocks;
Nursing mothers point a sly
Index finger at a sky,
Crimson with the setting sun;
In the valley of the fox
Gleams the barrel of a gun.

Once we could have made the docks,
Now it is too late to fly;
Once too often you and I

Did what we should not have done;
Round the rampant rugged rocks
Rude and ragged rascals run.

X *

Lady, weeping at the crossroads
Would you meet your love
In the twilight with his greyhounds,
And the hawk on his glove?

Bribe the birds then on the branches,
Bribe them to be dumb,
Stare the hot sun out of heaven
That the night may come.

Starless are the nights of travel,
Bleak the winter wind;
Run with terror all before you
And regret behind.

Run until you hear the ocean's
Everlasting cry;
Deep though it may be and bitter
You must drink it dry.

Wear out patience in the lowest
Dungeons of the sea,
Searching through the stranded shipwrecks
For the golden key.

Push onto the world's end, pay the
Dread guard with a kiss;
Cross the rotten bridge that totters
Over the abyss.

There stands the deserted castle
Ready to explore;
Enter, climb the marble staircase
Open the locked door.

Cross the silent empty ballroom,
Doubt and danger past;
Blow the cobwebs from the mirror
See yourself at last.

Put your hand behind the wainscot,
You have done your part;
Find the penknife there and plunge it
Into your false heart.

XI

Lay your sleeping head, my love,
Human on my faithless arm;
Time and fevers burn away
Individual beauty from
Thoughtful children, and the grave
Proves the child ephemeral:
But in my arms till break of day
Let the living creature lie,
Mortal, guilty, but to me
The entirely beautiful.

Soul and body have no bounds:
To lovers as they lie upon
Her tolerant enchanted slope
In their ordinary swoon,
Grave the vision Venus sends
Of supernatural sympathy,

Universal love and hope;
While an abstract insight wakes
Among the glaciers and the rocks
The hermit's sensual ecstasy.

Certainty, fidelity
On the stroke of midnight pass
Like vibrations of a bell,
And fashionable madmen raise
Their pedantic boring cry:
Every farthing of the cost,
All the dreaded cards foretell,
Shall be paid, but from this night
Not a whisper, not a thought,
Not a kiss nor look be lost.

Beauty, midnight, vision dies:
Let the winds of dawn that blow
Softly round your dreaming head
Such a day of sweetness show
Eye and knocking heart may bless,
Find the mortal world enough;
Noons of dryness see you fed
By the involuntary powers,
Nights of insult let you pass
Watched by every human love.

XII

(Tune: St. James' Infirmary)

Let me tell you a little story
    About Miss Edith Gee;
She lived in Clevedon Terrace
    At Number 83.

She'd a slight squint in her left eye,
    Her lips they were thin and small,
She had narrow sloping shoulders
    And she had no bust at all..

She'd a velvet hat with trimmings,
    And a dark-grey serge costume;
She lived in Clevedon Terrace
    In a small bed-sitting room.

She'd a purple mac for wet days,
    A green umbrella too to take,
She'd a bicycle with shopping basket
    And a harsh back-pedal brake.

The Church of Saint Aloysius
    Was not so very far;
She did a lot of knitting,
    Knitting for that Church Bazaar.

Miss Gee looked up at the starlight
    And said: "Does anyone care
That I live in Clevedon Terrace
    On one hundred pounds a year?"

She dreamed a dream one evening
    That she was the Queen of France
And the Vicar of Saint Aloysius
    Asked Her Majesty to dance.

But a storm blew down the palace,
    She was biking through a field of corn,
And a bull with the face of the Vicar
    Was charging with lowered horn.

She could feel his hot breath behind her,
  He was going to overtake;
And the bicycle went slower and slower
  Because of that back-pedal brake.

Summer made the trees a picture,
  Winter made them a wreck;
She bicycled to the evening service
  With her clothes buttoned up to her neck.

She passed by the loving couples,
  She turned her head away;
She passed by the loving couples
  And they didn't ask her to stay.

Miss Gee sat down in the side-aisle,
  She heard the organ play;
And the choir it sang so sweetly
  At the ending of the day,

Miss Gee knelt down in the side-aisle,
  She knelt down on her knees;
"Lead me not into temptation
  But make me a good girl, please."

The days and nights went by her
  Like waves round a Cornish wreck;
She bicycled down to the doctor
  With her clothes buttoned up to her neck.

She bicycled down to the doctor,
  And rang the surgery bell;
"O, doctor, I've a pain inside me,
  And I don't feel very well."

Doctor Thomas looked her over,
   And then he looked some more;
Walked over to his wash-basin,
   Said, "Why didn't you come before?"

Doctor Thomas sat over his dinner,
   Though his wife was waiting to ring;
Rolling his bread into pellets,
   Said, "Cancer's a funny thing.

"Nobody knows what the cause is,
   Though some pretend they do;
It's like some hidden assassin
   Waiting to strike at you.

"Childless women get it,
   And men when they retire;
It's as if there had to be some outlet
   For their foiled creative fire."

His wife she rang for the servant,
   Said, "Don't be so morbid, dear,"
He said; "I saw Miss Gee this evening
   And she's a goner, I fear."

They took Miss Gee to the hospital,
   She lay there a total wreck,
Lay in the ward for women
   With the bedclothes right up to her neck.

They laid her on the table,
   The students began to laugh;
And Mr. Rose the surgeon
   He cut Miss Gee in half.

Mr. Rose he turned to his students,
   Said; "Gentlemen, if you please,
We seldom see a sarcoma
   As far advanced as this."

They took her off the table,
   They wheeled away Miss Gee
Down to another department
   Where they study Anatomy.

They hung her from the ceiling,
   Yes, they hung up Miss Gee;
And a couple of Oxford Groupers
   Carefully dissected her knee.

XIII

Let the florid music praise,
   The flute and the trumpet,
Beauty's conquest of your face:
In that land of flesh and bone,
Where from citadels on high
Her imperial standards fly,
     Let the hot sun
     Shine on, shine on.

O but the unloved have had power,
   The weeping and striking,
Always: time will bring their hour;
Their secretive children walk
Through your vigilance of breath
To unpardonable death,
     And my vows break
     Before his look.

XIV

Look, stranger, on this island now
The leaping light for your delight discovers,
Stand stable here
And silent be,
That through the channels of the ear
May wander like a river
The swaying sound of the sea.

Here at the small field's ending pause
When the chalk wall falls to the foam and its tall ledges
Oppose the pluck
And knock of the tide,
And the shingle scrambles after the suck-
-ing surf,
And the gull lodges
A moment on its sheer side.

Far off like floating seeds the ships
Diverge on urgent voluntary errands,
And the full view
Indeed may enter
And move in memory as now these clouds do,
That pass the harbour mirror
And all the summer through the water saunter.

XV

May with its light behaving
Stirs vessel, eye, and limb;
The singular and sad
Are willing to recover,
And to the swan-delighting river

The careless picnics come,
The living white and red.

The dead remote and hooded
In their enclosures rest; but we
From the vague woods have broken,
Forests where children meet
And the white angel-vampires flit;
We stand with shaded eye,
The dangerous apple taken.

The real world lies before us,
Animal motions of the young,
The common wish for death,
The pleasured and the haunted;
The dying master sinks tormented
In the admirers' ring;
The unjust walk the earth.

And love that makes impatient
The tortoise and the roe, and lays
The blonde beside the dark,
Urges upon our blood,
Before the evil and the good
How insufficient is
The endearment and the look.

XVI *

My second thoughts condemn
And wonder how I dare
To look you in the eye.
What right have I to swear

Even at one a.m.
To love you till I die?

Earth meets too many crimes
For fibs to interest her;
If I can give my word,
Forgiveness can recur
Any number of times
In Time. Which is absurd.

Tempus fugit. Quite.
So finish up your drink.
All flesh is grass. It is.
But who on earth can think
With heavy heart or light
Of what will come of this?

XVII

Not, Father, further do prolong
   Our necessary defeat;
Spare us the numbing zero-hour,
   The desert-long retreat.

Against Your direct light, displayed,
   Regardant, absolute,
In person stubborn and oblique
   We set our maddened foot.

These nissen huts, if hide we could
   Your eye inseeing from,
Firm fenders were, but lo! to us
   Your loosened angers come.

Against Your accusations
   Though ready wit devise,
Nor magic countersigns prevail
   Nor airy sacrifice.

Weaker we are, and strict within
   Your organized blockade,
And from our desperate shore the last
   Few pallid youngsters fade.

Be not another than our hope;
   Expect we routed shall
Upon your peace; with ray disarm,
   Illumine, and not kill.

XVIII

Now the leaves are falling fast,
Nurse's flowers will not last;
Nurses to the graves are gone,
And the prams go rolling on.

Whispering neighbours, left and right,
Pluck us from the real delight;
And the active hands must freeze
Lonely on the separate knees.

Dead in hundreds at the back
Follow wooden in our track,
Arms raised stiffly to reprove
In false attitudes of love.

Starving through the leafless wood
Trolls run scolding for their food;

And the nightingale is dumb,
And the angel will not come.

Cold, impossible, ahead
Lifts the mountain's lovely head
Whose white waterfall could bless
Travellers in their last distress.

XIX

Now through night's caressing grip
Earth and all her oceans slip,
Capes of China slide away
From her fingers into day,
And the Americas incline
Coasts toward her shadow line.
Now the ragged vagrants creep
Into crooked holes to sleep;
Just and unjust, worst and best,
Change their places as they rest;
Awkward lovers lie in fields
Where disdainful beauty yields;
While the splendid and the proud
Naked stand before the crowd,
And the losing gambler gains,
And the beggar entertains.
May sleep's healing power extend
Through these hours to each friend;
Unpursued by hostile force
Traction engine bull or horse
Or revolting succubus;
Calmly till the morning break
Let them lie, then gently wake.

XX

—"O for doors to be open and an invite with gilded edges
 To dine with Lord Lobcock and Count Asthma on the
  platinum benches,
 With the somersaults and fireworks, the roast and the
  smacking kisses"—
   Cried the cripples to the silent statue,
   The six beggared cripples.

—"And Garbo's and Cleopatra's wits to go astraying,
 In a feather ocean with me to go fishing and playing,
 Still jolly when the cock has burst himself with crowing"—
   Cried the cripples to the silent statue,
   The six beggared cripples.

'–"And to stand on green turf among the craning yellow faces
 Dependent on the chestnut, the sable, and Arabian horses,
 And me with a magic crystal to foresee their places"—
   Cried the cripples to the silent statue,
   The six beggared cripples.

—"And this square to be deck and these pigeons sails to rig,
 And to follow the delicious breeze like a tantony pig
 To the shaded feverless islands where the melons
  are big"—
   Cried the cripples to the silent statue,
   The six beggared cripples.

—"And these shops to be turned to tulips in a garden bed,
 And me with my crutch to thrash each merchant dead
 As he pokes from a flower his bald and wicked head"—
   Cried the cripples to the silent statue,
   The six beggared cripples.

—"And a hole in the bottom of heaven, and Peter and Paul
And each smug surprised saint like parachutes to fall,
And every one-legged beggar to have no legs at all"—
Cried the cripples to the silent statue,
The six beggared cripples.

XXI

O lurcher-loving collier, black as night,
Follow your love across the smokeless hill;
Your lamp is out and all the cages still;
Course for her heart and do not miss,
For Sunday soon is past and, Kate, fly not so fast,
For Monday comes when none may kiss:
Be marble to his soot, and to his black be white.

XXII

O the valley in the summer where I and my John
Beside the deep river would walk on and on
While the flowers at our feet and the birds up above
Argued so sweetly on reciprocal love,
And I leaned on his shoulder; "O Johnny, let's play":
But he frowned like thunder and he went away.

O that Friday near Christmas as I well recall
When we went to the Charity Matinee Ball,
The floor was so smooth and the band was so loud
And Johnny so handsome I felt so proud;
"Squeeze me tighter, dear Johnny, let's dance till it's day":
But he frowned like thunder and he went away.

Shall I ever forget at the Grand Opera
When music poured out of each wonderful star?

Diamonds and pearls they hung dazzling down
Over each silver or golden silk gown;
"O John I'm in heaven," I whispered to say:
But he frowned like thunder and he went away.

O but he was as fair as a garden in flower,
As slender and tall as the great Eiffel Tower,
When the waltz throbbed out on the long promenade
O his eyes and his smile they went straight to my heart;
"O marry me, Johnny, I'll love and obey":
But he frowned like thunder and he went away.

O last night I dreamed of you, Johnny, my lover,
You'd the sun on one arm and the moon on the other,
The sea it was blue and the grass it was green,
Every star rattled a round tambourine;
Ten thousand miles deep in a pit there I lay:
But you frowned like thunder and you went away.

XXIII

Over the heather the wet wind blows,
I've lice in my tunic and a cold in my nose.

The rain comes pattering out of the sky,
I'm a Wall soldier, I don't know why.

The mist creeps over the hard grey stone,
My girl's in Tungria; I sleep alone.

Aulus goes hanging around her place,
I don't like his manners, I don't like his face.

Piso's a Christian, he worships a fish;
There'd be no kissing if he had his wish.

221

She gave me a ring but I diced it away;
I want my girl and I want my pay.

When I'm a veteran with only one eye
I shall do nothing but look at the sky.

XXIV

O what is that sound which so thrills the ear
   Down in the valley drumming, drumming?
Only the scarlet soldiers, dear,
   The soldiers coming.

O what is that light I see flashing so clear
   Over the distance brightly, brightly?
Only the sun on their weapons, dear,
   As they step lightly.

O what are they doing with all that gear,
   What are they doing this morning, this morning?
Only their usual manoeuvres, dear,
   Or perhaps a warning.

O why have they left the road down there,
   Why are they suddenly wheeling, wheeling?
Perhaps a change in their orders, dear.
   Why are you kneeling?

O haven't they stopped for the doctor's care,
   Haven't they reined their horses, their horses?
Why, they are none of them wounded, dear,
   None of these forces.

O is it the parson they want, with white hair,
   Is it the parson, is it, is it?

No, they are passing his gateway, dear,
    Without a visit.

O it must be the farmer who lives so near.
    It must be the farmer so cunning, so cunning?
They have passed the farmyard already, dear,
    And now they are running.

O where are you going? Stay with me here!
    Were the vows you swore deceiving, deceiving?
No, I promised to love you, dear,
    But I must be leaving.

O it's broken the lock and splintered the door,
    O it's the gate where they're turning, turning;
Their boots are heavy on the floor
    And their eyes are burning.

XXV

"O where are you going?" said reader to rider,
"That valley is fatal when furnaces burn,
Yonder's the midden whose odours will madden,
That gap is the grave where the tall return."

"O do you imagine," said fearer to farer,
"That dusk will delay on your path to the pass,
Your diligent looking discover the lacking
Your footsteps feel from granite to grass?"

"O what was that bird," said horror to hearer,
"Did you see that shape in the twisted trees?
Behind you swiftly the figure comes softly,
The spot on your skin is a shocking disease?"

"Out of this house"—said rider to reader,
"Yours never will"—said farer to fearer,
"They're looking for you"—said hearer to horror,
As he left them there, as he left them there.

XXVI

"O who can ever gaze his fill,"
　　Farmer and fisherman say,
"On native shore and local hill,
Grudge aching limb or callus on the hand?
Fathers, grandfathers stood upon this land,
And here the pilgrims from our loins shall stand."
　　So farmer and fisherman say
　　In their fortunate heyday:
　　But Death's soft answer drifts across
　　Empty catch or harvest loss
　　　Or an unlucky May.
The earth is an oyster with nothing inside it,
　　Not to be born is the best for man;
The end of toil is a bailiff's order,
　　Throw down the mattock and dance while you can.

"O life's too short for friends who share,"
　　Travellers think in their hearts,
"The city's common bed, the air,
The mountain bivouac and the bathing beach,
Where incidents draw every day from each
Memorable gesture and witty speech."
　　So travellers think in their hearts,
　　Till malice or circumstance parts
　　Them from their constant humour:
　　And slyly Death's coercive rumour
　　　In the silence starts.

A friend is the old old tale of Narcissus,
    Not to be born is the best for man;
An active partner in something disgraceful,
    Change your partner, dance while you can.

"O stretch your hands across the sea,"
    The impassioned lover cries,
"Stretch them towards your harm and me.
Our grass is green, and sensual our brief bed,
The stream sings at its foot, and at its head
The mild and vegetarian beasts are fed."
    So the impassioned lover cries
    Till his storm of pleasure dies:
    From the bedpost and the rocks
    Death's enticing echo mocks,
        And his voice replies.
The greater the love, the more false to its object,
    Not to be born is the best for man;
After the kiss comes the impulse to throttle,
    Break the embraces, dance while you can.

"I see the guilty world forgiven,"
    Dreamer and drunkard sing,
"The ladders let down out of heaven,
The laurel springing from the martyrs' blood,
The children skipping where the weepers stood,
The lovers natural and the beasts all good."
    So dreamer and drunkard sing
    Till day their sobriety bring:
    Parrotwise with death's reply
    From whelping fear and nesting lie,
        Woods and their echoes ring.
The desires of the heart are as crooked as corkscrews,
    Not to be born is the best for man;

The second-best is a formal order,
  The dance's pattern: Dance while you can.
Dance, dance, for the figure is easy,
  The tune is catching and will not stop;
Dance till the stars come down with the rafters;
  Dance, dance, dance till you drop.

XXVII

O who can ever praise enough
The world of his belief?
Harum-scarum childhood plays
In the meadows near his home,
In his woods love knows no wrong,
Travellers ride their placid ways,
In the cool shade of the tomb
Age's trusting footfalls ring.
O who can paint the vivid tree
And grass of phantasy?

But to create it and to guard
Shall be his whole reward:
He shall watch and he shall weep,
All his father's love deny,
To his mother's womb be lost,
Eight nights with a wanton sleep,
Then upon the ninth shall be
Bride and victim to a ghost,
And in the pit of terror thrown
Shall bear the wrath alone.

XXVIII

Say this city has ten million souls,
Some are living in mansions, some are living in holes:
Yet there's no place for us, my dear, yet there's no place for us.

Once we had a country and we thought it fair,
Look in the atlas and you'll find it there:
We cannot go there now, my dear, we cannot go there now.

In the village churchyard there grows an old yew,
Every spring it blossoms anew:
Old passports can't do that, my dear, old passports can't do that.

The consul banged the table and said;
"If you've got no passport you're officially dead":
But we are still alive, my dear, but we are still alive.

Went to a committee; they offered me a chair;
Asked me politely to return next year:
But where shall we go today, my dear, but where shall we
        go today?

Came to a public meeting; the speaker got up and said:
"If we let them in, they will steal our daily bread";
He was talking of you and me, my dear, he was talking of
        you and me.

Thought I heard the thunder rumbling in the sky;
It was Hitler over Europe, saying: "They must die";
O we were in his mind, my dear, O we were in his mind.

Saw a poodle in a jacket fastened with a pin,
Saw a door opened and a cat let in:

But they weren't German Jews, my dear, but they weren't
    German Jews.

Went down the harbour and stood upon the quay,
Saw the fish swimming as if they were free:
Only ten feet away, my dear, only ten feet away.

Walked through a wood, saw the birds in the trees;
They had no politicians and sang at their ease:
They weren't the human race, my dear, they weren't the
    human race.

Dreamed I saw a building with a thousand floors,
A thousand windows and a thousand doors;
Not one of them was ours, my dear, not one of them was ours.

Stood on a great plain in the falling snow;
Ten thousand soldiers marched to and fro:
Looking for you and me, my dear, looking for you and me.

XXIX

Seen when night is silent,
The bean-shaped island
And our ugly comic servant,
Who was observant.

O the verandah and the fruit,
The tiny steamer in the bay
Startling summer with its hoot: —
You have gone away.

XXX

Stop all the clocks, cut off the telephone,
Prevent the dog from barking with a juicy bone,

Silence the pianos and with muffled drum
Bring out the coffin, let the mourners come.

Let aeroplanes circle moaning overhead
Scribbling on the sky the message He Is Dead,
Put crêpe bows round the white necks of the public doves,
Let the traffic policemen wear black cotton gloves.

He was my North, my South, my East and West,
My working week and my Sunday rest,
My noon, my midnight, my talk, my song;
I thought that love would last for ever: I was wrong.

The stars are not wanted now; put out every one:
Pack up the moon and dismantle the sun;
Pour away the ocean and sweep up the woods:
For nothing now can ever come to any good.

XXXI

That night when joy began
Our narrowest veins to flush,
We waited for the flash
Of morning's levelled gun.

But morning let us pass,
And day by day relief
Outgrows his nervous laugh,
Grows credulous of peace,

As mile by mile is seen
No trespasser's reproach,

And love's best glasses reach
No fields but are his own.

XXXII *

Dog   The single creature leads a partial life,
Man by his mind, and by his nose the hound;
He needs the deep emotions I can give,
I scent in him a vaster hunting ground.

Cats   Like calls to like, to share is to relieve
And sympathy the root bears love the flower;
He feels in us, and we in him perceive
A common passion for the lonely hour.

Cats   We move in our apartness and our pride
About the decent dwellings he has made:
Dog   In all his walks I follow at his side,
His faithful servant and his loving shade.

XXXIII

The summer quickens all,
Scatters its promises
To you and me no less,
Though neither can compel

The wish to last the year,
The longest look to live,
The urgent word survive
The movement of the air.

But, loving now, let none
Think of divided days

When we shall choose from ways,
All of them evil, one;

Look on with stricter brows
The sacked and burning town,
The ice-sheet moving down,
The fall of an old house.

XXXIV *

Though determined Nature can
Only offer human eyes
One alternative to sleep,
Opportunity to weep,
    Who can refuse her?
Error does not end with youth
But increases in the man;
    All truth, only truth,
Carries the ambiguous lies
    Of the Accuser.

Though some sudden fire of grace
Visit our mortality
Till a whole life tremble for
Swans upon a river or
    Some passing stranger,
Hearts by envy are possessed
From the moment that they praise;
    To rejoice, to be blessed,
Places us immediately
    In mortal danger

Though we cannot follow how
Evil miracles are done

Through the medium of a kiss,
Aphrodite's garden is
    A haunted region;
For the very signs whereby
Lovers register their vow,
    With a look, with a sigh,
Summon to their meetings One
    Whose name is Legion.

We, my darling, for our sins
Suffer in each other's woe,
Read in injured eyes and hands
How we broke divine commands
    And served the Devil.
Who is passionate enough
When the punishment begins?
    O my love, O my love,
In the night of fire and snow
    Save me from evil.

XXXV

Underneath the abject willow,
    Lover, sulk no more:
Act from thought should quickly follow.
    What is thinking for?
Your unique and moping station
    Proves you cold;
    Stand up and fold
Your map of desolation.

Bells that toll across the meadows
    From the sombre spire

Toll for these unloving shadows
   Love does not require.
All that lives may love; why longer
   Bow to loss
   With arms across?
Strike and you shall conquer.

Geese in flocks above you flying
   Their direction know,
Brooks beneath the thin ice flowing
   To their oceans go.
Dark and dull is your distraction,
   Walk then, come,
   No longer numb
Into your satisfaction.

XXXVI

(Tune: Frankie & Johnny)

Victor was a little baby,
   Into this world he came;
His father took him on his knee and said:
   "Don't dishonour the family name."

Victor looked up at his father
   Looked up with big round eyes:
His father said; "Victor, my only son,
   Don't you ever ever tell lies."

Victor and his father went riding
   Out in a little dog-cart;
His father took a Bible from his pocket and read;
   "Blessed are the pure in heart."

It was a frosty December,
　　　　It wasn't the season for fruits;
His father fell dead of heart disease
　　　　While lacing up his boots.

It was a frosty December
　　　　When into his grave he sank;
His uncle found Victor a post as cashier
　　　　In the Midland Counties Bank.

It was a frosty December
　　　　Victor was only eighteen,
But his figures were neat and his margins straight
　　　　And his cuffs were always clean.

He took a room at the Peveril,
　　　　A respectable boarding-house;
And Time watched Victor day after day
　　　　As a cat will watch a mouse.

The clerks slapped Victor on the shoulder;
　　　　"Have you ever had a woman?" they said,
"Come down town with us on Saturday night."
　　　　Victor smiled and shook his head.

The manager sat in his office,
　　　　Smoked a Corona cigar:
Said; "Victor's a decent fellow but
　　　　He's too mousey to go far."

Victor went up to his bedroom,
　　　　Set the alarum bell;
Climbed into bed, took his Bible and read
　　　　Of what happened to Jezebel.

234

It was the First of April,
      Anna to the Peveril came;
Her eyes, her lips, her breasts, her hips
      And her smile set men aflame.

She looked as pure as a schoolgirl
      On her First Communion day,
But her kisses were like the best champagne
      When she gave herself away.

It was the Second of April,
      She was wearing a coat of fur;
Victor met her upon the stairs
      And he fell in love with her.

The first time he made his proposal,
      She laughed, said; "I'll never wed";
The second time there was a pause;
      Then she smiled and shook her head.

Anna looked into her mirror,
      Pouted and gave a frown:
Said; "Victor's as dull as a wet afternoon
      But I've got to settle down."

The third time he made his proposal,
      As they walked by the Reservoir:
She gave him a kiss like a blow on the head,
      Said; "You are my heart's desire."

They were married early in August,
      She said; "Kiss me, you funny boy":
Victor took her in his arms and said;
      "O my Helen of Troy."

It was the middle of September,
  Victor came to the office one day;
He was wearing a flower in his buttonhole,
  He was late but he was gay.

The clerks were talking of Anna,
  The door was just ajar:
One said; "Poor old Victor, but where ignorance
  Is bliss, etcetera."

Victor stood still as a statue,
  The door was just ajar:
One said; "God, what fun I had with her
  In that Baby Austin car."

Victor walked out into the High Street,
  He walked to the edge of the town;
He came to the allotments and the rubbish heaps
  And his tears came tumbling down.

Victor looked up at the sunset
  As he stood there all alone;
Cried: "Are you in Heaven, Father?"
  But the sky said "Address not known."

Victor looked up at the mountains,
  The mountains all covered with snow:
Cried; "Are you pleased with me, Father?"
  And the answer came back, No.

Victor came to the forest,
  Cried: "Father, will she ever be true?"
And the oaks and the beeches shook their heads
  And they answered: "Not to you."

Victor came to the meadow
     Where the wind went sweeping by:
Cried; "O Father, I love her so,"
     But the wind said, "She must die."

Victor came to the river
     Running so deep and so still:
Crying; "O Father, what shall I do?"
     And the river answered, "Kill."

Anna was sitting at table,
     Drawing cards from a pack;
Anna was sitting at table
     Waiting for her husband to come back.

It wasn't the Jack of Diamonds
     Nor the Joker she drew at first;
It wasn't the King or the Queen of Hearts
     But the Ace of Spades reversed.

Victor stood in the doorway,
     He didn't utter a word:
She said; "What's the matter, darling?"
     He behaved as if he hadn't heard.

There was a voice in his left ear,
     There was a voice in his right,
There was a voice at the base of his skull
     Saying, "She must die tonight."

Victor picked up a carving-knife,
     His features were set and drawn,
Said; "Anna, it would have been better for you
     If you had not been born."

Anna jumped up from the table,
    Anna started to scream,
But Victor came slowly after her
    Like a horror in a dream.

She dodged behind the sofa,
    She tore down a curtain rod,
But Victor came slowly after her:
    Said; "Prepare to meet thy God."

She managed to wrench the door open,
    She ran and she didn't stop.
But Victor followed her up the stairs
    And he caught her at the top.

He stood there above the body,
    He stood there holding the knife;
And the blood ran down the stairs and sang,
    "I'm the Resurrection and the Life."

They tapped Victor on the shoulder,
    They took him away in a van;
He sat as quiet as a lump of moss
    Saying, "I am the Son of Man."

Victor sat in a corner
    Making a woman of clay:
Saying; "I am Alpha and Omega, I shall come
    To judge the earth one day."

XXXVII

Warm are the still and lucky miles,
White shores of longing stretch away,

The light of recognition fills
    The whole great day, and bright
The tiny world of lovers' arms.

Silence invades the breathing wood
Where drowsy limbs a treasure keep,
Now greenly falls the learned shade
    Across the sleeping brows
And stirs their secret to a smile.

Restored! Returned! The lost are born
On seas of shipwreck home at last:
See! In the fire of praising burns
    The dry dumb past, and we
The life-day long shall part no more.

XXXVIII

What's in your mind, my dove, my coney;
Do thoughts grow like feathers, the dead end of life;
Is it making of love or counting of money,
Or raid on the jewels, the plans of a thief?

Open your eyes, my dearest dallier;
Let hunt with your hands for escaping me;
Go through the motions of exploring the familiar;
Stand on the brink of the warm white day.

Rise with the wind, my great big serpent;
Silence the birds and darken the air;
Change me with terror, alive in a moment;
Strike for the heart and have me there.

Part IV

DEPRAVITY

A Sermon

Note

I can only hope that this piece will seem meaningless to those who are not professing Christians, and that those who are, and consequently know that it is precisely in their religious life that the worst effects of the Fall are manifested, will not misinterpret it as simple anticlericalism which always implies a flattery of the laity.

It is concerned with two temptations: the constant tendency of the spiritual life to degenerate into an aesthetic performance; and the fatal ease with which Conscience, i.e., the voice of God, is replaced by "my conscience," i.e., the Super-Ego which, as a writer in Punch remarked some years ago, "is very genteel," and holds one variant or another of the Dualist heresy.

Depravity : A Sermon

What was the weather on Eternity's worst day? And where was that Son of God during the fatal second: pausing before a mirror in an anteroom, or in the Supreme Presence Itself, in the middle of an awful crescendo of praise, or again, withdrawn apart, regarding pensively the unspeakable beauties of the heavenly landscape?

The divinest of books says nothing. Of the primary crises of the soul no history is ever written. Yon citizen crossing the street while the policeman holds up the traffic like the Red Sea: he leaves one curb an honest man; but, ah, quickly, Constable, handcuffs out! Roll on, you heavy lorries! He is Pharaoh! Mercifully exterminate this pest! Too late, the warning cannot be given. It's done, the poison administered, the soul infected. The other curb is reached and our John Bull, honest-seeming, unsuspected, is free to walk away, within a few years to involve widows in financial ruin or a party of school children in some frightful accident.

So, on this inconceivably more catastrophic occasion, no door banged, no dog barked. There was no alarm of any kind. But consider its importance! No judge's sentence had yet been passed. Basedow's Disease had not occurred. Love. Joy. Peace. God. No words but these. No population but angels. And after . . . the whole lexicon of sin: the sullen proletariat of hell!

What, then, of the central figure in the tragedy: First among the Sons of God? Power? No Caliph or Mikado had one grain of it. Beauty? Alcibiades beside him were extraordinarily plain. Wits? Einstein were a stammerer. But for him it was not enough. For him, nothing was enough, but the unique majority of God. That or nothing! That or (ah, had he reckoned with the dread alternative!) unqualified ruin. Alas, for us he raised the question; but the answer was to lie with another!

O, even then, when the first thought tempted, was all irrevocably lost? Was there not still time, wonderful creature, to cast it from you with a phew of disgust? It doesn't matter now. Altered for ever and for the worse, he went out to corrupt others, to form his notorious and infamous societies. Gone for ever was the frank handshake, the obvious look, the direct and simple speech. The Golden Age was definitely over. Language had become symbolic, gesture a code of signals. The arrangement of books on a table conveyed a shame-faced message: flowers in a vase expressed some unsavoury *double entendre*. Personalities acquired a new and sinister significance, lost all but that. For or against: On this side of the ledger or on that. Gabriel and Michael: Out of the question. What glorious praise! Demagorgan: Safe. What a shameful comment! Abdiel and Azazael: Perhaps. Oh, beware, you unsuspecting pair! This is a terrible examination, decisive of your everlasting career. This is your only chance. There are but two colours for you to choose, the whitest white or the blackest black; salvation or damnation at one hundred per cent. Azazael chooses. What? The Black. Miserable, unlucky he! He's failed. Now, Abdiel! You hesitate? Quick, man, the White! Bravissimo, he passes! Baffled, they slink away to make their preparations. Too late for diplomacy or apologetic telegrams. It is war.

On the details of that appalling combat, History is mercifully silent. To the vanquished, unable to consider such reminiscences without a shudder, the subject is tabu: And the victors, to whom all boasting is by nature abhorrent, have been content to leave the matter in a decent obscurity. Remember, they were divine, and therefore omniscient, omnipotent. No new-fangled auxiliary arms, the value of which is realised only by the few enthusiastic subalterns, no depth-charges or detectors, no camouflage, no poison-gas which in times of peace even generals do not see how they could bring themselves to use, no technique of deployment or barrage can have been unknown to them. It was conflict on an astronomical scale and with the gloves off. Here were no Quakers, strikers or International Red Cross, no questions of colonies or reparations. Where all were committed absolutely, there could be no ironic misgivings.

Every schoolboy knows the result. To the rebels it was destruction. The reservoirs of the Divine Wrath were inexhaustible. Nothing was signed. There was no one left to discharge so unnecessary an office. Into the fosse of Hell they fell like water.

Yet, my friends, you and I know that the events I have just narrated were not the last. Would God they had been! The scene of operations was transferred to another front, to us. Impotent to attack Him directly, the defeated sought to strike at God through His creatures, to wound where it was most tender, His artist's love. And, to our shame, they succeeded. The world became an everlasting invalid. Of course, God could have dismissed us with a snap of His fingers. One little stellar collision and . . . no more trouble for him. Why not? All reason was for it. It would have been quite cricket. But God is no eugenist. There was no talk of sterilisation, euthanasia. Only the treatment of a very merciful and loving physician. He set over us a kindly strictness, appointed His authorities, severe but just, a kind of martial law. He gave them power to govern in His name and access to His presence in their prayers, to make their reports and ask for help and guidance, that through them the people might learn His primary will.

And so, today, we are here for a very good reason. His enemies have launched another offensive, on the grandest scale, perhaps, that this poor planet of ours has ever witnessed. As on the first awful occasion in Eden, so now: under the same deluding banner of Freedom. For their technique of propaganda has never varied; it has been far too successful for them to need to change it, to suggest that it is in the human interest to destroy God. In silk-clad China or the naked archipelagos, in the Bermudas or Brighton, in the stone hamlet among the beechwoods or the steel flats of the metropolis, that three-syllable whisper: "You are God," has been, is and, alas, will be sufficient to convert in an instant the chapped-handed but loyal ploughboy, the patient sufferer from incurable disease, the tired economical student or the beautiful juvenile mama into a very spiteful maniac indeed, into whose hands modern science has placed an all-too-efficient axe.

I should like just to try and imagine for one moment what the world would be like if this lunacy with its grim fanatic theories were to spread over the civilised globe. I tell you there would exist a tyranny compared with which a termite colony would seem dangerously lax. No family love. Sons would inform against fathers, cheerfully send them to the execution cellars. Mothers send their daughters to the mines. No romance. Even the peasant must beget that standard child under laboratory conditions. Motherhood would be by licence. Truth and Beauty would be proscribed as dangerously obstructive. To be beautiful would be treason against the State, Thought a sabotage deadly to the thinker. No books, no art, no music. A year of this, I say, and even the grass would cease to grow, flowers would not risk appearance, heifers would not dare to calve.

So you see our job. God has given us extraordinary privileges, but if there be any doubters, cowards wavering like to cowl on an oast-house, to these I say: "Go out of that door before it is too late!" Only those whose decisions are swift as the sirocco, senses keen as the finest mirror galvanometer, will constant as the standard inch and of a chemical purity need apply. As for the enemy, those rats! they shall skedaddle like a brook. Nature herself is on our side. Their boasts are vain. You cannot threaten a thunderstorm with a revolver. They shall be trapped by the stalks of flowers. Sheep shall chase them away. Useless for them to imitate natural objects: a boulder or a tree. Even the spade-handed moles shall declare their folly!

But mind, God first! To God the glory and let Him reward! God is no summer tourist. We're more than scenery to Him. He has a farmer's eye for ergot and tares. Oh delight higher than Everest and deeper than the Challenger Gulf! His commodores come into His council and His lieutenants know His love. Lord, I confess! I confess! I am all too weak and utterly unworthy. There is no other want. All actions and diversions of the people, their greyhound races, their football competitions, their clumsy acts of love, what are they but the pitiful, maimed expression of that entire passion, the positive tropism of the soul to God?

Oh Father, I am praising Thee, I have always praised Thee, I shall always praise Thee! Listen to the wooden sabots of Thy eager child running to Thy arms! Admit him to the fairs of that blessed country where Thy saints move happily about their neat, clean houses under the blue sky! O windmills, O cocks, O clouds and ponds! Mother is waving from the tiny door! The quilt is turned down in my beautiful blue and gold room! Father, I thank Thee in advance! Everything has been grand! I am coming home!

Part V

THE QUEST

A Sonnet Sequence

The Door

Out of it steps the future of the poor,
Enigmas, executioners and rules,
Her Majesty in a bad temper or
The red-nosed Fool who makes a fool of fools.

Great persons eye it in the twilight for
A past it might so carelessly let in,
A widow with a missionary grin,
The foaming inundation at a roar.

We pile our all against it when afraid,
And beat upon its panels when we die:
By happening to be open once, it made

Enormous Alice see a wonderland
That waited for her in the sunshine, and,
Simply by being tiny, made her cry.

The Preparations

All had been ordered weeks before the start
From the best firms at such work; instruments
To take the measure of all queer events,
And drugs to move the bowels or the heart.

A watch, of course, to watch impatience fly,
Lamps for the dark and shades against the sun;
Foreboding, too, insisted on a gun
And coloured beads to soothe a savage eye.

In theory they were sound on Expectation
Had there been situations to be in;
Unluckily they were their situation:

251

One should not give a poisoner medicine,
A conjurer fine apparatus, nor
A rifle to a melancholic bore.

The Crossroads

The friends who met here and embraced are gone,
Each to his own mistake; one flashes on
To fame and ruin in a rowdy lie,
A village torpor holds the other one,
Some local wrong where it takes time to die:
The empty junction glitters in the sun.

So at all quays and crossroads: who can tell,
O places of decision and farewell,
To what dishonor all adventure leads,
What parting gift could give that friend protection,
So orientated, his salvation needs
The Bad Lands and the sinister direction?

All landscapes and all weathers freeze with fear,
But none have ever thought, the legends say,
The time allowed made it impossible;
For even the most pessimistic set
The limit of their errors at a year.
What friends could there be left then to betray,
What joy take longer to atone for? Yet
Who would complete without the extra day
The journey that should take no time at all?

The Pilgrim

No window in his suburb lights that bedroom where
A little fever heard large afternoons at play:

His meadows multiply; that mill, though, is not there
Which went on grinding at the back of love all day.

Nor all his weeping ways through weary wastes have found
The castle where his Greater Hallows are interned;
For broken bridges halt him, and dark thickets round
Some ruin where an evil heritage was burned.

Could he forget a child's ambition to be old
And institutions where it learned to wash and lie,
He'd tell the truth for which he thinks himself too young,

That everywhere on the horizon of his sigh
Is now, as always, only waiting to be told
To be his father's house and speak his mother tongue.

The City

In villages from which their childhoods came
Seeking Necessity, they had been taught
Necessity by nature is the same,
No matter how or by whom it be sought.

The city, though, assumed no such belief,
But welcomed each as if he came alone,
The nature of Necessity like grief
Exactly corresponding to his own.

And offered them so many, every one
Found some temptation fit to govern him;
And settled down to master the whole craft

Of being nobody; sat in the sun
During the lunch-hour round the fountain rim;
And watched the country kids arrive, and laughed.

The First Temptation

Ashamed to be the darling of his grief
He joined a gang of rowdy stories where
His gift for magic quickly made him chief
Of all these boyish powers of the air;

Who turned his hungers into Roman food,
The town's asymmetry into a park;
All hours took taxis; any solitude
Became his flattered duchess in the dark.

But if he wished for anything less grand,
The nights came padding after him like wild
Beasts that meant harm, and all the doors cried Thief;

And when Truth met him and put out her hand,
He clung in panic to his tall belief
And shrank away like an ill-treated child.

The Second Temptation

The library annoyed him with its look
Of calm belief in being really there;
He threw away a rival's silly book,
And clattered panting up the spiral stair.

Swaying upon the parapet he cried:
"O Uncreated Nothing, set me free,
Now let Thy perfect be identified,
Unending passion of the Night, with Thee."

And his long suffering flesh, that all the time
Had felt the simple cravings of the stone
And hoped to be rewarded for her climb,

Took it to be a promise when he spoke
That now at last she would be left alone,
And plunged into the college quad, and broke.

The Third Temptation

He watched with all his organs of concern
How princes walk, what wives and children say;
Reopened old graves in his heart to learn
What laws the dead had died to disobey.

And came reluctantly to his conclusion:
"All the arm-chair philosophers are false;
To love another adds to the confusion;
The song of pity is the Devil's Waltz."

And bowed to fate and was successful so
That soon he was the king of all the creatures:
Yet, shaking in an autumn nightmare, saw,

Approaching down a ruined corridor,
A figure with his own distorted features
That wept, and grew enormous, and cried Woe.

The Tower

This is an architecture for the odd;
Thus heaven was attacked by the afraid,
So once, unconsciously, a virgin made
Her maidenhead conspicuous to a god.

Here on dark nights while worlds of triumph sleep
Lost Love in abstract speculation burns,
And exiled Will to politics returns
In epic verse that lets its traitors weep.

Yet many come to wish their tower a well;
For those who dread to drown of thirst may die,
Those who see all become invisible:

Here great magicians, caught in their own spell,
Long for a natural climate as they sigh
"Beware of Magic" to the passer-by.

The Presumptuous

They noticed that virginity was needed
To trap the unicorn in every case,
But not that, of those virgins who succeeded,
A high percentage had an ugly face.

The hero was as daring as they thought him,
But his peculiar boyhood missed them all;
The angel of a broken leg had taught him
The right precautions to avoid a fall.

So in presumption they set forth alone
On what, for them, was not compulsory:
And stuck halfway to settle in some cave
With desert lions to domesticity;

Or turned aside to be absurdly brave,
And met the ogre and were turned to stone.

The Average

His peasant parents killed themselves with toil
To let their darling leave a stingy soil
For any of those smart professions which
Encourage shallow breathing, and grow rich.

The pressure of their fond ambition made
Their shy and country-loving child afraid
No sensible career was good enough,
Only a hero could deserve such love.

So here he was without maps or supplies,
A hundred miles from any decent town;
The desert glared into his blood-shot eyes;

The silence roared displeasure: looking down,
He saw the shadow of an Average Man
Attempting the Exceptional, and ran.

Vocation

Incredulous, he stared at the amused
Official writing down his name among
Those whose request to suffer was refused.

The pen ceased scratching: though he came too late
To join the martyrs, there was still a place
Among the tempters for a caustic tongue

To test the resolution of the young
With tales of the small failings of the great,
And shame the eager with ironic praise.

Though mirrors might be hateful for a while,
Women and books should teach his middle age
The fencing wit of an informal style
To keep the silences at bay and cage
His pacing manias in a worldly smile.

The Useful

The over-logical fell for the witch
Whose argument converted him to stone;
Thieves rapidly absorbed the over-rich;
The over-popular went mad alone,
And kisses brutalised the over-male.

As agents their effectiveness soon ceased;
Yet, in proportion as they seemed to fail,
Their instrumental value was increased
To those still able to obey their wish.

By standing stones the blind can feel their way,
Wild dogs compel the cowardly to fight,
Beggars assist the slow to travel light,
And even madmen manage to convey
Unwelcome truths in lonely gibberish.

The Way

Fresh addenda are published every day
To the encyclopaedia of the Way.

Linguistic notes and scientific explanations,
And texts for schools with modernised spelling and illustrations.

Now everyone knows the hero must choose the old horse,
Abstain from liquor and sexual intercourse,

And look out for a stranded fish to be kind to:
Now everyone thinks he could find, had he a mind to,

The way through the waste to the chapel in the rock
For a vision of the Triple Rainbow or the Astral Clock.

Forgetting his information comes mostly from married men
Who liked fishing and a flutter on the horses now and then.

And how reliable can any truth be that is got
By observing oneself and then just inserting a Not?

The Lucky

Suppose he'd listened to the erudite committee,
He would have only found where not to look;
Suppose his terrier when he whistled had obeyed,
It would not have unearthed the buried city;
Suppose he had dismissed the careless maid,
The cryptogram would not have fluttered from the book.

"It was not I," he cried as, healthy and astounded,
He stepped across a predecessor's skull;
"A nonsense jingle simply came into my head
And left the intellectual Sphinx dumbfounded;
I won the Queen because my hair was red;
The terrible adventure is a little dull."

Hence Failure's torment: "Was I doomed in any case,
Or would I not have failed had I believed in Grace?"

The Hero

He parried every question that they hurled:
"What did the Emperor tell you?" "Not to push?"
"What is the greatest wonder of the world?"
"The bare man Nothing in the Beggar's Bush."

Some muttered, "He is cagey for effect.
A hero owes a duty to his fame.
He looks too like a grocer for respect."
Soon they slipped back into his Christian name.

The only difference that could be seen
From those who'd never risked their lives at all
Was his delight in details and routine.

For he was always glad to mow the grass,
Pour liquids from large bottles into small,
Or look at clouds through bits of colored glass.

Adventure

Others had swerved off to the left before,
But only under protest from outside,
Embittered robbers outlawed by the Law,
Lepers in terror of the terrified.

Now no one else accused these of a crime;
They did not look ill: old friends, overcome,
Stared as they rolled away from talk and time
Like marbles out into the blank and dumb.

The crowd clung all the closer to convention,
Sunshine and horses, for the sane know why
The even numbers should ignore the odd:

The Nameless is what no free people mention;
Successful men know better than to try
To see the face of their Absconded God.

The Adventurers

Spinning upon their central thirst like tops,
They went the Negative Way toward the Dry;
By empty caves beneath an empty sky
They emptied out their memories like slops

Which made a foul marsh as they dried to death,
Where monsters bred who forced them to forget
The lovelies their consent avoided; yet,
Still praising the Absurd with their last breath,

They seeded out into their miracles:
The images of each grotesque temptation
Became some painter's happiest inspiration;

And barren wives and burning virgins came
To drink the pure cold water of their wells,
And wish for beaux and children in their name.

The Waters

Poet, oracle and wit
Like unsuccessful anglers by
The ponds of apperception sit,
Baiting with the wrong request
The vectors of their interest;
At nightfall tell the angler's lie.

With time in tempest everywhere,
To rafts of frail assumption cling
The saintly and the insincere;
Enraged phenomena bear down

In overwhelming waves to drown
Both sufferer and suffering.

The waters long to hear our question put
Which would release their longed-for answer, but.

The Garden

Within these gates all opening begins:
White shouts and flickers through its green and red,
Where children play at seven earnest sins
And dogs believe their tall conditions dead.

Here adolescence into number breaks
The perfect circle time can draw on stone,
And flesh forgives division as it makes
Another's moment of consent its own.

All journeys die here; wish and weight are lifted:
Where often round some old maid's desolation
Roses have flung their glory like a cloak,

The gaunt and great, the famed for conversation
Blushed in the stare of evening as they spoke,
And felt their center of volition shifted.

Part VI

NEW YEAR LETTER

(January 1, 1940)

TO ELIZABETH MAYER

Part I

Under the familiar weight
Of winter, conscience and the State,
In loose formations of good cheer,
Love, language, loneliness and fear,
Towards the habits of next year,
Along the streets the people flow,
Singing or sighing as they go:
Exalté, piano, or in doubt,
All our reflections turn about
A common meditative norm,
Retrenchment, Sacrifice, Reform.

Twelve months ago in Brussels, I
Heard the same wishful-thinking sigh
As round me, trembling on their beds,
Or taut with apprehensive dreads,
The sleepless guests of Europe lay
Wishing the centuries away,
And the low mutter of their vows
Went echoing through her haunted house,
As on the verge of happening
There crouched the presence of The Thing.
All formulas were tried to still
The scratching on the window-sill,
All bolts of custom made secure
Against the pressure on the door,
But up the staircase of events
Carrying his special instruments,
To every bedside all the same
The dreadful figure swiftly came.

Yet Time can moderate his tone
When talking to a man alone,

And the same sun whose neutral eye
All florid August from the sky
Had watched the earth behave and seen
Strange traffic on her brown and green,
Obedient to some hidden force
A ship abruptly change her course,
A train make an unwonted stop,
A little crowd smash up a shop,
Suspended hatreds crystallise
In visible hostilities,
Vague concentrations shrink to take
The sharp crude patterns generals make,
The very morning that the war
Took action on the Polish floor,
Lit up America and on
A cottage in Long Island shone
Where Buxtehude as we played
One of his *passacaglias* made
Our minds a *civitas* of sound
Where nothing but assent was found,
For art had set in order sense
And feeling and intelligence,
And from its ideal order grew
Our local understanding too.

To set in order—that's the task
Both Eros and Apollo ask;
For Art and Life agree in this
That each intends a synthesis,
That order which must be the end
That all self-loving things intend
Who struggle for their liberty,
Who use, that is, their will to be.
Though order never can be willed

But is the state of the fulfilled,
For will but wills its opposite
And not the whole in which they fit,
The symmetry disorders reach
When both are equal each to each,
Yet in intention all are one,
Intending that their wills be done
Within a peace where all desires
Find each in each what each requires,
A true *Gestalt* where indiscrete
Perceptions and extensions meet.
Art in intention is mimesis
But, realised, the resemblance ceases;
Art is not life and cannot be
A midwife to society.
For art is a *fait accompli*.
What they should do, or how or when
Life-order comes to living men
It cannot say, for it presents
Already lived experience
Through a convention that creates
Autonomous completed states.
Though their particulars are those
That each particular artist knows,
Unique events that once took place
Within a unique time and space,
In the new field they occupy,
The unique serves to typify,
Becomes, though still particular,
An algebraic formula,
An abstract model of events
Derived from dead experiments,
And each life must itself decide
To what and how it be applied.

Great masters who have shown mankind
An order it has yet to find,
What if all pedants say of you
As personalities be true?
All the more honor to you then
If, weaker than some other men,
You had the courage that survives
Soiled, shabby, egotistic lives,
If poverty or ugliness,
Ill-health or social unsuccess
Hunted you out of life to play
At living in another way;
Yet the live quarry all the same
Were changed to huntsmen in the game,
And the wild furies of the past,
Tracked to their origins at last,
Trapped in a medium's artifice,
To charity, delight, increase.
Now large, magnificent, and calm,
Your changeless presences disarm
The sullen generations, still
The fright and fidget of the will,
And to the growing and the weak
Your final transformations speak,
Saying to dreaming "I am deed."
To striving "Courage. I succeed."
To mourning "I remain. Forgive."
And to becoming "I am. Live."

They challenge, warn and witness. Who
That ever has the rashness to
Believe that he is one of those
The greatest of vocations chose,
Is not perpetually afraid

That he's unworthy of his trade,
As round his tiny homestead spread
The grand constructions of the dead,
Nor conscious, as he works, of their
Complete uncompromising stare,
And the surveillance of a board
Whose warrant cannot be ignored?
O often, often must he face,
Whether the critics blame or praise,
Young, high-brow, popular or rich,
That summary tribunal which
In a perpetual session sits,
And answer, if he can, to its
Intense interrogation. Though
Considerate and mild and low
The voices of the questioners,
Although they delegate to us
Both prosecution and defence,
Accept our rules of evidence
And pass no sentence but our own,
Yet, as he faces them alone,
O who can show convincing proof
That he is worthy of their love?
Who ever rose to read aloud
Before that quiet attentive crowd
And did not falter as he read,
Stammer, sit down, and hang his head?
Each one, so liberal is the law,
May choose whom he appears before,
Pick any influential ghost
From those whom he admires the most.
So, when my name is called, I face,
Presiding coldly on my case,
That lean hard-bitten pioneer

Who spoiled a temporal career
And to the supernatural brought
His passion, senses, will and thought,
By Amor Rationalis led
Through the three kingdoms of the dead,
In concrete detail saw the whole
Environment that keeps the soul,
And grasped in its complexity
The Catholic ecology,
Described the savage fauna he
In Malebolge's fissure found,
And fringe of blessed flora round
A juster nucleus than Rome,
Where love had its creative home.
Upon his right appears, as I
Reluctantly must testify
And weigh the sentence to be passed,
A choleric enthusiast,
Self-educated WILLIAM BLAKE,
Who threw his spectre in the lake,
Broke off relations in a curse
With the Newtonian Universe,
But even as a child would pet
The tigers Voltaire never met,
Took walks with them through Lambeth, and
Spoke to Isaiah in the Strand,
And heard inside each mortal thing
Its holy emanation sing.
While to his left upon the bench,
Muttering that terror is not French,
Frowns the young RIMBAUD guilt demands,
The adolescent with red hands,
Skilful, intolerant and quick,
Who strangled an old rhetoric.
The court is full; I catch the eyes

Of several I recognise,
For as I look up from the dock
Embarrassed glances interlock.
There DRYDEN sits with modest smile,
The master of the middle style,
Conscious CATULLUS who made all
His gutter-language musical,
Black TENNYSON whose talents were
For an articulate despair,
Trim, dualistic BAUDELAIRE,
Poet of cities, harbours, whores,
Acedia, gaslight and remorse,
HARDY whose Dorset gave much joy
To one unsocial English boy,
And RILKE whom *die Dinge* bless,
The Santa Claus of loneliness.
And many others, many times,
For I relapse into my crimes,
Time and again have slubbered through
With slip and slapdash what I do,
Adopted what I would disown,
The preacher's loose immodest tone;
Though warned by a great sonneteer
Not to sell cheap what is most dear,
Though horrible old KIPLING cried
"One instant's toil to Thee denied
Stands all eternity's offence,"
I would not give them audience.
Yet still the weak offender must
Beg still for leniency and trust
His power to avoid the sin
Peculiar to his discipline.

The situation of our time
Surrounds us like a baffling crime.

There lies the body half-undressed,
We all had reason to detest,
And all are suspects and involved
Until the mystery is solved
And under lock and key the cause
That makes a nonsense of our laws.
O Who is trying to shield Whom?
Who left a hairpin in the room?
Who was the distant figure seen
Behaving oddly on the green?
Why did the watchdog never bark?
Why did the footsteps leave no mark?
Where were the servants at that hour?
How did a snake get in the tower?
Delayed in the democracies
By departmental vanities,
The rival sergeants run about
But more to squabble than find out,
Yet where the Force has been cut down
To one inspector dressed in brown,
He makes the murderer whom he pleases
And all investigation ceases.
Yet our equipment all the time
Extends the area of the crime
Until the guilt is everywhere,
And more and more we are aware,
However miserable may be
Our parish of immediacy,
How small it is, how, far beyond,
Ubiquitous within the bond
Of one impoverishing sky,
Vast spiritual disorders lie.
Who, thinking of the last ten years,
Does not hear howling in his ears

The Asiatic cry of pain,
The shots of executing Spain
See stumbling through his outraged mind
The Abyssinian, blistered, blind,
The dazed uncomprehending stare
Of the Danubian despair,
The Jew wrecked in the German cell,
Flat Poland frozen into hell,
The silent dumps of unemployed
Whose areté has been destroyed,
And will not feel blind anger draw
His thoughts towards the Minotaur,
To take an early boat for Crete
And rolling, silly, at its feet
Add his small tidbit to the rest?
It lures us all; even the best,
Les hommes de bonne volonté, feel
Their politics perhaps unreal
And all they have believed untrue,
Are tempted to surrender to
The grand apocalyptic dream
In which the persecutors scream
As on the evil Aryan lives
Descends the night of the long knives;
The bleeding tyrant dragged through all
The ashes of his capitol.

Though language may be useless, for
No words men write can stop the war
Or measure up to the relief
Of its immeasurable grief,
Yet truth, like love and sleep, resents
Approaches that are too intense,
And often when the searcher stood

Before the Oracle, it would
Ignore his grown-up earnestness
But not the child of his distress,
For through the Janus of a joke
The candid psychopompos spoke.
May such heart and intelligence
As huddle now in conference
Whenever an impasse occurs
Use the good offices of verse;
May an Accord be reached, and may
This *aide-mémoire* on what they say,
This private minute for a friend,
Be the dispatch that I intend;
Although addressed to a Whitehall
Be under Flying Seal to all
Who wish to read it anywhere,
And, if they open it, *En Clair.*

Part II

Tonight a scrambling decade ends,
And strangers, enemies and friends
Stand once more puzzled underneath
The signpost on the barren heath
Where the rough mountain track divides
To silent valleys on all sides,
Endeavouring to decipher what
Is written on it but cannot,
Nor guess in what direction lies
The overhanging precipice.
Through the pitch-darkness can be heard
Occasionally a muttered word,
And intense in the mountain frost

The heavy breathing of the lost;
Far down below them whence they came
Still flickers feebly a red flame,
A tiny glow in the great void
Where an existence was destroyed;
And now and then a nature turns
To look where her whole system burns
And with a last defiant groan
Shudders her future into stone.

How hard it is to set aside
Terror, concupiscence and pride,
Learn who and where and how we are,
The children of a modest star,
Frail, backward, clinging to the granite
Skirts of a sensible old planet,
Our placid and suburban nurse
In SITTER's swelling universe,
How hard to stretch imagination
To live according to our station.
For we are all insulted by
The mere suggestion that we die
Each moment and that each great I
Is but a process in a process
Within a field that never closes;
As proper people find it strange
That we are changed by what we change,
That no event can happen twice
And that no two existences
Can ever be alike; we'd rather
Be perfect copies of our father,
Prefer our *idées fixes* to be
True of a fixed Reality.
No wonder, then, we lose our nerve

And blubber when we should observe
The patriots of an old idea
No longer sovereign this year,
Get angry like LABELLIÈRE,
Who, finding no invectives hurled
Against a topsy-turvy world
Would right it, earn a quaint renown
By being buried upside-down:
Unwilling to adjust belief,
Go mad in a fantastic grief
Where no adjustment need be done,
Like SARAH WHITEHEAD, the Bank Nun,
For, loving a live brother, she
Wed an impossibility,
Pacing Threadneedle Street in tears,
She watched one door for twenty years
Expecting, what she dared not doubt,
Her hanged embezzler to walk out.

But who, though, is the Prince of Lies
If not the Spirit-that-denies,
The shadow just behind the shoulder
Claiming it's wicked to grow older,
Though we are lost if we turn round
Thinking salvation has been found?
Yet in his very effort to
Prevent the actions we could do,
He has to make the here and now
As marvellous as he knows how
And so engrossing we forget
To drop attention for regret;
Defending relaxation, he
Must show impassioned energy,

And all through tempting us to doubt
Point us the way to find truth out.
Poor cheated MEPHISTOPHELES,
Who think you're doing as you please
In telling us by doing ill
To prove that we possess free will,
Yet do not will the will you do,
For the Determined uses you,
Creation's errand-boy creator,
Diabolus egredietur
Ante pedes ejus—foe,
But so much more effective, though,
Than our well-meaning stupid friends
In driving us towards good ends.
Lame fallen shadow, *retro me,*
Retro but do not go away:
Although, for all your fond insistence,
You have no positive existence,
Are only a recurrent state
Of fear and faithlessness and hate,
That takes on from becoming me
A legal personality,
Assuming your existence is
A rule-of-thumb hypostasis,
For, though no person, you can damn,
So, *credo ut intelligam.*
For how could we get on without you
Who give the *savoir-faire* to doubt you
And keep you in your proper place,
Which is, to push us into grace?

Against his paralysing smile
And honest realistic style

Our best protection is that we
In fact live in eternity.
The sleepless counter of our breaths
That chronicles the births and deaths
Of pious hopes, the short careers
Of dashing promising ideas,
Each congress of the Greater Fears,
The emigration of beliefs,
The voyages of hopes and griefs,
Has no direct experience
Of discontinuous events,
And all our intuitions mock
The formal logic of the clock.
All real perception, it would seem,
Has shifting contours like a dream,
Nor have our feelings ever known
Any discretion but their own.
Suppose we love, not friends or wives,
But certain patterns in our lives,
Effects that take the cause's name,
Love cannot part them all the same;
If in this letter that I send
I write "Elizabeth's my friend,"
I cannot but express my faith
That I is Not-Elizabeth.
For though the intellect in each
Can only think in terms of speech
We cannot practise what we preach.
The cogitations of Descartes
Are where all sound semantics start;
In Ireland the great Berkeley rose
To add new glories to our prose,
But when in the pursuit of knowledge,

Risking the future of his college,
The bishop hid his anxious face,
'Twas more by grammar than by grace
His modest Church-of-England God
Sustained the fellows and the quad.

But the Accuser would not be
In his position, did not he,
Unlike the big-shots of the day,
Listen to what his victims say.
Observing every man's desire
To warm his bottom by the fire
And state his views on Education,
Art, Women, and The Situation,
Has learnt what every woman knows,
The wallflower can become the rose,
Penelope the homely seem
The Helen of Odysseus' dream
If she will look as if she were
A fascinated listener,
Since men will pay large sums to whores
For telling them they are not bores.
So when with overemphasis
We contradict a lie of his,
The great Denier won't deny
But purrs: "You're cleverer than I;
Of course you're absolutely right,
I never saw it in that light.
I see it now: The intellect
That parts the Cause from the Effect
And thinks in terms of Space and Time
Commits a legalistic crime,
For such an unreal severance

Must falsify experience.
Could one not almost say that the
Cold serpent on the poisonous tree
Was *l'esprit de géométrie*,
That Eve and Adam till the Fall
Were totally illogical,
But as they tasted of the fruit
The syllogistic sin took root?
Abstracted, bitter refugees,
They fought over their premises,
Shut out from Eden by the bar
And Chinese Wall of *Barbara*.
O foolishness of man to seek
Salvation in an *ordre logique!*
O cruel intellect that chills
His natural warmth until it kills
The roots of all togetherness!
Love's vigour shrinks to less and less,
On sterile acres governed by
Wage's abstract prudent tie
The hard self-conscious particles
Collide, divide like numerals
In knock-down drag-out *laissez-faire*,
And build no order anywhere.
O when will men show common sense
And throw away intelligence,
That killjoy which discriminates,
Recover what appreciates,
The deep unsnobbish instinct which
Alone can make relation rich,
Upon the *Beischlaf* of the blood
Establish a real neighbourhood
Where art and industry and *mœurs*
Are governed by an *ordre du cœur?*"

The Devil, as is not surprising —
His business is self-advertising —
Is a first-rate psychologist
Who keeps a conscientious list,
To help him in his ticklish deals,
Of what each client thinks and feels,
His school, religion, birth and breeding,
Where he has dined and what he's reading,
By every name he makes a note
Of what quotations to misquote,
And flings at every author's head
Something a favorite author said.
"The Arts? Well, FLAUBERT didn't say
Of artists: *'Ils sont dans le vrai.'*
Democracy? Ask BAUDELAIRE:
'Un esprit Belge,' a soiled affair
Of gas and steam and table-turning.
Truth? ARISTOTLE was discerning:
'In crowds I am a friend of myth.'"
Then, as I start protesting, with
The air of one who understands
He puts a RILKE in my hands.
"You know the *Elegies*, I'm sure —
O Seligkeit der Kreatur
Die immer bleibt in Schoosse — womb,
In English, is a rhyme to tomb."
He moves on tiptoe round the room,
Turns on the radio to mark
Isolde's *Sehnsucht* for the dark.

But all his tactics are dictated
By problems he himself created,
For as the great schismatic who
First split creation into two

He did what it could never do,
Inspired it with the wish to be
Diversity in unity,
An action which has put him in,
Pledged as he is to Rule-by-Sin,
As ambiguous a position
As any Irish politician,
For, torn between conflicting needs,
He's doomed to fail if he succeeds,
And his neurotic longing mocks
Him with its self-made paradox
To be both god and dualist.
For, if dualities exist,
What happens to the god? If there
Are any cultures anywhere
With other values than his own,
How can it possibly be shown
That his are not subjective or
That all life is a state of war?
While, if the monist view be right,
How is it possible to fight?
If love has been annihilated
There's only hate left to be hated.
To say two different things at once,
To wage offensives on two fronts,
And yet to show complete conviction,
Requires the purpler kinds of diction,
And none appreciate as he
Polysyllabic oratory.
All vague idealistic art
That coddles the uneasy heart
Is up his alley, and his pigeon
The woozier species of religion,
Even a novel, play or song,

If loud, lugubrious and long;
He knows the bored will not unmask him
But that he's lost if someone ask him
To come the hell in off the links
And say exactly what he thinks.
To win support of any kind
He has to hold before the mind
Amorphous shadows it can hate,
Yet constantly postpone the date
Of what he's made The Grand Attraction,
Putting an end to them by action
Because he knows, were he to win,
Man could do evil but not sin.
To sin is to act consciously
Against what seems necessity,
A possibility cut out
In any world that excludes doubt.
So victory could do no more
Than make us what we were before,
Beasts with a Rousseauistic charm
Unconscious we were doing harm.
Politically, then, he's right
To keep us shivering all night,
Watching for dawn from Pisgah's height,
And to sound earnest as he paints
The new Geneva of the saints,
To strike the poses as he speaks
Of David's too too Empire Greeks,
Look forward with the cheesecake air
Of one who crossed the Delaware.
A realist, he has always said:
"It is Utopian to be dead,
For only on the Other Side
Are Absolutes all satisfied

Where, at the bottom of the graves,
Low Probability behaves."

The False Association is
A favorite strategy of his:
Induce men to associate
Truth with a lie, then demonstrate
The lie and they will, in truth's name,
Treat babe and bath-water the same,
A trick that serves him in good stead
At all times. It was thus he led
The early Christians to believe
All Flesh unconscious on the eve
Of the Word's temporal interference
With the old Adam of Appearance;
That almost any moment they
Would see the trembling consuls pray,
Knowing that as their hope grew less
So would their heavenly worldliness,
Their early agapë decline
To a late lunch with Constantine.
Thus WORDSWORTH fell into temptation
In France during a long vacation,
Saw in the fall of the Bastille
The Parousia of liberty,
And weaving a platonic dream
Round a provisional régime
That sloganised the Rights of Man,
A liberal fellow-traveller ran
With Sans-culotte and Jacobin,
Nor guessed what circles he was in,
But ended as the Devil knew
An earnest Englishman would do,
Left by Napoleon in the lurch,

Supporting the Established Church,
The Congress of Vienna and
The Squire's paternalistic hand.

Like his, our lives have been coeval
With a political upheaval,
Like him, we had the luck to see
A rare discontinuity,
Old Russia suddenly mutate
Into a proletarian state,
The odd phenomenon, the strange
Event of qualitative change.
Some dreamed, as students always can,
It realised the potential Man,
A higher species brought to birth
Upon a sixth part of the earth,
While others settled down to read
The theory that forecast the deed
And found their humanistic view
In question from the German who,
Obscure in gaslit London, brought
To human consciousness a thought
It thought unthinkable, and made
Another consciousness afraid.
What if his hate distorted? Much
Was hateful that he had to touch.
What if he erred? He flashed a light
On facts where no one had been right.
The father-shadow that he hated
Weighed like an Alp; his love, frustrated,
Negating as it was negated,
Burst out in boils; his animus
Outlawed him from himself; but thus,
And only thus, perhaps, could he

Have come to his discovery.
Heroic charity is rare;
Without it, what except despair
Can shape the hero who will dare
The desperate catabasis
Into the snarl of the abyss
That always lies just underneath
Our jolly picnic on the heath
Of the agreeable, where we bask,
Agreed on what we will not ask,
Bland, sunny and adjusted by
The light of the accepted lie?
As he explored the muttering tomb
Of a museum reading room,
The Dagon of the General Will
Fell in convulsions and lay still;
The tempting Contract of the rich,
Revealed as an abnormal witch,
Fled with a shriek, for as he spoke
The justifying magic broke;
The garden of the Three Estates
Turned desert, and the Ivory Gates
Of Pure Idea to gates of horn
Through which the Governments are born.
But his analysis reveals
The other side to Him-who-steals
Is He-who-makes-what-is-of-use,
Since, to consume, man must produce;
By Man the Tough Devourer sets
The nature his despair forgets
Of Man Prolific since his birth,
A race creative on the earth,
Whose love of money only shows
That in his heart of hearts he knows

His love is not determined by
A personal or tribal tie
Or color, neighbourhood, or creed,
But universal, mutual need;
Loosed from its shroud of temper, his
Determinism comes to this:
None shall receive unless they give;
All must coöperate to live.
Now he is one with all of those
Who brought an epoch to a close,
With him who ended as he went
Past an archbishop's monument
The slaveowners' mechanics, one
With the ascetic farmer's son
Who, while the Great Plague ran its course,
Drew up a Roman code of Force,
One with the naturalist, who fought
Pituitary headaches, brought
Man's pride to heel at last and showed
His kinship with the worm and toad,
And Order as one consequence
Of the unfettered play of Chance.
Great sedentary Caesars who
Have pacified some dread tabu,
Whose wits were able to withdraw
The *numen* from some local law
And with a single concept brought
Some ancient rubbish heap of thought
To rational diversity,
You are betrayed unless we see
No *codex gentium* we make
It is difficult for Truth to break;
The *Lex Abscondita* evades
The vigilantes in the glades;

Now here, now there, one leaps and cries
"I've got her and I claim the prize,"
But when the rest catch up, he stands
With just a torn blouse in his hands.

We hoped; we waited for the day
The State would wither clean away,
Expecting the Millennium
That theory promised us would come,
It didn't. Specialists must try
To detail all the reasons why;
Meanwhile at least the layman knows
That none are lost so soon as those
Who overlook their crooked nose,
That they grow small who imitate
The mannerisms of the great,
Afraid to be themselves, or ask
What acts are proper to their task,
And that a tiny trace of fear
Is lethal in man's atmosphere.
The rays of Logos take effect,
But not as theory would expect,
For, sterile and diseased by doubt,
The dwarf mutations are thrown out
From Eros' weaving centrosome.

O Freedom still is far from home,
For Moscow is as far as ROME
Or PARIS. Once again we wake
With swimming heads and hands that shake
And stomachs that keep nothing down.
Here's where the devil goes to town
Who knows that nothing suits his book
So well as the hang-over look,

That few drunks feel more awful than
The Simon-pure Utopian.
He calls at breakfast in the rôle
Of blunt but sympathetic soul:
"Well, how's our Socialist this morning?
I could say 'Let this be a warning,'
But no, why should I? Students must
Sow their wild oats at times or bust.
Such things have happened in the lives
Of all the best Conservatives.
I'll fix you something for your liver."
And thus he sells us down the river.
Repenting of our last infraction
We seek atonement in reaction
And cry, nostalgic like a whore,
"I was a virgin still at four."
Perceiving that by sailing near
The Hegelian whirlpool of Idea
Some foolish aliens have gone down,
Lest our democracy should drown
We'd wreck her on the solid rock
Of genteel anarchists like Locke,
Wave at the mechanised barbarian
The vorpal sword of an Agrarian.

O how the devil who controls
The moral asymmetric souls
The either-ors, the mongrel halves
Who find truth in a mirror, laughs.
Yet time and memory are still
Limiting factors on his will;
He cannot always fool us thrice,
For he may never tell us lies,
Just half-truths we can synthesise.

So, hidden in his hocus-pocus,
There lies the gift of double focus,
That magic lamp which looks so dull
And utterly impractical
Yet, if Aladdin use it right,
Can be a sesame to light.

Part III

Across East River in the night
Manhattan is ablaze with light.
No shadow dares to criticise
The popular festivities,
Hard liquor causes everywhere
A general *détente,* and Care
For this state function of Good Will
Is diplomatically ill:
The Old Year dies a noisy death.

Warm in your house, Elizabeth,
A week ago at the same hour
I felt the unexpected power
That drove our ragged egos in
From the dead-ends of greed and sin
To sit down at the wedding feast,
Put shining garments on the least,
Arranged us so that each and all,
The erotic and the logical,
Each felt the *placement* to be such
That he was honored overmuch,
And SCHUBERT sang and MOZART played
And GLUCK and food and friendship made
Our privileged community

That real republic which must be
The State all politicians claim,
Even the worst, to be their aim.

O but it happens every day
To someone. Suddenly the way
Leads straight into their native lands,
The *temenos'* small wicket stands
Wide open, shining at the centre
The well of life, and they may enter.
Though compasses and stars cannot
Direct to that magnetic spot,
Nor Will nor willing-not-to-will,
For there is neither good nor ill,
But free rejoicing energy.
Yet anytime, how casually,
Out of his organised distress
An accidental happiness,
Catching man off his guard, will blow him
Out of his life in time to show him
The field of Being where he may,
Unconscious of Becoming, play
With the Eternal Innocence
In unimpeded utterance.
But perfect Being has ordained
It must be lost to be regained,
And in its orchards grow the tree
And fruit of human destiny,
And man must eat it and depart
At once with gay and grateful heart,
Obedient, reborn, re-aware;
For, if he stop an instant there,
The sky grows crimson with a curse,
The flowers change colour for the worse,

He hears behind his back the wicket
Padlock itself, from the dark thicket
The chuckle with no healthy cause,
And, helpless, sees the crooked claws
Emerging into view and groping
For handholds on the low round coping,
As Horror clambers from the well:
For he has sprung the trap of Hell.

Hell is the being of the lie
That we become if we deny
The laws of consciousness and claim
Becoming and Being are the same,
Being in time, and man discrete
In will, yet free and self-complete;
Its fire the pain to which we go
If we refuse to suffer, though
The one unnecessary grief
Is the vain craving for relief,
When to the suffering we could bear
We add intolerable fear,
Absconding from remembrance, mocked
By our own partial senses, locked
Each in a stale uniqueness, lie
Time-conscious for eternity.

We cannot, then, will Heaven where
Is perfect freedom; our wills there
Must lose the will to operate.
But will is free not to negate
Itself in Hell; we're free to will
Ourselves up Purgatory still,
Consenting parties to our lives,
To love them like attractive wives

Whom we adore but do not trust,
Who cannot love without their lust,
And need their stratagems to win
Truth out of Time. In Time we sin.
But Time is sin and can forgive;
Time is the life with which we live
At least three quarters of our time,
The purgatorial hill we climb,
Where any skyline we attain
Reveals a higher ridge again.
Yet since, however much we grumble,
However painfully we stumble,
Such mountaineering all the same
Is, it would seem, the only game
At which we show a natural skill,
The hardest exercises still
Just those our muscles are the best
Adapted to, its grimmest test
Precisely what our fear suspected,
We have no cause to look dejected
When, wakened from a dream of glory,
We find ourselves in Purgatory,
Back on the same old mountain side
With only guessing for a guide.
To tell the truth, although we stifle
The feeling, are we not a trifle
Relieved to wake on its damp earth?
It's been our residence since birth,
Its inconveniences are known,
And we have made its flaws our own.
Is it not here that we belong,
Where everyone is doing wrong,
And normal our freemartin state,
Half angel and half *petite bête?*

So, perched upon the sharp arête,
When if we do not move we fall,
Yet movement is heretical,
Since over its ironic rocks
No route is truly orthodox,
O once again let us set out,
Our faith well balanced by our doubt,
Admitting every step we make
Will certainly be a mistake,
But still believing we can climb
A little higher every time,
And keep in order, that we may
Ascend the penitential way
That forces our wills to be free,
A reverent frivolity
That suffers each unpleasant test
With scientific interest,
And finds romantic, *faute de mieux,*
Its sad *nostalgie des adieux.*

Around me, pausing as I write,
A tiny object in the night,
Whichever way I look, I mark
Importunate along the dark
Horizon of immediacies
The flares of desperation rise
From signallers who justly plead
Their cause is piteous indeed:
Bewildered, how can I divine
Which is my true Socratic Sign,
Which of these calls to conscience is
For me the *casus fœderis,*
From all the tasks submitted, choose
The *athlon* I must not refuse?

A particle, I must not yield
To particles who claim the field,
Nor trust the demagogue who raves,
A quantum speaking for the waves,
Nor worship blindly the ornate
Grandezza of the Sovereign State.
Whatever wickedness we do
Need not be, orators, for you;
We can at least serve other ends,
Can love the *polis* of our friends
And pray that loyalty may come
To serve mankind's *imperium*.

But why and where and when and how?
O none escape these questions now:
The future which confronts us has
No likeness to that age when, as
Rome's huggermugger unity
Was slowly knocked to pieces by
The uncoördinated blows
Of artless and barbaric foes,
The stressed and rhyming measures rose;
The cities we abandon fall
To nothing primitive at all;
This lust in action to destroy
Is not the pure instinctive joy
Of animals, but the refined
Creation of machines and mind.
We face our self-created choice
As out of Europe comes a voice,
A theologian who denies
What more than twenty centuries
Of Europe have assumed to be
The basis of civility,

Our evil *Daimon* to express
In all its ugly nakedness
What none before dared say aloud,
The metaphysics of the Crowd,
The Immanent Imperative
By which the lost and injured live
In mechanised societies
Where natural intuition dies,
The hitherto-unconscious creed
Of little men who half succeed,
The international result
Of Industry's *Quicunque vult.*

Yet maps and languages and names
Have meaning and their proper claims.
There are two atlases: the one
The public space where acts are done,
In theory common to us all,
Where we are needed and feel small,
The *agora* of work and news
Where each one has the right to choose
His trade, his corner and his way,
And can, again in theory, say
For whose protection he will pay,
And loyalty is help we give
The place where we prefer to live;
The other is the inner space
Of private ownership, the place
That each of us is forced to own,
Like his own life from which it's grown,
The landscape of his will and need
Where he is sovereign indeed,
The state created by his acts
Where he patrols the forest tracts

Planted in childhood, farms the belt
Of doings memorised and felt,
And even if he find it hell
May neither leave it nor rebel.
Two worlds describing their rewards,
That one in tangents, this in chords;
Each lives in one, all in the other,
Here all are kings, there each a brother:
In politics the Fall of Man
From natural liberty began
When, loving power or sloth, he came
Like Burke to think them both the same.

England to me is my own tongue,
And what I did when I was young.
If now, two aliens in New York,
We meet, Elizabeth, and talk
Of friends who suffer in the torn
Old Europe where we both were born,
What this refutes or that confirms,
I can but think our talk in terms
Of images that I have seen,
And England tells me what we mean.
Thus, squalid beery Burton stands
For shoddy thinking of all brands;
The wreck of Rhondda for the mess
We make when for a short success
We split our symmetry apart,
Deny the Reason or the Heart;
Ye Olde Tudor Tea-Shoppe for
The folly of dogmatic law,
While graceless Bournemouth is the sloth
Of men or bureaucrats or both.

No matter where, or whom I meet,
Shop-gazing in a Paris street,
Bumping through Iceland in a bus,
At teas when clubwomen discuss
The latest Federation Plan,
In Pullman washrooms, man to man,
Hearing how circumstance has vexed
A broker who is oversexed,
In houses where they do not drink,
Whenever I begin to think
About the human creature we
Must nurse to sense and decency,
An English area comes to mind,
I see the nature of my kind
As a locality I love,
Those limestone moors that stretch from BROUGH
To HEXHAM and the ROMAN WALL,
There is my symbol of us all.
There, where the EDEN leisures through
Its sandstone valley, is my view
Of green and civil life that dwells
Below a cliff of savage fells
From which original address
Man faulted into consciousness.
Along the line of lapse the fire
Of life's impersonal desire
Burst through his sedentary rock
And, as at DUFTON and at KNOCK,
Thrust up between his mind and heart
Enormous cones of myth and art.
Always my boy of wish returns
To those peat-stained deserted burns
That feed the WEAR and TYNE and TEES,

And, turning states to strata, sees
How basalt long oppressed broke out
In wild revolt at CAULDRON SNOUT,
And from the relics of old mines
Derives his algebraic signs
For all in man that mourns and seeks,
For all of his renounced techniques,
Their tramways overgrown with grass,
For lost belief, for all Alas,
The derelict lead-smelting mill,
Flued to its chimney up the hill,
That smokes no answer any more
But points, a landmark on BOLTS LAW,
The finger of all questions. There
In ROOKHOPE I was first aware
Of Self and Not-self, Death and Dread:
Adits were entrances which led
Down to the Outlawed, to the Others,
The Terrible, the Merciful, the Mothers;
Alone in the hot day I knelt
Upon the edge of shafts and felt
The deep *Urmutterfurcht* that drives
Us into knowledge all our lives,
The far interior of our fate
To civilise and to create,
Das Weibliche that bids us come
To find what we're escaping from.
There I dropped pebbles, listened, heard
The reservoir of darkness stirred;
"O deine Mutter kehrt dir nicht
Wieder. Du selbst bin ich, dein' Pflicht
Und Liebe. Brach sie nun mein Bild."
And I was conscious of my guilt.

But such a bond is not an Ought,
Only a given mode of thought,
Whence my imperatives were taught.
Now in that other world I stand
Of fully alienated land,
An earth made common by the means
Of hunger, money, and machines,
Where each determined nature must
Regard that nature as a trust
That, being chosen, he must choose,
Determined to become of use;
For we are conscripts to our age
Simply by being born; we wage
The war we are, and may not die
With POLYCARP's despairing cry,
Desert or become ill: but how
To be the patriots of the Now?
Here all, by rights, are volunteers,
And anyone who interferes
With how another wills to fight
Must base his action, not on right,
But on the power to compel;
Only the "Idiot" can tell
For which state office he should run,
Only the Many make the One.

Eccentric, wrinkled, and ice-capped,
Swarming with parasites and wrapped
In a peculiar atmosphere,
Earth wabbles on down her career
With no ambition in her heart;
Her loose land-masses drift apart,
Her zone of shade and silence crawls
Steadily westward. Daylight falls

On Europe's frozen soldiery
And millions brave enough to die
For a new day; for each one knows
A day is drawing to a close.
Yes, all of us at least know that,
All from the seasoned diplomat
Used to the warm Victorian summers
Down to the juveniles and drummers.
Whatever nonsense we believe,
Whomever we can still deceive,
Whatever language angers us,
Whoever seems the poisonous
Old dragon to be killed if men
Are ever to be rich again,
We know no fuss or pain or lying
Can stop the moribund from dying,
That all the special tasks begun
By the Renaissance have been done.

When unity has come to grief
Upon professional belief,
Another unity was made
By equal amateurs in trade.
Out of the noise and horror, the
Opinions of artillery,
The barracks chatter and the yell
Of charging cavalry, the smell
Of poor opponents roasting, out
Of LUTHER's faith and MONTAIGNE's doubt,
The epidemic of translations,
The Councils and the navigations,
The confiscations and the suits,
The scholars' scurrilous disputes
Over the freedom of the Will

And right of Princes to do ill,
Emerged a new *Anthropos,* an
Empiric Economic Man,
The urban, prudent, and inventive,
Profit his rational incentive
And Work his whole *exercitus,*
The individual let loose
To guard himself, at liberty
To starve or be forgotten, free
To feel in splendid isolation
Or drive himself about creation
In the closed cab of Occupation.
He did what he was born to do,
Proved some assumptions were untrue.
He had his half-success; he broke
The silly and unnatural yoke
Of famine and disease that made
A false necessity obeyed;
A Protestant, he found the key
To Catholic economy,
Subjected earth to the control
And moral choices of the soul;
And in the training of each sense
To serve with joy its evidence
He founded a new discipline
To fight an intellectual sin,
Reason's depravity that takes
The useful concepts that she makes
As universals, as the *kitsch,*
But worshipped statues upon which
She leaves her effort and her crown,
And if his half-success broke down,
All failures have one good result:
They prove the Good is difficult.

He never won complete support;
However many votes he bought.
He could not silence all the cliques,
And no miraculous techniques
Could sterilise all discontent
Or dazzle it into assent,
But at the very noon and arch
Of his immense triumphal march
Stood prophets pelting him with curses
And sermons and satiric verses,
And ostentatious beggars slept.
BLAKE shouted insults, ROUSSEAU wept,
Ironic KIERKEGAARD stared long
And muttered "All are in the wrong,"
While BAUDELAIRE went mad protesting
That progress is not interesting
And thought he was an albatross,
The great Erotic on the cross
Of Science, crucified by fools
Who sit all day on office stools,
Are fairly faithful to their wives
And play for safety all their lives,
For whose *Verbürgerlichung* of
All joy and suffering and love
Let the grand pariah atone
By dying hated and alone.

The World ignored them; they were few.
The careless victor never knew
Their grapevine rumour would grow true,
Their alphabet of warning sounds
The common grammar all have grounds
To study; for their guess is proved:
It is the Mover that is moved.

Whichever way we turn, we see
Man captured by his liberty,
The measurable taking charge
Of him who measures, set at large
By his own actions, useful facts
Become the user of his acts,
And Chance the choices of his soul;
The beggar put out by his bowl,
Boys trained by factories for leading
Unusual lives as nurses, feeding
Helpless machines, girls married off
To typewriters, old men in love
With prices they can never get,
Homes blackmailed by a radio set,
Children inherited by slums
And idiots by enormous sums.
We see, we suffer, we despair:
The well-armed children everywhere
Who envy the self-governed beast
Now know that they are bound at least,
Die Aufgeregten without pity
Destroying the historic city,
The ruined showering with honors
The blind Christs and the mad Madonnas,
The Gnostics in the brothels treating
The flesh as secular and fleeting,
The *dialegesthai* of the rich
At cocktail parties as to which
Technique is most effective in
Enforcing labour discipline,
What Persian Apparatus will
Protect their privileges still
And safely keep the living dead
Entombed, hilarious, and fed,

The Disregarded in their shacks
Upon the wrong side of the tracks,
Poisoned by reasonable hate,
Are symptoms of one common fate.
All in their morning mirrors face
A member of a governed race.
Each recognises what LEAR saw,
The *homo* THURBER likes to draw,
The neuter outline that's the plan
And icon of Industrial Man,
The Unpolitical afraid
Of all that has to be obeyed.

But still each private citizen
Thanks God he's not as other men.
O all too easily we blame
The politicians for our shame
And the hired officers of state
For all those customs that frustrate
Our own intention to fulfil
Eros's legislative will.
Yet who must not, if he reflect,
See how unserious the effect
That he to love's volition gives,
On what base compromise he lives?
Even true lovers on some bed
The graceful god has visited
Find faults at which to hang the head,
And know the morphon full of guilt
Whence all community is built,
The cryptozoön with two backs
Whose sensibility that lacks
True reverence contributes much
Towards the soldier's violent touch.

For, craving language and a myth
And hands to shape their purpose with,
In shadow round the fond and warm
The possible societies swarm,
Because their freedom as their form
Upon our sense of style depends,
Whose eyes alone can seek their ends,
And they are impotent if we
Decline responsibility.
O what can love's intention do
If all his agents are untrue?
The politicians we condemn
Are nothing but our L. C. M.
The average of the average man
Becomes the dread Leviathan,
Our million individual deeds,
Omissions, vanities, and creeds,
Put through the statistician's hoop
The gross behaviour of a group:
Upon each English conscience lie
Two decades of hypocrisy,
And not a German can be proud
Of what his apathy allowed.

The flood of tyranny and force
Arises at a double source:
In PLATO's lie of intellect
That all are weak but the Elect
Philosophers who must be strong,
For, knowing Good, they will no Wrong,
United in the abstract Word
Above the low anarchic herd;
Or ROUSSEAU's falsehood of the flesh
That stimulates our pride afresh

306

To think all men identical
And strong in the Irrational.
And yet, although the social lie
Looks double to the dreamer's eye,
The rain to fill the mountain streams
That water the opposing dreams
By turns in favour with the crowd
Is scattered from one common cloud.
Up in the Ego's atmosphere
And higher altitudes of fear
The particles of error form
The shepherd-killing thunderstorm,
And our political distress
Descends from her self-consciousness,
Her cold *concupiscence d'esprit*
That looks upon her liberty
Not as a gift from life with which
To serve, enlighten, and enrich
The total creature that could use
Her function of free-will to choose
The actions that this world requires
To educate its blind desires,
But as the right to lead alone
An attic life all on her own,
Unhindered, unrebuked, unwatched,
Self-known, self-praising, self-attached.
All happens as she wishes till
She ask herself why she should will
This more than that, or who would care
If she were dead or gone elsewhere,
And on her own hypothesis
Is powerless to answer this.
Then panic seizes her; the glance
Of mirrors shows a countenance

Of wretched empty-brilliance. How
Can she escape self-loathing now?
What is there left for pride to do
Except plunge headlong *vers la boue*,
For freedom except suicide,
The self-asserted, self-denied?
A witch self-tortured as she spins
Her whole devotion widdershins,
She worships in obscene delight
The Not, the Never, and the Night,
The formless Mass without a Me,
The Midnight Women and the Sea.
The genius of the loud Steam Age,
Loud WAGNER, put it on the stage:
The mental hero who has swooned
With sensual pleasure at his wound,
His intellectual life fulfilled
In knowing that his doom is willed,
Exists to suffer; borne along
Upon a timeless tide of song,
The huge doll roars for death or mother,
Synonymous with one another;
And Woman, passive as in dreams,
Redeems, redeems, redeems, redeems.

Delighted with their takings, bars
Are closing under fading stars;
The revellers go home to change
Back into something far more strange,
The tightened self in which they may
Walk safely through their bothered day,
With formal purpose up and down
The crowded fatalistic town,
And dawn sheds its calm candour now

On monasteries where they vow
An economic abstinence.
Modern in their impenitence,
Blonde, naked, paralysed, alone,
Like rebel angels turned to stone
The secular cathedrals stand
Upon their valuable land,
Frozen forever in a lie,
Determined always to deny
That man is weak and has to die,
And hide the huge phenomena
Which must decide America,
That culture that had worshipped no
Virgin before the Dynamo,
Held no Nicea nor Canossa,
Hat keine verfallenen Schlösser,
Keine Basalte, the great Rome
To all who lost or hated home.

A long time since it seems today
The Saints in Massachusetts Bay
Heard theocratic COTTON preach
And legal WINTHROP's Little Speech;
Since MISTRESS HUTCHINSON was tried
By those her Inner Light defied,
And WILLIAMS questioned Moses' law
But in Rhode Island waited for
The Voice of the Beloved to free
Himself and the Democracy;
Long since inventive JEFFERSON
Fought realistic HAMILTON,
Pelagian versus Jansenist;
But the same heresies exist.
Time makes old formulas look strange,

309

Our properties and symbols change,
But round the freedom of the Will
Our disagreements centre still,
And now as then the voter hears
The battle cries of two ideas.
Here, as in Europe, is dissent,
This raw untidy continent
Where the Commuter can't forget
The Pioneer; and even yet
A *Völkerwanderung* occurs:
Resourceful manufacturers
Trek southward by progressive stages
For sites with no floor under wages,
No ceiling over hours; and by
Artistic souls in towns that lie
Out in the weed and pollen belt
The need for sympathy is felt,
And east to hard New York they come;
And self-respect drives Negroes from
The one-crop and race-hating delta
To northern cities helter-skelter;
And in jalopies there migrates
A rootless tribe from windblown states
To suffer further westward where
The tolerant Pacific air
Makes logic seem so silly, pain
Subjective, what he seeks so vain
The wanderer may die; and kids,
When their imagination bids,
Hitch-hike a thousand miles to find
The Hesperides that's on their mind,
Some Texas where real cowboys seem
Lost in a movie-cowboy's dream.
More even than in Europe, here

The choice of patterns is made clear
Which the machine imposes, what
Is possible and what is not,
To what conditions we must bow
In building the Just City now.

However we decide to act,
Decision must accept the fact
That the machine has now destroyed
The local customs we enjoyed,
Replaced the bonds of blood and nation
By personal confederation.
No longer can we learn our good
From chances of a neighbourhood
Or class or party, or refuse
As individuals to choose
Our loves, authorities, and friends,
To judge our means and plan our ends;
For the machine has cried aloud
And publicised among the crowd
The secret that was always true
But known once only to the few,
Compelling all to the admission,
Aloneness is man's real condition,
That each must travel forth alone
In search of the Essential Stone,
"The Nowhere-without-No" that is
The justice of societies.
Each salesman now is the polite
Adventurer, the landless knight
GAWAINE-QUIXOTE, and his goal
The *Frauendienst* of his weak soul;
Each biggie in the Canning Ring
An unrobust lone FISHER-KING;

Each subway face the PEQUOD of
Some ISHMAEL hunting his lost love,
To harpoon his unhappiness
And turn the whale to a princess;
In labs the puzzled KAFKAS meet
The inexplicable defeat:
The odd behaviour of the law,
The facts that suddenly withdraw,
The path that twists away from the
Near-distant CASTLE they can see,
The Truth where they will be denied
Permission ever to reside;
And all the operatives know
Their factory is the *champ-clos*
And drawing-room of HENRY JAMES,
Where the *débat* decides the claims
Of liberty and justice; where,
Like any Jamesian character,
They learn to draw the careful line,
Develop, understand, refine.

A weary Asia out of sight
Is tugging gently at the night,
Uncovering a restless race;
Clocks shoo the childhood from its face,
And accurate machines begin
To concentrate its adults in
A narrow day to exercise
Their gifts in some cramped enterprise.
How few pretend to like it: O
Three quarters of these people know
Instinctively what ought to be
The nature of society
And how they'd live there if they could.

If it were easy to be good,
And cheap, and plain as evil how,
We all would be its members now:
How readily would we become
The seamless live continuum
Of supple and coherent stuff,
Whose form is truth, whose content love,
Its pluralist interstices
The homes of happiness and peace,
Where in a unity of praise
The largest *publicum's* a *res,*
And the least *res* a *publicum;*
How grandly would our virtues bloom
In a more conscionable dust
Where Freedom dwells because it must,
Necessity because it can,
And men confederate in Man.

But wishes are not horses, this
Annus is not *mirabilis;*
Day breaks upon the world we know
Of war and wastefulness and woe;
Ashamed civilians come to grief
In brotherhoods without belief,
Whose good intentions cannot cure
The actual evils they endure,
Nor smooth their practical career,
Nor bring the far horizon near.
The New Year brings an earth afraid,
Democracy a ready-made
And noisy tradesman's slogan, and
The poor betrayed into the hand
Of lackeys with ideas, and truth
Whipped by their elders out of youth,

The peaceful fainting in their tracks
With martyrs' tombstones on their backs,
And culture on all fours to greet
A butch and criminal élite,
While in the vale of silly sheep
Rheumatic old patricians weep.

Our news is seldom good: the heart,
As ZOLA said, must always start
The day by swallowing its toad
Of failure and disgust. Our road
Gets worse and we seem altogether
Lost as our theories, like the weather,
Veer round completely every day,
And all that we can always say
Is: true democracy begins
With free confession of our sins.
In this alone are all the same,
All are so weak that none dare claim
"I have the right to govern," or
"Behold in me the Moral Law,"
And all real unity commences
In consciousness of differences,
That all have needs to satisfy
And each a power to supply.
We need to love all since we are
Each a unique particular
That is no giant, god, or dwarf,
But one odd human isomorph;
We can love each because we know
All, all of us, that this is so:
Can live since we are lived, the powers
That we create with are not ours.

O Unicorn among the cedars,
To whom no magic charm can lead us,
White childhood moving like a sigh
Through the green woods unharmed in thy
Sophisticated innocence,
To call thy true love to the dance,
O Dove of science and of light,
Upon the branches of the night,
O Ichthus playful in the deep
Sea-lodges that forever keep
Their secret of excitement hidden,
O sudden Wind that blows unbidden,
Parting the quiet reeds, O Voice
Within the labyrinth of choice
Only the passive listener hears,
O Clock and Keeper of the years,
O Source of equity and rest,
Quando non fuerit, non est,
It without image, paradigm
Of matter, motion, number, time,
The grinning gap of Hell, the hill
Of Venus and the stairs of Will,
Disturb our negligence and chill,
Convict our pride of its offence
In all things, even penitence,
Instruct us in the civil art
Of making from the muddled heart
A desert and a city where
The thoughts that have to labour there
May find locality and peace,
And pent-up feelings their release,
Send strength sufficient for our day,
And point our knowledge on its way,
O da quod jubes, Domine.

Dear friend Elizabeth, dear friend
These days have brought me, may the end
I bring to the grave's dead-line be
More worthy of your sympathy
Than the beginning; may the truth
That no one marries lead my youth
Where you already are and bless
Me with your learned peacefulness,
Who on the lives about you throw
A calm *solificatio,*
A warmth throughout the universe
That each for better or for worse
Must carry round with him through life,
A judge, a landscape, and a wife.
We fall down in the dance, we make
The old ridiculous mistake,
But always there are such as you
Forgiving, helping what we do.
O every day in sleep and labour
Our life and death are with our neighbour,
And love illuminates again
The city and the lion's den,
The world's great rage, the travel of young men.

Part VII

IN TIME OF WAR

A Sonnet Sequence
with a verse commentary

I

So from the years the gifts were showered; each
Ran off with his at once into his life:
Bee took the politics that make a hive,
Fish swam as fish, peach settled into peach.

And were successful at the first endeavour;
The hour of birth their only time at college,
They were content with their precocious knowledge,
And knew their station and were good for ever.

Till finally there came a childish creature
On whom the years could model any feature,
And fake with ease a leopard or a dove;

Who by the lightest wind was changed and shaken,
And looked for truth and was continually mistaken,
And envied his few friends and chose his love.

II

They wondered why the fruit had been forbidden;
It taught them nothing new. They hid their pride,
But did not listen much when they were chidden;
They knew exactly what to do outside.

They left: immediately the memory faded
Of all they'd learnt; they could not understand
The dogs now who, before, had always aided;
The stream was dumb with whom they'd always planned.

They wept and quarrelled: freedom was so wild.
In front, maturity, as he ascended,
Retired like a horizon from the child;

The dangers and the punishments grew greater;
And the way back by angels was defended
Against the poet and the legislator.

III

Only a smell had feelings to make known,
Only an eye could point in a direction;
The fountain's utterance was itself alone;
The bird meant nothing: that was his projection

Who named it as he hunted it for food.
He felt the interest in his throat, and found
That he could send his servant to the wood,
Or kiss his bride to rapture with a sound.

They bred like locusts till they hid the green
And edges of the world: and he was abject,
And to his own creation became subject;

And shook with hate for things he'd never seen,
And knew of love without love's proper object,
And was oppressed as he had never been.

IV

He stayed: and was imprisoned in possession.
The seasons stood like guards about his ways,
The mountains chose the mother of his children,
And like a conscience the sun ruled his days.

Beyond him his young cousins in the city
Pursued their rapid and unnatural course,
Believed in nothing but were easy-going,
And treated strangers like a favourite horse.

And he changed little,
But took his colour from the earth,
And grew in likeness to his sheep and cattle.

The townsman thought him miserly and simple,
The poet wept and saw in him the truth,
And the oppressor held him up as an example.

V

His generous bearing was a new invention:
For life was slow; earth needed to be careless:
With horse and sword he drew the girls' attention;
He was the Rich, the Bountiful, the Fearless.

And to the young he came as a salvation;
They needed him to free them from their mothers,
And grew sharp-witted in the long migration,
And round his camp fires learnt all men are brothers.

But suddenly the earth was full: he was not wanted.
And he became the shabby and demented,
And took to drink to screw his nerves to murder;

Or sat in offices and stole,
And spoke approvingly of Law and Order,
And hated life with all his soul.

VI

He watched the stars and noted birds in flight;
The rivers flooded or the Empire fell:
He made predictions and was sometimes right;
His lucky guesses were rewarded well.

And fell in love with Truth before he knew her,
And rode into imaginary lands,
With solitude and fasting hoped to woo her,
And mocked at those who served her with their hands.

But her he never wanted to despise,
But listened always for her voice; and when
She beckoned to him, he obeyed in meekness,

And followed her and looked into her eyes;
Saw there reflected every human weakness,
And saw himself as one of many men.

VII

He was their servant—some say he was blind—
And moved among their faces and their things;
Their feeling gathered in him like a wind
And sang: they cried—"It is a God that sings"—

And worshipped him and set him up apart,
And made him vain, till he mistook for song
The little tremors of his mind and heart
At each domestic wrong.

Songs came no more: he had to make them.
With what precision was each strophe planned.
He hugged his sorrow like a plot of land,

And walked like an assassin through the town,
And looked at men and did not like them,
But trembled if one passed him with a frown.

VIII

He turned his field into a meeting-place,
And grew the tolerant ironic eye,
And formed the mobile money-changer's face,
And found the notion of equality.

And strangers were as brothers to his clocks,
And with his spires he made a human sky;
Museums stored his learning like a box,
And paper watched his money like a spy.

It grew so fast his life was overgrown,
And he forgot what once it had been made for,
And gathered into crowds and was alone,

And lived expensively and did without,
And could not find the earth which he had paid for,
Nor feel the love that he knew all about.

IX

They died and entered the closed life like nuns:
Even the very poor lost something; oppression
Was no more a fact; and the self-centred ones
Took up an even more extreme position.

And the kingly and the saintly also were
Distributed among the woods and oceans,
And touch our open sorrow everywhere,
Airs, waters, places, round our sex and reasons;

Are what we feed on as we make our choice.
We bring them back with promises to free them,
But as ourselves continually betray them:

They hear their deaths lamented in our voice,
But in our knowledge know we could restore them;
They could return to freedom; they would rejoice.

X

As a young child the wisest could adore him;
He felt familiar to them like their wives:
The very poor saved up their pennies for him,
And martyrs brought him presents of their lives.

But who could sit and play with him all day?
Their other needs were pressing, work, and bed:
The beautiful stone courts were built where they
Could leave him to be worshipped and well fed.

But he escaped. They were too blind to tell
That it was he who came with them to labour,
And talked and grew up with them like a neighbour:

To fear and greed those courts became a centre;
The poor saw there the tyrant's citadel,
And martyrs the lost face of the tormentor.

XI

He looked in all His wisdom from the throne
Down on the humble boy who kept the sheep,
And sent a dove; the dove returned alone:
Youth liked the music, but soon fell asleep.

But He had planned such future for the youth:
Surely His duty now was to compel;
For later he would come to love the truth,
And own his gratitude. The eagle fell.

It did not work: his conversation bored
The boy who yawned and whistled and made faces,
And wriggled free from fatherly embraces;

But with the eagle he was always willing
To go where it suggested, and adored
And learnt from it the many ways of killing.

XII

And the age ended, and the last deliverer died
In bed, grown idle and unhappy; they were safe:
The sudden shadow of the giant's enormous calf
Would fall no more at dusk across the lawn outside.

They slept in peace: in marshes here and there no doubt
A sterile dragon lingered to a natural death,
But in a year the spoor had vanished from the heath;
The kobold's knocking in the mountain petered out.

Only the sculptors and the poets were half sad,
And the pert retinue from the magician's house
Grumbled and went elsewhere. The vanquished powers
    were glad

To be invisible and free: without remorse
Struck down the sons who strayed into their course,
And ravished the daughters, and drove the fathers mad.

XIII

Certainly praise: let the song mount again and again
For life as it blossoms out in a jar or a face,
For the vegetable patience, the animal grace;
Some people have been happy; there have been great men.

But hear the morning's injured weeping, and know why:
Cities and men have fallen; the will of the Unjust
Has never lost its power; still, all princes must
Employ the Fairly-Noble unifying Lie.

History opposes its grief to our buoyant song:
The Good Place has not been; our star has warmed
        to birth
A race of promise that has never proved its worth;

The quick new West is false; and prodigious, but wrong
This passive flower-like people who for so long
In the Eighteen Provinces have constructed the earth.

XIV

Yes, we are going to suffer, now; the sky
Throbs like a feverish forehead; pain is real;
The groping searchlights suddenly reveal
The little natures that will make us cry,

Who never quite believed they could exist,
Not where we were. They take us by surprise
Like ugly long-forgotten memories,
And like a conscience all the guns resist.

Behind each sociable home-loving eye
The private massacres are taking place;
All Women, Jews, the Rich, the Human Race.

The mountains cannot judge us when we lie:
We dwell upon the earth; the earth obeys
The intelligent and evil till they die.

XV

Engines bear them through the sky: they're free
And isolated like the very rich;
Remote like savants, they can only see
The breathing city as a target which

Requires their skill; will never see how flying
Is the creation of ideas they hate,
Nor how their own machines are always trying
To push through into life. They chose a fate

The islands where they live did not compel.
Though earth may teach our proper discipline,
At any time it will be possible

To turn away from freedom and become
Bound like the heiress in her mother's womb,
And helpless as the poor have always been.

XVI

Here war is simple like a monument:
A telephone is speaking to a man;
Flags on a map assert that troops were sent;
A boy brings milk in bowls. There is a plan

For living men in terror of their lives,
Who thirst at nine who were to thirst at noon,
And can be lost and are, and miss their wives,
And, unlike an idea, can die too soon.

But ideas can be true although men die,
And we can watch a thousand faces
Made active by one lie:

And maps can really point to places
Where life is evil now:
Nanking; Dachau.

XVII

They are and suffer; that is all they do;
A bandage hides the place where each is living,
His knowledge of the world restricted to
The treatment that the instruments are giving.

And lie apart like epochs from each other
—Truth in their sense is how much they can bear;
It is not talk like ours, but groans they smother—
And are remote as plants; we stand elsewhere.

For who when healthy can become a foot?
Even a scratch we can't recall when cured,
But are boist'rous in a moment and believe

In the common world of the uninjured, and cannot
Imagine isolation. Only happiness is shared,
And anger, and the idea of love.

XVIII

Far from the heart of culture he was used:
Abandoned by his general and his lice,
Under a padded quilt he closed his eyes
And vanished. He will not be introduced

When this campaign is tidied into books:
No vital knowledge perished in his skull;

328

His jokes were stale; like wartime, he was dull;
His name is lost for ever like his looks.

He neither knew nor chose the Good, but taught us,
And added meaning like a comma, when
He turned to dust in China that our daughters

Be fit to love the earth, and not again
Disgraced before the dogs; that, where are waters,
Mountains and houses, may be also men.

XIX

But in the evening the oppression lifted;
The peaks came into focus; it had rained:
Across the lawns and cultured flowers drifted
The conversation of the highly trained.

The gardeners watched them pass and priced their shoes;
A chauffeur waited, reading in the drive,
For them to finish their exchange of views;
It seemed a picture of the private life.

Far off, no matter what good they intended,
The armies waited for a verbal error
With all the instruments for causing pain:

And on the issue of their charm depended
A land laid waste, with all its young men slain,
The women weeping, and the towns in terror.

XX

They carry terror with them like a purse,
And flinch from the horizon like a gun;

And all the rivers and the railways run
Away from Neighbourhood as from a curse.

They cling and huddle in the new disaster
Like children sent to school, and cry in turn;
For Space has rules they cannot hope to learn,
Time speaks a language they will never master.

We live here. We lie in the Present's unopened
Sorrow; its limits are what we are.
Ought the prisoner ever to pardon his cell,

Can future ages ever escape so far,
Yet feel derived from everything that happened,
Even from us, that even this was well?

XXI

The life of man is never quite completed;
The daring and the chatter will go on:
But, as an artist feels his power gone,
These walk the earth and know themselves defeated.

Some could not bear nor break the young and mourn for
The wounded myths that once made nations good,
Some lost a world they never understood,
Some saw too clearly all that man was born for.

Loss is their shadow-wife, Anxiety
Receives them like a grand hotel; but where
They may regret they must; their life, to hear

The call of the forbidden cities, see
The stranger watch them with a happy stare,
And Freedom hostile in each home and tree.

XXII

Simple like all dream wishes, they employ
The elementary language of the heart,
And speak to muscles of the need for joy;
The dying and the lovers soon to part

Hear them and have to whistle. Always new,
They mirror every change in our position;
They are our evidence of what we do;
They speak directly to our lost condition.

Think in this year what pleased the dancers best:
When Austria died and China was forsaken,
Shanghai in flames and Teruel retaken,

France put her case before the world: "Partout
Il y a de la joie." America addressed
The earth: "Do you love me as I love you?"

XXIII

When all the apparatus of report
Confirms the triumph of our enemies;
Our bastion pierced, our army in retreat,
Violence successful like a new disease,

And Wrong a charmer everywhere invited;
When we regret that we were ever born:
Let us remember all who seemed deserted.
Tonight in China let me think of one,

Who through ten years of silence worked and waited,
Until in Muzot all his powers spoke,
And everything was given once for all:

331

And with the gratitude of the Completed
He went out in the winter night to stroke
That little tower like a great animal.

XXIV

No, not their names. It was the others who built
Each great coercive avenue and square,
Where man can only recollect and stare,
The really lonely with the sense of guilt

Who wanted to persist like that for ever;
The unloved had to leave material traces:
But these need nothing but our better faces,
And dwell in them, and know that we shall never

Remember who we are nor why we're needed.
Earth grew them as a bay grows fishermen
Or hills a shepherd; they grew ripe and seeded;

And the seeds clung to us; even our blood
Was able to revive them; and they grew again;
Happy their wish and mild to flower and flood.

XXV

Nothing is given: we must find our law.
Great buildings jostle in the sun for domination;
Behind them stretch like sorry vegetation
The low recessive houses of the poor.

We have no destiny assigned us:
Nothing is certain but the body; we plan

To better ourselves; the hospitals alone remind us
Of the equality of man.

Children are really loved here, even by police:
They speak of years before the big were lonely,
And will be lost.

                    And only
The brass bands throbbing in the parks foretell
Some future reign of happiness and peace.

We learn to pity and rebel.

XXVI

Always far from the centre of our names,
The little workshop of love: yes, but how wrong
We were about the old manors and the long
Abandoned Folly and the children's games.

Only the acquisitive expects a quaint
Unsalable product, something to please
An artistic girl; it's the selfish who sees
In every impractical beggar a saint.

We can't believe that we ourselves designed it,
A minor item of our daring plan
That caused no trouble; we took no notice of it.

Disaster comes, and we're amazed to find it
The single project that since work began
Through all the cycle showed a steady profit.

XXVII

Wandering lost upon the mountains of our choice,
Again and again we sigh for an ancient South,
For the warm nude ages of instinctive poise,
For the taste of joy in the innocent mouth.

Asleep in our huts, how we dream of a part
In the glorious balls of the future; each intricate maze
Has a plan, and the disciplined movements of the heart
Can follow for ever and ever its harmless ways.

We envy streams and houses that are sure:
But we are articled to error; we
Were never nude and calm like a great door,

And never will be perfect like the fountains;
We live in freedom by necessity,
A mountain people dwelling among mountains.

COMMENTARY

Season inherits legally from dying season;
Protected by the wide peace of the sun, the planets
Continue their circulations; and the galaxy

Is free for ever to revolve like an enormous biscuit:
With all his engines round him and the summer flowers,
Little upon his little earth, man contemplates

The universe of which he is both judge and victim;
A rarity in an uncommon corner, gazes
On the great trackways where his tribe and truth are nothing.

Certainly the growth of the fore-brain has been a success:
He has not got lost in a backwater like the lampshell
Or the limpet; he has not died out like the super-lizards.

His boneless worm-like ancestors would be amazed
At the upright position, the breasts, the four-chambered heart,
The clandestine evolution in the mother's shadow.

"Sweet is it," say the doomed, "to be alive though wretched,"
And the young emerging from the closed parental circle,
To whose uncertainty the certain years present

Their syllabus of limitless anxiety and labour,
At first feel nothing but the gladness of their freedom,
Are happy in the new embraces and the open talk.

But liberty to be and weep has never been sufficient;
The winds surround our griefs, the unfenced sky
To all our failures is a taciturn unsmiling witness.

And not least here, among this humorous and hairless people
Who like a cereal have inherited these valleys:
Tarim nursed them; Thibet was the tall rock of their protection,

And where the Yellow River shifts its course, they learnt
How to live well, though ruin threatened often.
For centuries they looked in fear towards the northern defiles,

But now must turn and gather like a fist to strike
Wrong coming from the sea, from those whose paper houses
Tell of their origin among the coral islands;

Who even to themselves deny a human freedom,
And dwell in the estranging tyrant's vision of the earth
In a calm stupor under their blood-spotted flag.

Here danger works a civil reconciliation,
Interior hatreds are resolved upon this foreign foe,
And will-power to resist is growing like a prosperous city.

For the invader now is deadly and impartial as a judge:
Down country footpaths, from each civic sky,
His anger blows alike upon the rich, and all

Who dwell within the crevices of destitution,
On those with a laborious lifetime to recall, and those,
The innocent and short whose dreams contain no children.

While in an international and undamaged quarter,
Casting our European shadows on Shanghai,
Walking unhurt among the banks, apparently immune

Below the monuments of an acquisitive society,
With friends and books and money and the traveller's freedom,
We are compelled to realize that our refuge is a sham.

For this material contest that has made Hongkew
A terror and a silence, and Chapei a howling desert,
Is but the local variant of a struggle in which all,

The elderly, the amorous, the young, the handy and
    the thoughtful,
Those to whom feeling is a science, those to whom study
Of all that can be added and compared is a consuming love,

With those whose brains are empty as a school in August,
And those in whom the urge to action is so strong
They cannot read a letter without whispering, all

In cities, deserts, ships, in lodgings near the port,
Discovering the past of strangers in a library,
Creating their own future on a bed, each with his treasure,

Self-confident among the laughter and the *petits verres,*
Or motionless and lonely like a moping cormorant,
In all their living are profoundly implicated.

This is one sector and one movement of the general war
Between the dead and the unborn, the Real and the Pretended,
Which for the creature who creates, communicates, and chooses,

The only animal aware of lack of finish,
In essence is eternal. When we emerged from holes
And blinked in the warm sunshine of the Laufen Ice Retreat,

Thinking of Nature as a close and loyal kinsman,
On every acre the opponents faced each other,
And we were far within the zone where casualties begin.

Now in a world that has no localized events,
Where not a tribe exists without its dossier,
And the machine has taught us how, to the Non-Human,

That unprogressive blind society that knows
No argument except the absolute and violent veto,
Our colours, creeds and sexes are identical,

The issue is the same. Some uniforms are new,
Some have changed sides; but the campaign continues:
Still unachieved is *Jen*, the Truly Human.

This is the epoch of the Third Great Disappointment:
The First was the collapse of that slave-owning empire
Whose yawning magistrate asked, "What is truth?"

Upon its ruins rose the Plainly Visible Churches:
Men camped like tourists under their tremendous shadows,
United by a common sense of human failure,

Their certain knowledge only of the timeless fields
Where the Unchanging Happiness received the faithful,
And the Eternal Nightmare waited to devour the doubters.

In which a host of workers, famous and obscure,
Meaning to do no more than use their eyes,
Not knowing what they did, then sapped belief;

Put in its place a neutral dying star,
Where Justice could not visit. Self was the one city,
The cell where each must find his comfort and his pain,

The body nothing but a useful favourite machine
To go upon errands of love and to run the house,
While the mind in its study spoke with its private God.

But now that wave which already was washing the heart,
When the cruel Turk stormed the gates of Constantine's city,
When Galileo muttered to himself, *"sed movet,"*

And Descartes thought, "I am because I think,"
Today, all spent, is silently withdrawing itself:
Unhappy he or she who after it is sucked.

Never before was the Intelligence so fertile,
The Heart more stunted. The human field became
Hostile to brotherhood and feeling like a forest.

Machines devised by harmless clergymen and boys
Attracted men like magnets from the marl and clay
Into towns on the coal-measures, to a kind of freedom,

Where the abstinent with the landless drove a bitter bargain,
But sowed in that act the seeds of an experienced hatred,
Which, germinating long in tenement and gas-lit cellar,

Is choking now the aqueducts of our affection.
Knowledge of their colonial suffering has cut off
The Hundred Families like an attack of shyness;

The apprehensive rich pace up and down
Their narrow compound of success; in every body
The ways of living are disturbed; intrusive as a sill,

Fear builds enormous ranges casting shadows,
Heavy, bird-silencing, upon the outer world,
Hills that our grief sighs over like a Shelley, parting

All that we feel from all that we perceive,
Desire from Data; and the Thirteen gay Companions
Grow sullen now and quarrelsome as mountain tribes.

We wander on the earth, or err from bed to bed
In search of home, and fail, and weep for the lost ages
Before Because became As If, or rigid Certainty

The Chances Are. The base hear us, and the violent
Who long to calm our guilt with murder, and already
Have not been slow to turn our wish to their advantage.

On every side they make their brazen offer:
Now in that Catholic country with the shape of Cornwall,
Where Europe first became a term of pride,

North of the Alps where dark hair turns to blonde,
In Germany now loudest, land without a centre
Where the sad plains are like a sounding rostrum,

And on these tidy and volcanic summits near us now,
From which the Black Stream hides the Tuscarora Deep,
The voice is quieter but the more inhuman and triumphant.

By wire and wireless, in a score of bad translations,
They give their simple message to the world of man:
"Man can have Unity if Man will give up Freedom.

The State is real, the Individual is wicked;
Violence shall synchronize your movements like a tune,
And Terror like a frost shall halt the flood of thinking.

Barrack and bivouac shall be your friendly refuge,
And racial pride shall tower like a public column
And confiscate for safety every private sorrow.

Leave Truth to the police and us; we know the Good;
We build the Perfect City time shall never alter;
Our Law shall guard you always like a cirque of mountains,

Your ignorance keep off evil like a dangerous sea;
You shall be consummated in the General Will,
Your children innocent and charming as the beasts."

All the great conquerors sit upon their platform,
Lending their sombre weight of practical experience:
Ch'in Shih Huang Ti, who burnt the scholars' books,

Chaka the mad, who segregated the two sexes,
And *Genghis Khan,* who thought mankind should be destroyed,
And *Diocletian* the administrator, make impassioned speeches.

Napoleon claps who found religion useful,
And all who passed deception of the People, or who said
Like Little *Frederick,* "I shall see that it is done."

While many famous clerks support their programme:
Plato the good, despairing of the average man,
With sad misgiving signs their manifesto;

Shang-tzu approves their principle of Nothing Private;
The author of *The Prince* will heckle; *Hobbes* will canvass,
With generalizing *Hegel* and quiet *Bosanquet.*

And every family and every heart is tempted:
The earth debates; the Fertile Crescent argues;
Even the little towns upon the way to somewhere,

Those desert flowers the aeroplane now fertilizes,
Quarrel on this; in England far away,
Behind the high tides and the navigable estuaries;

In the Far West, in absolutely free America,
In melancholy Hungary, and clever France
Where ridicule has acted a historic rôle,

And here where the rice-grain nourishes these patient households
The ethic of the feudal citadel has impregnated,
Thousands believe, and millions are half-way to a conviction.

Nor do our leaders help; we know them now
For humbugs full of vain dexterity, invoking
A gallery of ancestors, pursuing still the mirage

343

Of long dead grandeurs whence the interest has absconded,
As Fahrenheit in an odd corner of great Celsius' kingdom
Might mumble of the summers measured once by him.

Yet all the same we have our faithful sworn supporters
Who never lost their faith in knowledge or in man,
But worked so eagerly that they forgot their food

And never noticed death or old age coming on,
Prepared for freedom as *Kuo Hsi* for inspiration,
Waiting it calmly like the coming of an honoured guest.

Some looked at falsehood with the candid eyes of children,
Some had a woman's ear to catch injustice,
Some took Necessity, and knew her, and she brought
        forth Freedom.

Some of our dead are famous, but they would not care:
Evil is always personal and spectacular,
But goodness needs the evidence of all our lives,

And, even to exist, it must be shared as truth,
As freedom or as happiness. (For what is happiness
If not to witness joy upon the features of another?)

They did not live to be remembered specially as noble,
Like those who cultivated only cucumbers and melons
To prove that they were rich; and when we praise their names,

They shake their heads in warning, chiding us to give
Our gratitude to the Invisible College of the Humble,
Who through the ages have accomplished everything essential.

And stretch around our struggle as the normal landscape,
And mingle, fluent with our living, like the winds and waters,
The dust of all the dead that reddens every sunset;

Giving us courage to confront our enemies,
Not only on the Grand Canal, or in Madrid,
Across the campus of a university city,

But aid us everywhere, that in the lovers' bedroom,
The white laboratory, the school, the public meeting,
The enemies of life may be more passionately attacked.

And, if we care to listen, we can always hear them:
"Men are not innocent as beasts and never can be,
Man can improve but never will himself be perfect,

Only the free have disposition to be truthful,
Only the truthful have the interest to be just,
Only the just possess the will-power to be free.

For common justice can determine private freedom,
As a clear sky can tempt men to astronomy,
Or a peninsula persuade them to be sailors.

You talked of Liberty, but were not just; and now
Your enemies have called your bluff; for in your city,
Only the man behind the rifle had free-will.

One wish is common to you both, the wish to build
A world united as that Europe was in which
The flint-faced exile wrote his three-act comedy.

Lament not its decay; that shell was too constricting:
The years of private isolation had their lesson,
And in the interest of intelligence were necessary.

Now in the clutch of crisis and the bloody hour
You must defeat your enemies or perish, but remember,
Only by those who reverence it can life be mastered;

345

Only a whole and happy conscience can stand up
And answer their bleak lie; among the just,
And only there, is Unity compatible with Freedom."

Night falls on China; the great arc of travelling shadow
Moves over land and ocean, altering life:
Thibet already silent, the packed Indias cooling,

Inert in the paralysis of caste. And though in Africa
The vegetation still grows fiercely like the young,
And in the cities that receive the slanting radiations

The lucky are at work, and most still know they suffer.
The dark will touch them soon: night's tiny noises
Will echo vivid in the owl's developed ear,

Vague in the anxious sentry's; and the moon look down
On battlefields and dead men lying, heaped like treasure,
On lovers ruined in a brief embrace, on ships

Where exiles watch the sea: and in the silence
The cry that streams out into the indifferent spaces,
And never stops or slackens, may be heard more clearly,

Above the everlasting murmur of the woods and rivers,
And more insistent than the lulling answer of the waltzes,
Or hum of printing-presses turning forests into lies;

As now I hear it, rising round me from Shanghai,
And mingling with the distant mutter of guerrilla fighting,
The voice of Man: *"O teach us to outgrow our madness.*

Ruffle the perfect manners of the frozen heart,
And once again compel it to be awkward and alive,
To all it suffered once a weeping witness.

346

Clear from the head the masses of impressive rubbish;
Rally the lost and trembling forces of the will,
Gather them up and let them loose upon the earth,

Till, as the contribution of our star, we follow
The clear instructions of that Justice, in the shadow
Of Whose uplifting, loving, and constraining power
All human reasons do rejoice and operate."

Part VIII

THE SEA AND THE MIRROR

A Commentary on Shakespeare's The Tempest

TO JAMES AND TANIA STERN

And am I wrong to worship where
Faith cannot doubt nor Hope despair
Since my own soul can grant my prayer?
Speak, God of Visions, plead for me
And tell why I have chosen thee.
                    EMILY BRONTË

Preface

(The Stage Manager to the Critics)

The aged catch their breath,
For the nonchalant couple go
Waltzing across the tightrope
As if there were no death
Or hope of falling down;
The wounded cry as the clown
Doubles his meaning, and O
How the dear little children laugh
When the drums roll and the lovely
Lady is sawn in half.

O what authority gives
Existence its surprise?
Science is happy to answer
That the ghosts who haunt our lives
Are handy with mirrors and wire,
That song and sugar and fire,
Courage and come-hither eyes
Have a genius for taking pains.
But how does one think up a habit?
Our wonder, our terror remains.

Art opens the fishiest eye
To the Flesh and the Devil who heat
The Chamber of Temptation
Where heroes roar and die.
We are wet with sympathy now;
Thanks for the evening; but how
Shall we satisfy when we meet,
Between Shall-I and I-Will,
The lion's mouth whose hunger
No metaphors can fill?

Well, who in his own backyard
Has not opened his heart to the smiling
Secret he cannot quote?
Which goes to show that the Bard
Was sober when he wrote
That this world of fact we love
Is unsubstantial stuff:
All the rest is silence
On the other side of the wall;
And the silence ripeness,
And the ripeness all.

I

Prospero to Ariel

Stay with me, Ariel, while I pack, and with your first free act
   Delight my leaving; share my resigning thoughts
As you have served my revelling wishes: then, brave spirit,
   Ages to you of song and daring, and to me
Briefly Milan, then earth. In all, things have turned out better
   Than I once expected or ever deserved;
I am glad that I did not recover my dukedom till
   I do not want it; I am glad that Miranda
No longer pays me any attention; I am glad I have freed you,
   So at last I can really believe I shall die.
For under your influence death is inconceivable:
   On walks through winter woods, a bird's dry carcass
Agitates the retina with novel images,
   A stranger's quiet collapse in a noisy street
Is the beginning of much lively speculation,
   And every time some dear flesh disappears
What is real is the arriving grief; thanks to your service,
   The lonely and unhappy are very much alive.

But now all these heavy books are no use to me any more, for
  Where I go, words carry no weight: it is best,
Then, I surrender their fascinating counsel
  To the silent dissolution of the sea
Which misuses nothing because it values nothing;
  Whereas man overvalues everything
Yet, when he learns the price is pegged to his valuation,
  Complains bitterly he is being ruined which, of course, he is.
So kings find it odd they should have a million subjects
  Yet share in the thoughts of none, and seducers
Are sincerely puzzled at being unable to love
  What they are able to possess; so, long ago,
In an open boat, I wept at giving a city,
  Common warmth and touching substance, for a gift
In dealing with shadows. If age, which is certainly
  Just as wicked as youth, look any wiser,
It is only that youth is still able to believe
  It will get away with anything, while age
Knows only too well that it has got away with nothing:
  The child runs out to play in the garden, convinced
That the furniture will go on with its thinking lesson,
  Who, fifty years later, if he plays at all,
Will first ask its kind permission to be excused.

  When I woke into my life, a sobbing dwarf
Whom giants served only as they pleased, I was not what
    I seemed;
  Beyond their busy backs I made a magic
To ride away from a father's imperfect justice,
  Take vengeance on the Romans for their grammar,
Usurp the popular earth and blot out for ever
  The gross insult of being a mere one among many:
Now, Ariel, I am that I am, your late and lonely master,
  Who knows now what magic is;—the power to enchant

That comes from disillusion. What the books can teach one
    Is that most desires end up in stinking ponds,
But we have only to learn to sit still and give no orders,
    To make you offer us your echo and your mirror;
We have only to believe you, then you dare not lie;
    To ask for nothing, and at once from your calm eyes,
With their lucid proof of apprehension and disorder,
    All we are not stares back at what we are. For all things
In your company, can be themselves: historic deeds
    Drop their hauteur and speak of shabby childhoods
When all they longed for was to join in the gang of doubts
    Who so tormented them; sullen diseases
Forget their dreadful appearance and make silly jokes;
    Thick-headed goodness for once is not a bore.
No one but you had sufficient audacity and eyesight
    To find those clearings where the shy humiliations
Gambol on sunny afternoons, the waterhole to which
    The scarred rogue sorrow comes quietly in the small hours:
And no one but you is reliably informative on hell;
    As you whistle and skip past, the poisonous
Resentments scuttle over your unrevolted feet,
    And even the uncontrollable vertigo,
Because it can scent no shame, is unobliged to strike.

> *Could he but once see Nature as*
>   *In truth she is for ever,*
> *What oncer would not fall in love?*
> *Hold up your mirror, boy, to do*
>   *Your vulgar friends this favour:*
> *One peep, though, will be quite enough;*
>   *To those who are not true,*
> *A statue with no figleaf has*
>   *A pornographic flavour.*

Inform my hot heart straight away
  Its treasure loves another,
But turn to neutral topics then,
Such as the pictures in this room,
  Religion or the Weather;
Pure scholarship in Where and When,
  How Often and With Whom,
Is not for Passion that must play
  The Jolly Elder Brother.

Be frank about our heathen foe,
  For Rome will be a goner
If you soft-pedal the loud beast;
Describe in plain four-letter words
  This dragon that's upon her:
But should our beggars ask the cost,
  Just whistle like the birds;
Dare even Pope or Caesar know
  The price of faith and honour?

Today I am free and no longer need your freedom:
You, I suppose, will be off now to look for likely victims;
  Crowds chasing ankles, lone men stalking glory,
Some feverish young rebel among amiable flowers
  In consultation with his handsome envy,
A punctual plump judge, a fly-weight hermit in a dream
  Of gardens that time is for ever outside—
To lead absurdly by their self-important noses.
  Are you malicious by nature? I don't know.
Perhaps only incapable of doing nothing or of
  Being by yourself, and, for all your wry faces
May secretly be anxious and miserable without
  A master to need you for the work you need.
Are all your tricks a test? If so, I hope you find, next time,
  Someone in whom you cannot spot the weakness

Through which you will corrupt him with your charm. Mine
        you did
    And me you have: thanks to us both, I have broken
Both of the promises I made as an apprentice;—
    To hate nothing and to ask nothing for its love.
All by myself I tempted Antonio into treason;
    However that could be cleared up; both of us know
That both were in the wrong, and neither need be sorry:
    But Caliban remains my impervious disgrace.
We did it, Ariel, between us; you found on me a wish
    For absolute devotion; result—his wreck
That sprawls in the weeds and will not be repaired:
    My dignity discouraged by a pupil's curse,
I shall go knowing and incompetent into my grave.

    The extravagant children, who lately swaggered
Out of the sea like gods, have, I think, been soundly hunted
    By their own devils into their human selves:
To all, then, but me, their pardons. Alonso's heaviness
    Is lost; and weak Sebastian will be patient
In future with his slothful conscience—after all, it pays;
    Stephano is contracted to his belly, a minor
But a prosperous kingdom; stale Trinculo receives,
    Gratis, a whole fresh repertoire of stories, and
Our younger generation its independent joy.
    Their eyes are big and blue with love; its lighting
Makes even us look new: yes, today it all looks so easy.
    Will Ferdinand be as fond of a Miranda
Familiar as a stocking? Will a Miranda who is
    No longer a silly lovesick little goose,
When Ferdinand and his brave world are her profession,
    Go into raptures over existing at all?
Probably I over-estimate their difficulties;
    Just the same, I am very glad I shall never

Be twenty and have to go through that business again,
  The hours of fuss and fury, the conceit, the expense.

  Sing first that green remote Cockagne
    Where whiskey-rivers run,
  And every gorgeous number may
    Be laid by anyone;
  For medicine and rhetoric
    Lie mouldering on shelves,
  While sad young dogs and stomach-aches
    Love no one but themselves.

  Tell then of witty angels who
    Come only to the beasts,
  Of Heirs Apparent who prefer
    Low dives to formal feasts;
  For shameless Insecurity
    Prays for a boot to lick,
  And many a sore bottom finds
    A sorer one to kick.

  Wind up, though, on a moral note;—
    That Glory will go bang,
  Schoolchildren shall coöperate,
    And honest rogues must hang;
  Because our sound committee man
    Has murder in his heart:
  But should you catch a living eye,
    Just wink as you depart.

Now our partnership is dissolved, I feel so peculiar:
  As if I had been on a drunk since I was born
And suddenly now, and for the first time, am cold sober,
  With all my unanswered wishes and unwashed days

357

Stacked up all round my life; as if through the ages I
    had dreamed
  About some tremendous journey I was taking,
Sketching imaginary landscapes, chasms and cities,
  Cold walls, hot spaces, wild mouths, defeated backs,
Jotting down fictional notes on secrets overheard
  In theatres and privies, banks and mountain inns,
And now, in my old age, I wake, and this journey really exists,
  And I have actually to take it, inch by inch,
Alone and on foot, without a cent in my pocket,
  Through a universe where time is not foreshortened,
No animals talk, and there is neither floating nor flying.

  When I am safely home, oceans away in Milan, and
Realise once and for all I shall never see you again,
  Over there, maybe, it won't seem quite so dreadful
Not to be interesting any more, but an old man
  Just like other old men, with eyes that water
Easily in the wind, and a head that nods in the sunshine,
  Forgetful, maladroit, a little grubby,
And to like it. When the servants settle me into a chair
  In some well-sheltered corner of the garden,
And arrange my muffler and rugs, shall I ever be able
  To stop myself from telling them what I am doing,—
Sailing alone, out over seventy thousand fathoms—?
  Yet if I speak, I shall sink without a sound
Into unmeaning abysses. Can I learn to suffer
  Without saying something ironic or funny
On suffering? I never suspected the way of truth
  Was a way of silence where affectionate chat
Is but a robbers' ambush and even good music
  In shocking taste; and you, of course, never told me.
If I peg away at it honestly every moment,
  And have luck, perhaps by the time death pounces

His stumping question, I shall just be getting to know
  The difference between moonshine and daylight. . . .
I see you starting to fidget. I forgot. To you
  That doesn't matter. My dear, here comes Gonzalo
With a solemn face to fetch me. O Ariel, Ariel,
  How I shall miss you. Enjoy your element. Good-bye.

> Sing, Ariel, sing,
> Sweetly, dangerously
> Out of the sour
> And shiftless water,
> Lucidly out
> Of the dozing tree,
> Entrancing, rebuking
> The raging heart
> With a smoother song
> Than this rough world,
> Unfeeling god.
>
> O brilliantly, lightly,
> Of separation,
> Of bodies and death,
> Unanxious one, sing
> To man, meaning me,
> As now, meaning always,
> In love or out,
> Whatever that mean,
> Trembling he takes
> The silent passage
> Into discomfort.

The Supporting Cast, Sotto Voce

Antonio

As all the pigs have turned back into men
And the sky is auspicious and the sea
Calm as a clock, we can all go home again.

Yes, it undoubtedly looks as if we
Could take life as easily now as tales
Write ever-after: not only are the

Two heads silhouetted against the sails
—And kissing, of course—well-built, but the lean
Fool is quite a person, the fingernails

Of the dear old butler for once quite clean,
And the royal passengers quite as good
As rustics, perhaps better, for they mean

What they say, without, as a rustic would,
Casting reflections on the courtly crew.
Yes, Brother Prospero, your grouping could

Not be more effective: given a few
Incomplete objects and a nice warm day,
What a lot a little music can do.

Dotted about the deck they doze or play,
Your loyal subjects all, grateful enough
To know their place and believe what you say.

Antonio, sweet brother, has to laugh.
How easy you have made it to refuse
Peace to your greatness! Break your wand in half,

The fragments will join; burn your books or lose
Them in the sea, they will soon reappear,
Not even damaged: as long as I choose

To wear my fashion, whatever you wear
Is a magic robe; while I stand outside
Your circle, the will to charm is still there.

As I exist so you shall be denied,
Forced to remain our melancholy mentor,
The grown-up man, the adult in his pride,

Never have time to curl up at the centre
Time turns on when completely reconciled,
Never become and therefore never enter
The green occluded pasture as a child.

    Your all is partial, Prospero;
      My will is all my own:
    Your need to love shall never know
    Me: I am I, Antonio,
      By choice myself alone.

Ferdinand

Flesh, fair, unique, and you, warm secret that my kiss
Follows into meaning Miranda, solitude
Where my omissions are, still possible, still good,
Dear Other at all times, retained as I do this,

From moment to moment as you enrich them so
Inherit me, my cause, as I would cause you now
With mine your sudden joy, two wonders as one vow
Pre-empting all, here, there, for ever, long ago.

361

I would smile at no other promise than touch, taste, sight,
Were there not, my enough, my exaltation, to bless
As world is offered world, as I hear it tonight

Pleading with ours for us, another tenderness
That neither without either could or would possess,
The Right Required Time, The Real Right Place, O Light.

> One bed is empty, Prospero,
>   My person is my own;
> Hot Ferdinand will never know
> The flame with which Antonio
>   Burns in the dark alone.

Stephano

Embrace me, belly, like a bride;
Dear daughter, for the weight you drew
From humble pie and swallowed pride,
Believe the boast in which you grew:
Where mind meets matter, both should woo;
Together let us learn that game
The high play better than the blue:
A lost thing looks for a lost name.

Behind your skirts your son must hide
When disappointments bark and boo;
Brush my heroic ghosts aside,
Wise nanny, with a vulgar pooh:
Exchanging cravings we pursue
Alternately a single aim:
Between the bottle and the "loo"
A lost thing looks for a lost name.

Though in the long run satisfied,
The will of one by being two
At every moment is denied;
Exhausted glasses wonder who
Is self and sovereign, I or You?
We cannot both be what we claim,
The real Stephano— Which is true?
A lost thing looks for a lost name.

Child? Mother? Either grief will do;
The need for pardon is the same,
The contradiction is not new:
A lost thing looks for a lost name.

One glass is untouched, Prospero,
My nature is my own;
Inert Stephano does not know
The feast at which Antonio
Toasts One and One alone.

Gonzalo

Evening, grave, immense, and clear,
Overlooks our ship whose wake
Lingers undistorted on
Sea and silence; I look back
For the last time as the sun
Sets behind that island where
All our loves were altered: yes,
My prediction came to pass,
Yet I am not justified,
And I weep but not with pride.
Not in me the credit for
Words I uttered long ago

Whose glad meaning I betrayed;
Truths today admitted, owe
Nothing to the councillor
In whose booming eloquence
Honesty became untrue.
Am I not Gonzalo who
By his self-reflection made
Consolation an offence?

There was nothing to explain:
Had I trusted the Absurd
And straightforward note by note
Sung exactly what I heard,
Such immediate delight
Would have taken there and then
Our common welkin by surprise,
All would have begun to dance
Jigs of self-deliverance.
It was I prevented this,
Jealous of my native ear,
Mine the art which made the song
Sound ridiculous and wrong,
I whose interference broke
The gallop into jog-trot prose
And by speculation froze
Vision into an idea,
Irony into a joke,
Till I stood convicted of
Doubt and insufficient love.

Farewell, dear island of our wreck:
All have been restored to health,
All have seen the Commonwealth,
There is nothing to forgive.

Since a storm's decision gave
His subjective passion back
To a meditative man,
Even reminiscence can
Comfort ambient troubles like
Some ruined tower by the sea
Whence boyhoods growing and afraid
Learn a formula they need
In solving their mortality,
Even rusting flesh can be
A simple locus now, a bell
The Already There can lay
Hands on if at any time
It should feel inclined to say
To the lonely—"Here I am,"
To the anxious—"All is well."

One tongue is silent, Prospero,
 My language is my own;
Decayed Gonzalo does not know
The shadow that Antonio
 Talks to, at noon, alone.

Adrian and Francisco

Good little sunbeams must learn to fly,
But it's madly ungay when the goldfish die.

One act is censored, Prospero,
 My audience is my own;
Nor Adrian nor Francisco know
The drama that Antonio
 Plays in his head alone.

Alonso

Dear Son, when the warm multitudes cry,
Ascend your throne majestically,
But keep in mind the waters where fish
See sceptres descending with no wish
To touch them; sit regal and erect,
But imagine the sands where a crown
Has the status of a broken-down
Sofa or mutilated statue:
Remember as bells and cannon boom
The cold deep that does not envy you,
The sunburnt superficial kingdom
Where a king is an object.

Expect no help from others, for who
Talk sense to princes or refer to
The scorpion in official speeches
As they unveil some granite Progress
Leading a child and holding a bunch
Of lilies? In their Royal Zoos the
Shark and the octopus are tactfully
Omitted; synchronised clocks march on
Within their powers: without, remain
The ocean flats where no subscription
Concerts are given, the desert plain
Where there is nothing for lunch.

Only your darkness can tell you what
A prince's ornate mirror dare not,
Which you should fear more—the sea in which
A tyrant sinks entangled in rich
Robes while a mistress turns a white back
Upon his splutter, or the desert

Where an emperor stands in his shirt
While his diary is read by sneering
Beggars, and far off he notices
A lean horror flapping and hopping
Toward him with inhuman swiftness:
Learn from your dreams what you lack,

For as your fears are, so must you hope.
The Way of Justice is a tightrope
Where no prince is safe for one instant
Unless he trust his embarrassment,
As in his left ear the siren sings
Meltingly of water and a night
Where all flesh had peace, and on his right
The efreet offers a brilliant void
Where his mind could be perfectly clear
And all his limitations destroyed:
Many young princes soon disappear
To join all the unjust kings.

So, if you prosper, suspect those bright
Mornings when you whistle with a light
Heart. You are loved; you have never seen
The harbour so still, the park so green,
So many well-fed pigeons upon
Cupolas and triumphal arches,
So many stags and slender ladies
Beside the canals. Remember when
Your climate seems a permanent home
For marvellous creatures and great men,
What griefs and convulsions startled Rome,
Ecbatana, Babylon.

How narrow the space, how slight the chance
For civil pattern and importance

Between the watery vagueness and
The triviality of the sand,
How soon the lively trip is over
From loose craving to sharp aversion,
Aimless jelly to paralysed bone:
At the end of each successful day
Remember that the fire and the ice
Are never more than one step away
From the temperate city; it is
But a moment to either.

But should you fail to keep your kingdom
And, like your father before you, come
Where thought accuses and feeling mocks,
Believe your pain: praise the scorching rocks
For their desiccation of your lust,
Thank the bitter treatment of the tide
For its dissolution of your pride,
That the whirlwind may arrange your will
And the deluge release it to find
The spring in the desert, the fruitful
Island in the sea, where flesh and mind
Are delivered from mistrust.

Blue the sky beyond her humming sail
As I sit today by our ship's rail
Watching exuberant porpoises
Escort us homeward and writing this
For you to open when I am gone:
Read it, Ferdinand, with the blessing
Of Alonso, your father, once King
Of Naples, now ready to welcome
Death, but rejoicing in a new love,
A new peace, having heard the solemn

Music strike and seen the statue move
To forgive our illusion.

> *One crown is lacking, Prospero,*
> *My empire is my own;*
> *Dying Alonso does not know*
> *The diadem Antonio*
> *Wears in his world alone.*

Master and Boatswain

At Dirty Dick's and Sloppy Joe's
  We drank our liquor straight,
Some went upstairs with Margery,
  And some, alas, with Kate;
And two by two like cat and mouse
The homeless played at keeping house.

There Wealthy Meg, the Sailor's Friend,
  And Marion, cow-eyed,
Opened their arms to me but I
  Refused to step inside;
I was not looking for a cage
In which to mope in my old age.

The nightingales are sobbing in
  The orchards of our mothers,
And hearts that we broke long ago
  Have long been breaking others;
Tears are round, the sea is deep:
Roll them overboard and sleep.

> *One gaze points elsewhere, Prospero,*
> *My compass is my own;*

369

Nostalgic sailors do not know
The waters where Antonio
Sails on and on alone.

Sebastian

My rioters all disappear, my dream
Where Prudence flirted with a naked sword,
Securely vicious, crumbles; it is day;
Nothing has happened; we are all alive:
I am Sebastian, wicked still, my proof
Of mercy that I wake without a crown.

What sadness signalled to our children's day
Where each believed all wishes wear a crown
And anything pretended is alive,
That one by one we plunged into that dream
Of solitude and silence where no sword
Will ever play once it is called a proof?

The arrant jewel singing in his crown
Persuaded me my brother was a dream
I should not love because I had no proof,
Yet all my honesty assumed a sword;
To think his death I thought myself alive
And stalked infected through the blooming day.

The lie of Nothing is to promise proof
To any shadow that there is no day
Which cannot be extinguished with some sword,
To want and weakness that the ancient crown
Envies the childish head, murder a dream
Wrong only while its victim is alive.

O blessed be bleak Exposure on whose sword,
Caught unawares, we prick ourselves alive!
Shake Failure's bruising fist! Who else would crown
Abominable error with a proof?
I smile because I tremble, glad today
To be ashamed, not anxious, not a dream.

Children are playing, brothers are alive,
And not a heart or stomach asks for proof
That all this dearness is no lovers' dream;
Just Now is what it might be every day,
Right Here is absolute and needs no crown,
Ermine or trumpets, protocol or sword.

In dream all sins are easy, but by day
It is defeat gives proof we are alive;
The sword we suffer is the guarded crown.

>   *One face cries nothing, Prospero,*
>   *My conscience is my own;*
>   *Pallid Sebastian does not know*
>   *The dream in which Antonio*
>   *Fights the white bull alone.*

Trinculo

>   Mechanic, merchant, king,
>   Are warmed by the cold clown
>   Whose head is in the clouds
>   And never can get down.

>   Into a solitude
>   Undreamed of by their fat
>   Quick dreams have lifted me;
>   The north wind steals my hat,

On clear days I can see
Green acres far below,
And the red roof where I
Was Little Trinculo.

There lies that solid world
These hands can never reach;
My history, my love,
Is but a choice of speech.

A terror shakes my tree,
A flock of words fly out,
Whereat a laughter shakes
The busy and devout.

Wild images, come down
Out of your freezing sky,
That I, like shorter men,
May get my joke and die.

One note is jarring, Prospero,
  My humour is my own;
Tense Trinculo will never know
The paradox Antonio
  Laughs at, in woods, alone.

Miranda

My Dear One is mine as mirrors are lonely,
As the poor and sad are real to the good king,
And the high green hill sits always by the sea.

Up jumped the Black Man behind the elder tree,
Turned a somersault and ran away waving;
My Dear One is mine as mirrors are lonely.

372

The Witch gave a squawk; her venomous body
Melted into light as water leaves a spring
And the high green hill sits always by the sea.

At his crossroads, too, the Ancient prayed for me;
Down his wasted cheeks tears of joy were running:
My Dear One is mine as mirrors are lonely.

He kissed me awake, and no one was sorry;
The sun shone on sails, eyes, pebbles, anything,
And the high green hill sits always by the sea.

So, to remember our changing garden, we
Are linked as children in a circle dancing:
My Dear One is mine as mirrors are lonely,
And the high green hill sits always by the sea.

> *One link is missing, Prospero,*
>   *My magic is my own;*
> *Happy Miranda does not know*
> *The figure that Antonio,*
> *The Only One, Creation's O*
>   *Dances for Death alone.*

III

Caliban to the Audience

If now, having dismissed your hired impersonators with
verdicts ranging from the laudatory orchid to the disgusted
and disgusting egg, you ask and, of course, notwithstanding
the conscious fact of his irrevocable absence, you instinctively *do* ask for our so good, so great, so dead author to stand
before the finally lowered curtain and take his shyly respon-

sible bow for this, his latest, ripest production, it is I—my reluctance is, I can assure you, co-equal with your dismay—who will always loom thus wretchedly into your confused picture, for, in default of the all-wise, all-explaining master you would speak *to,* who else at least can, who else indeed must respond to your bewildered cry, but its very echo, the begged question you would speak to him *about.*

*　　*　　*

We must own [*for the present I speak your echo*] to a nervous perplexity not unmixed, frankly, with downright resentment. How *can* we grant the indulgence for which in his epilogue your personified type of the creative so lamely, tamely pleaded? Imprisoned, by you, in the mood doubtful, loaded, by you, with distressing embarrassments, we are, we submit, in no position to set *anyone* free.

Our native Muse, heaven knows and heaven be praised, is not exclusive. Whether out of the innocence of a childlike heart to whom all things are pure, or with the serenity of a status so majestic that the mere keeping up of tones and appearances, the suburban wonder as to what the strait-laced Unities might possibly think, or sad sour Probability possibly say, are questions for which she doesn't because she needn't, she hasn't in her lofty maturity any longer to care a rap, she invites, dear generous-hearted creature that she is, just *tout le monde* to drop in at any time so that her famous, memorable, sought-after evenings present to the speculative eye an ever-shining, never-tarnished proof of her amazing unheard-of power to combine and happily contrast, to make *every* shade of the social and moral palette contribute to the general richness, of the skill, unapproached and unattempted by Grecian aunt or Gallic sister, with which she can skate full tilt toward the forbidden incoherence and then, in the last split second, on the shuddering edge of the bohemian standardless abyss effect her breathtaking triumphant turn.

No timid segregation by rank or taste for her, no prudent listing into those who will, who might, who certainly would not get on, no nicely graded scale of invitations to heroic formal Tuesdays, young comic Thursdays, al fresco farcical Saturdays. No, the real, the only test of the theatrical as of the gastronomic, her practice confidently wagers, is the mixed perfected brew.

As he looks in on her, so marvellously at home with all her cozy swarm about her, what accents will not assault the new arrival's ear, the magnificent tropes of tragic defiance and despair, the repartee of the high humour, the pun of the very low, cultured drawl and manly illiterate bellow, yet all of them gratefully doing their huge or tiny best to make the party go?

And if, assured by her smiling wave that of course he may, he should presently set out to explore her vast and rambling mansion, to do honour to its dear odd geniuses of local convenience and proportion, its multiplied deities of mysterious stair and interesting alcove, not one of the laughing groups and engrossed warmed couples that he keeps "surprising"—the never-ending surprise for him is that he doesn't seem to—but affords some sharper instance of relations he would have been the last to guess at, choleric prince at his ease with lymphatic butler, moist hand-taking so to dry, youth getting on quite famously with stingy cold old age, some stranger vision of the large loud liberty violently rocking yet never, he is persuaded, finally upsetting the jolly crowded boat.

What, he may well ask, has the gracious goddess done to all these people that, at her most casual hint, they should so trustingly, so immediately take off those heavy habits one thinks of them as having for their health and happiness day and night to wear, without in this unfamiliar unbuttoned state—the notable absence of the slighest shiver or not-quite-inhibited sneeze is indication positive—for a second feeling the draught? Is there, could there be, *any* miraculous suspension of the wearily historic, the dingily geographic, the dully drearily sensible beyond her faith, her charm, her love, to command? Yes, there could be, yes, alas, indeed yes, O there is, right here, right now before us, the situation present.

How *could* you, you who are one of the oldest habitués at these delightful functions, one, possibly the closest, of her trusted inner circle, how could you be guilty of the incredible unpardonable treachery of bringing along the one creature, as you above all men must have known, whom she cannot and will not under any circumstances stand, the solitary exception she is not at any hour of the day or night at home to, the unique case that her attendant spirits have absolute instructions never, neither at the front door nor at the back, to admit?

At Him and at Him only does she draw the line, not because there are any limits to her sympathy but precisely because there are none. Just because of all she is and all she means to be, she cannot conceivably tolerate in her presence the represented principle of *not* sympathising, *not* associating, *not* amusing, the only child of her Awful Enemy, the rival whose real name she will never sully her lips with—"that envious witch" is sign sufficient—who does not rule but defiantly is the unrectored chaos.

All along and only too well she has known what would happen if, by any careless mischance—of conscious malice she never dreamed till now—He should ever manage to get in. She foresaw what He would do to the conversation, lying in wait for its vision of private love or public justice to warm to an Egyptian brilliance and then with some fishlike odour or *bruit insolite* snatching the visionaries back tongue-tied

376

and blushing to the here and now; she foresaw what He would do to the arrangements, breaking, by a refusal to keep in step, the excellent order of the dancing ring, and ruining supper by knocking over the loaded appetising tray; worst of all, she foresaw, she dreaded what He would end up by doing to her, that, not content with upsetting her guests, with spoiling their fun, His progress from outrage to outrage would not relent before the gross climax of His making, horror unspeakable, a pass at her virgin self.

Let us suppose, even, that in your eyes she is by no means as we have always fondly imagined, your dear friend, that what we have just witnessed was not what it seemed to us, the inexplicable betrayal of a life-long sacred loyalty, but your long-premeditated just revenge, the final evening up of some ancient never-forgotten score, then even so, why make us suffer who have never, in all conscience, done you harm? Surely the theatrical relation, no less than the marital, is governed by the sanely decent general law that, before visitors, in front of the children or the servants, there shall be no indiscreet revelation of animosity, no "scenes," that, no matter to what intolerable degrees of internal tempera- ture and pressure restraint may raise both the injured and the guilty, nevertheless such restraint is applied to tones and topics, the exhibited picture must be still as always the calm and smiling one the most malicious observer can see nothing wrong with, and not until the last of those whom manifested anger or mistrust would embarrass or amuse or not be good for have gone away or out or up, is the voice raised, the table thumped, the suspicious letter snatched at or the outrageous bill furiously waved.

For we, after all—you cannot have forgotten this—are strangers to her. We have never claimed her acquaintance, knowing as well as she that we do not and never could belong on her side of the curtain. All we have ever asked for is that for a few hours the curtain should be left undrawn, so as to allow our humble ragged selves the privilege of craning and gaping at the splendid goings-on inside. We most emphatically do *not* ask that she should speak to us, or try to understand us; on the contrary our one desire has always been that she should preserve for ever her old high strangeness, for what delights us about her world is just that it neither is nor possibly could become one in which we could breathe or behave, that in her house the right of innocent passage should remain so universal that the same neutral space accommodates the conspirator and his victim; the generals of both armies, the chorus of patriots and the choir of nuns, palace and farmyard, cathedral and smugglers' cave, that time should never revert to that intransigent element we are so ineluctably and only too familiarly in, but remain the passive good-natured creature she and her friends can by common consent do anything they like with —(it is not surprising that they should take advantage of their strange power and so frequently skip hours and days and even years: the dramatic mystery is that they should always so unanimously agree upon exactly how many hours and days and years to skip)—that upon their special constitutions the moral law should continue to operate so exactly that the timid not only deserve but actually win the fair, and it is the socially and physically unemphatic David who lays low the gorilla-chested Goliath with one well-aimed custard pie, that in their blessed climate, the manifestation of the inner life should always remain so easy and habitual that a sudden eruption of musical and metaphorical power is instantly recognised as standing for grief and disgust, an elegant *contrapposto* for violent death, and that consequently the picture which they in there present to us out here is always that of the perfectly tidiable case of disorder, the beautiful and serious problem exquisitely set with-

378

out a single superfluous datum and insoluble with less, the expert landing of all the passengers with all their luggage safe and sound in the best of health and spirits and without so much as a scratch or a bruise.

Into that world of freedom without anxiety, sincerity without loss of vigour, feeling that loosens rather than ties the tongue, we are not, we reiterate, so blinded by presumption to our proper status and interest as to expect or even wish at any time to enter, far less to dwell there.

Must we—it seems oddly that we must—remind you that our existence does not, like hers, enjoy an infinitely indicative mood, an eternally present tense, a limitlessly active voice, for in our shambling, slovenly makeshift world any two persons, whether domestic first or neighbourly second, require and necessarily presuppose in both their numbers and in all their cases, the whole inflected gamut of an alien third since, without a despised or dreaded Them to turn the back *on*, there could be no intimate or affectionate Us to turn the eye *to*; that, *chez nous*, space is never the whole uninhibited circle but always some segment, its eminent domain upheld by two co-ordinates. There always has been and always will be not only the vertical boundary, the river on this side of which initiative and honesty stroll arm in arm wearing sensible clothes, and beyond which is a savage elsewhere swarming with contagious diseases, but also its horizontal counterpart, the railroad above which houses stand in their own grounds, each equipped with a garage and a beautiful woman, sometimes with several, and below which huddled shacks provide a squeezing shelter to collarless herds who eat blancmange and have never said anything witty. Make the case as special as you please; take the tamest congregation or the wildest faction; take, say, a college. What river and railroad did for the grosser instance, lawn and corridor do for the more refined, dividing the tender who value

379

from the tough who measure, the superstitious who still sacrifice to causation from the heretics who have already reduced the worship of truth to bare description, and so creating the academic fields to be guarded with umbrella and learned periodical against the trespass of any unqualified stranger, not a whit less jealously than the game-preserve is protected from the poacher by the unamiable shot-gun. For without these prohibitive frontiers we should never know who we were or what we wanted. It is they who donate to neighbourhood all its accuracy and vehemence. It is thanks to them that we do know with whom to associate, make love, exchange recipes and jokes, go mountain climbing or sit side by side fishing from piers. It is thanks to them, too, that we know against whom to rebel. We *can* shock our parents by visiting the dives below the railroad tracks, we *can* amuse ourselves on what would otherwise have been a very dull evening indeed, in plotting to seize the post office across the river.

Of course, these several private regions must together comprise one public whole—we would never deny that logic and instinct require that—of course, We and They are united in the candid glare of the same commercial hope by day, and the soft refulgence of the same erotic nostalgia by night but—and this is our point—without our privacies of situation, our local idioms of triumph and mishap, our different doctrines concerning the transubstantiation of the larger pinker bun on the terrestrial dish for which the mature sense may reasonably water and the adult fingers furtively or unabashedly go for, our specific choices of which hill it would be romantic to fly away over or what sea it would be exciting to run away to, our peculiar visions of the absolute stranger with a spontaneous longing for the lost who will adopt our misery not out of desire but pure compassion, without, in short, our devoted pungent expression of the partial and constrasted, the Whole would have no importance and its Day and Night no interest.

So, too, with Time who, in our auditorium, is not her dear old buffer so anxious to please everybody, but a prim magistrate whose court never adjourns, and from whose decisions, as he laconically sentences one to loss of hair and talent, another to seven days' chastity, and a third to boredom for life, there is no appeal. We should not be sitting here now, washed, warm, well-fed, in seats we have paid for, unless there were others who are not here; our liveliness and good-humour, such as they are, are those of survivors, conscious that there are others who have not been so fortunate, others who did not succeed in navigating the narrow passage or to whom the natives were not friendly, others whose streets were chosen by the explosion or through whose country the famine turned aside from ours to go, others who failed to repel the invasion of bacteria or to crush the insurrection of their bowels, others who lost their suit against their parents or were ruined by wishes they could not adjust or murdered by resentments they could not control; aware of some who were better and bigger but from whom, only the other day, Fortune withdrew her hand in sudden disgust, now nervously playing chess with drunken sea-captains in sordid cafés on the equator or the Arctic Circle, or lying, only a few blocks away, strapped and screaming on iron beds or dropping to naked pieces in damp graves. And shouldn't you too, dear master, reflect—forgive us for mentioning it—that we might very well not have been attending a production of yours this evening, had not some other and maybe—who can tell?—brighter talent married a barmaid or turned religious and shy or gone down in a liner with all his manuscripts, the loss recorded only in the corner of some country newspaper below A Poultry Lover's Jottings?

You yourself, we seem to remember, have spoken of the

conjured spectacle as "a mirror held up to nature," a phrase misleading in its aphoristic sweep but indicative at least of one aspect of the relation between the real and the imagined, their mutual reversal of value, for isn't the essential artistic strangeness to which your citation of the sinisterly biassed image would point just this: that on the far side of the mirror the general will to compose, to form at all costs a felicitous pattern becomes the *necessary cause* of any particular effort to live or act or love or triumph or vary, instead of being as, in so far as it emerges at all, it is on this side, their *accidental effect?*

Does Ariel—to nominate the spirit of reflection in your terms—call for manifestation? Then neither modesty nor fear of reprisals excuses the one so called on from publicly confessing that she cheated at croquet or that he committed incest in a dream. Does He demand concealment? Then their nearest and dearest must be deceived by disguises of sex and age which anywhere else would at once attract the attentions of the police or the derisive whistle of the awful schoolboy. That is the price asked, and how promptly and gladly paid, for universal reconciliation and peace, for the privilege of all galloping together past the finishing post neck and neck.

How then, we continue to wonder, knowing all this, could you act as if you did not, as if you did not realise that the embarrassing compresence of the absolutely natural, incorrigibly right-handed, and, to any request for co-operation, utterly negative, with the enthusiastically self-effacing would be a simultaneous violation of both worlds, as if you were not perfectly well aware that the magical musical condition, the orphic spell that turns the fierce dumb greedy beasts into grateful guides and oracles who will gladly take one anywhere and tell one everything free of charge, is precisely and simply that of his finite immediate note *not,* under any circumstances, being struck, of its not being tentatively whispered, far less positively banged.

Are we not bound to conclude, then, that, whatever snub to the poetic you may have intended incidentally to administer, your profounder motive in so introducing Him to them among whom, because He doesn't belong, He couldn't appear as anything but His distorted parody, a deformed and savage slave, was to deal a mortal face-slapping insult to us among whom He does and is, moreover, all grossness turned to glory, no less a person than the nude august elated archer of our heaven, the darling single son of Her who, in her right milieu, is certainly no witch but the most sensible of all the gods, whose influence is as sound as it is pandemic, on the race-track no less than in the sleeping cars of the Orient Express, our great white Queen of Love herself?

But even that is not the worst we suspect you of. If your words have not buttered any parsnips, neither have they broken any bones.

He, after all, can come back to us now to be comforted and respected, perhaps, after the experience of finding Himself for a few hours and for the first time in His life not wanted, more fully and freshly appreciative of our affection than He has always been in the past; as for His dear mother, She is far too grand and far too busy to hear or care what you say or think. If only we were certain that your malice was confined to the verbal affront, we should long ago have demanded our money back and gone whistling home to bed. Alas, in addition to resenting what you have openly said, we fear even more what you may secretly have done. Is it possible that, not content with inveigling Caliban into Ariel's kingdom, you have also let loose Ariel in Caliban's? We note with alarm that when the other members of the final tableau were dismissed, He was not returned to His arboreal con-finement as He should have been. Where is He now? For if the intrusion of the real has disconcerted and incommoded the poetic, that is a mere bagatelle compared to the damage which the poetic would inflict if it ever succeeded in intruding upon the real. We want no Ariel here, breaking down our picket fences in the name of fraternity, seducing our wives in the name of romance, and robbing us of our sacred pecuniary deposits in the name of justice. Where is Ariel? What have you done with Him? For we won't, we daren't leave until you give us a satisfactory answer.

*   *   *

Such (let me cease to play your echo and return to my officially natural role)—such are your questions, are they not, but before I try to deal with them, I must ask for your patience, while I deliver a special message for our late author to those few among you, if indeed there be any—I have certainly heard no comment yet from them—who have come here, not to be entertained but to learn; that is, to any gay apprentice in the magical art who may have chosen this specimen of the prestidigitatory genus to study this evening in the hope of grasping more clearly just how the artistic contraption works, of observing some fresh detail in the complex process by which the heady wine of amusement is distilled from the grape of composition. The rest of you I must beg for a little while to sit back and relax as the remarks I have now to make do not concern you; your turn will follow later.

*   *   *

So, strange young man,—it is at his command, remember, that I say this to you; whether I agree with it or not is neither here nor there—you have decided on the conjurer's profession. Somewhere, in the middle of a salt marsh or at the bottom of a kitchen garden or on the top of a bus, you

heard imprisoned Ariel call for help, and it is now a libera-
tor's face that congratulates you from your shaving mirror
every morning. As you walk the cold streets hatless, or sit
over coffee and doughnuts in the corner of a cheap restaurant, your secret has already set you apart from the howling
merchants and transacting multitudes to watch with fascinated distaste the bellowing barging banging passage of
the awkward profit-seeking elbow, the dazed eye of the
gregarious acquisitive condition. Lying awake at night in
your single bed you are conscious of a power by which you
will survive the wallpaper of your boardinghouse or the
expensive bourgeois horrors of your home. Yes, Ariel is
grateful; He does come when you call, He does tell you all
the gossip He overhears on the stairs, all the goings-on He
observes through the keyhole; He really is willing to arrange
anything you care to ask for, and you are rapidly finding
out the right orders to give—who should be killed in the
hunting accident, which couple to send into the cast-iron
shelter, what scent will arouse a Norwegian engineer, how
to get the young hero from the country lawyer's office to the
Princess' reception, when to mislay the letter, where the cabinet minister should be reminded of his mother, why the
dishonest valet must be a martyr to indigestion but immune
from the common cold.

As the gay productive months slip by, in spite of fretful
discouraged days, of awkward moments of misunderstanding or rather, seen retrospectively as happily cleared up and
got over, verily because of them, you are definitely getting
the hang of this, at first so novel and bewildering, relation-
ship between magician and familiar, whose duty it is to
sustain your infinite conceptual appetite with vivid concrete
experiences. And, as the months turn into years, your won-
der-working romance into an economic habit, the encoun-
tered case of good or evil in our wide world of property and

boredom which leaves you confessedly and unsympathet-
ically at a loss, the aberrant phase in the whole human cycle
of ecstasy and exhaustion with which you are imperfectly
familiar, become increasingly rare. No perception however
petite, no notion however subtle, escapes your attention or
baffles your understanding: on entering any room you immediately distinguish the wasters who throw away their
fruit half-eaten from the preservers who bottle all the summer; as the passengers file down the ship's gangway you
unerringly guess which suitcase contains indecent novels;
a five-minute chat about the weather or the coming elections
is all you require to diagnose any distemper, however self-
assured, for by then your eye has already spotted the tremor
of the lips in that infinitesimal moment while the lie was
getting its balance, your ear already picked up the heart's
low whimper which the capering legs were determined to
stifle, your nose detected on love's breath the trace of ennui
which foretells his early death, or the despair just starting
to smoulder at the base of the scholar's brain which years
hence will suddenly blow it up with one appalling laugh:
in every case you can prescribe the saving treatment called
for, knowing at once when it may be gentle and remedial
when all that is needed is soft music and a pretty girl, and
when it must be drastic and surgical, when nothing will do
any good but political disgrace or financial and erotic failure.
If I seem to attribute these powers to you when the eyes, the
ears, the nose, the putting two and two together are, of
course, all His, and yours only the primitive wish to know,
it is a rhetorical habit I have caught from your, in the main
juvenile and feminine, admirers whose naive unawareness
of whom they ought properly to thank and praise you see no
point in, for mere accuracy's stuffy sake, correcting.

Anyway, the partnership is a brilliant success. On you go
together to ever greater and faster triumphs; ever more

major grows the accumulated work, ever more masterly the manner, sound even at its pale sententious worst, and at its best the rich red personal flower of the grave and grand, until one day which you can never either at the time or later identify exactly, your strange fever reaches its crisis and from now on begins, ever so slowly, maybe to subside. At first you cannot tell what or why is the matter; you have only a vague feeling that it is no longer between you so smooth and sweet as it used to be. Sour silences appear, at first only for an occasional moment, but progressively more frequently and more prolonged, curdled moods in which you cannot for the life of you think of any request to make, and His dumb standing around, waiting for orders gets inexplicably but maddeningly on your nerves, until presently, to your amazement, you hear yourself asking Him if He wouldn't like a vacation and are shocked by your feeling of intense disappointment when He who has always hitherto so immediately and recklessly taken your slightest hint, says gauchely "No." So it goes on from exasperated bad to desperate worst until you realise in despair that there is nothing for it but you two to part. Collecting all your strength for the distasteful task, you finally manage to stammer or shout "You are free. Good-bye," but to your dismay He whose obedience through all the enchanted years has never been less than perfect, now refuses to budge. Striding up to Him in fury, you glare into His unblinking eyes and stop dead, transfixed with horror at seeing reflected there, not what you had always expected to see, a conqueror smiling at a conqueror, both promising mountains and marvels, but a gibbering fist-clenched creature with which you are all too unfamiliar, for this is the first time indeed that you have met the only subject that you have, who is not a dream amenable to magic but the all too solid flesh you must acknowledge as your own; at last you have come face to face with me, and are appalled to learn how far I am from being, in any sense, your dish; how completely lacking in that poise and calm and all-forgiving because all-understanding good nature which to the critical eye is so wonderfully and domestically present on every page of your published inventions.

But where, may I ask, should I have acquired them, when, like a society mother who, although she is, of course, as she tells everyone, absolutely *devoted* to her child, simply *cannot* leave the dinner table just now and really *must* be in Le Touquet tomorrow, and so leaves him in charge of servants she doesn't know or boarding schools she has never seen, you have never in all these years taken the faintest personal interest in me? "Oh!" you protestingly gasp, "but how can you say such a thing, after I've toiled and moiled and worked my fingers to the bone, trying to give you a good home, after all the hours I've spent planning wholesome nourishing meals for you, after all the things I've gone without so that you should have swimming lessons and piano lessons and a new bicycle. Have I ever let you go out in summer without your sun hat, or come in in winter without feeling your stockings and insisting, if they were the least bit damp, on your changing them at once? Haven't you always been allowed to do everything, in reason, that you liked?"

Exactly: even deliberate ill-treatment would have been less unkind. Gallows and battlefields are, after all, no less places of mutual concern than sofa and bridal-bed; the dashing flirtations of fighter pilots and the coy tactics of twirled moustache and fluttered fan, the gasping mudcaked wooing of the coarsest foes and the reverent rage of the highest-powered romance, the lover's nip and the grip of the torturer's tongs are all,—ask Ariel,—variants of one common type, the bracket within which life and death with such passionate gusto cohabit, to be distinguished solely by the plus or minus sign which stands before them, signs which He is able at any time and in either direction to switch, but the one exception, the sum no magic of His can ever transmute, is the indifferent zero. Had you tried to destroy me, had we wrestled through long dark hours, we might by daybreak have learnt something from each other; in some panting pause to recover breath for further more savage blows or in the moment before your death or mine, we might both have heard together that music which explains and pardons all.

Had you, on the other hand, really left me alone to go my whole free-wheeling way to disorder, to be drunk every day before lunch, to jump stark naked from bed to bed, to have a fit every week or a major operation every other year, to forge checks or water the widow's stock, I might, after countless skids and punctures, have come by the bumpy third-class road of guilt and remorse, smack into that very same truth which you were meanwhile admiring from your distant comfortable veranda but would never point out to me.

Such genuine escapades, though, might have disturbed the master at his meditations and even involved him in trouble with the police. The strains of oats, therefore, that you prudently permitted me to sow were each and all of an unmitigatedly minor wildness: a quick cold clasp now and then in some *louche* hotel to calm me down while you got on with the so thorough documentation of your great unhappy love for one who by being bad or dead or married provided you with the Good Right Subject that would never cease to bristle with importance; one bout of flu per winter, an occasional twinge of toothache, and enough tobacco to keep me in a good temper while you composed your melting eclogues of rustic piety; licence to break my shoelaces, spill soup on my tie, burn cigarette holes in the tablecloth, lose letters and borrowed books, and generally keep myself busy while you polished to a perfection your lyric praises of the more candid, more luxurious world to come.

Can you wonder then, when, as was bound to happen sooner or later, your charms, because they no longer amuse you, have cracked and your spirits, because you are tired of giving orders, have ceased to obey, and you are left alone with me, the dark thing you could never abide to be with, if I do not yield you kind answer or admire you for the achievements I was never allowed to profit from, if I resent hearing you speak of your neglect of me as your "exile," of the pains you never took with me as "all lost"?

But why continue? From now on we shall have, as we both know only too well, no company but each other's, and if I have had, as I consider, a good deal to put up with from you, I must own that, after all, I am not just the person I would have chosen for a life companion myself; so the only chance, which in any case is slim enough, of my getting a tolerably new master and you a tolerably new man, lies in our both learning, if possible and as soon as possible, to forgive and forget the past, and to keep our respective hopes for the future, within moderate, very moderate, limits.

*   *   *

And now at last it is you, assorted, consorted specimens of the general popular type, the major flock who have trotted trustingly hither but found, you reproachfully baah, no grazing, that I turn to and address on behalf of Ariel and myself. To your questions I shall attempt no direct reply, for the mere fact that you have been able so anxiously to put them is in itself sufficient proof that you possess their answers. All your clamour signifies is this: that your first big crisis, the breaking of the childish spell in which, so long as it enclosed you, there was, for you, no mirror, no magic, for everything that happened was a miracle—it was just as extraordinary for a chair to be a chair as for it to turn into a horse; it was no more absurd that the girding on of coal-scuttle and poker should transform you into noble Hector than that you should have a father and mother who called you Tommy—and it was therefore only necessary for you to presuppose one genius, one unrivalled I to wish these wonders in all their endless plenitude and novelty to be, is, in relation to your present, behind, that your singular transparent globes of enchantment have shattered one by one, and you have now all come together in the larger colder emptier room on this side of the mirror which *does* force your eyes to recognise and reckon with the two of us, your ears to detect the irreconcilable difference between my reiterated affirmation of what your furnished circumstances categorically are, and His successive propositions as to everything else which they conditionally might be. You have, as I say, taken your first step.

The Journey of life—the down-at-heels disillusioned figure can still put its characterisation across—is infinitely long and its possible destinations infinitely distant from one another, but the time spent in actual travel is infinitesimally small. The hours the traveller measures are those in which he is at rest between the three or four decisive instants of transportation which are all he needs and all he gets to carry him the whole of his way; the scenery he observes is the view, gorgeous or drab, he glimpses from platform and siding; the incidents he thrills or blushes to remember take place in waiting and washrooms, ticket queues and parcels offices: it is in those promiscuous places of random association, in that air of anticipatory fidget, that he makes friends and enemies, that he promises, confesses, kisses, and betrays until, either because it is the one he has been expecting, or because, losing his temper, he has vowed to take the first to come along, or because he has been given a free ticket, or simply by misdirection or mistake, a train arrives which he does get into: it whistles—at least he thinks afterwards he remembers it whistling—but before he can blink, it has come to a standstill àgain and there he stands clutching his battered bags, surrounded by entirely strange smells and noises—yet in their smelliness and noisiness how familiar— one vast important stretch the nearer Nowhere, that still smashed terminus at which he will, in due course, be deposited, seedy and by himself.

Yes, you have made a definite start; you *have* left your homes way back in the farming provinces or way out in the suburban tundras, but whether you have been hanging around for years or have barely and breathlessly got here on one of those locals which keep arriving minute after minute, this is still only the main depot, the Grandly Average Place from which at odd hours the expresses leave seriously and sombrely for Somewhere, and where it is still possible for me to posit the suggestion that you go no farther. You will never, after all, feel better than in your present shaved and breakfasted state which there are restaurants and barber shops here indefinitely to preserve; you will never feel more secure than you do now in your knowledge that you *have* your ticket, your passport *is* in order, you have *not* forgotten to pack your pyjamas and an extra clean shirt; you will never have the same opportunity of learning about *all* the holy delectable spots of current or historic interest—an insistence on reaching *one* will necessarily exclude the others—than you have in these bepostered halls; you will never meet a jollier, more various crowd than you see around you here, sharing with you the throbbing, suppressed excitement of those to whom the exciting thing is still, perhaps, to happen. But once you leave, no matter in which direction, your next

stop will be far outside this land of habit that so democrati-
cally stands up for your right to stagestruck hope, and well
inside one of those, all equally foreign, uncomfortable and
despotic, certainties of failure or success. Here at least I, and
Ariel too, are free to warn you not, should we meet again
there, to speak to either of us, not to engage either of us as
your guide, but there we shall no longer be able to refuse
you; then, unfortunately for you, we shall be compelled to
say nothing and obey your fatal foolish commands. Here,
whether you listen to me or not, and it's highly improbable
that you will, I can at least warn you what will happen if at
our next meeting you should insist—and that is all too
probable—on putting one of us in charge.

*   *   *

"Release us," you will beg, then, supposing it is I whom
you make for,—oh how awfully uniform, once one trans-
lates them out of your private lingoes of expression, all your
sorrows are and how awfully well I know them—"release
us from our minor roles. Carry me back, Master, to the
cathedral town where the canons run through the water
meadows with butterfly nets and the old women keep sweet-
shops in the cobbled side streets, or back to the upland mill
town (gunpowder and plush) with its grope-movie and its
poolroom lit by gas, carry me back to the days before my wife
had put on weight, back to the years when beer was cheap
and the rivers really froze in winter. Pity me, Captain, pity
a poor old stranded sea-salt whom an unlucky voyage has
wrecked on the desolate mahogany coast of this bar with
nothing left him but his big moustache. Give me my passage
home, let me see that harbour once again just as it was before I learned the bad words. Patriarchs wiser than Abraham
mended their nets on the modest wharf; white and wonderful beings undressed on the sand-dunes; sunset glittered on

the plate-glass windows of the Marine Biological Station; far off on the extreme horizon a whale spouted. Look, Uncle, look. They have broken my glasses and I have lost my silver whistle. Pick me up, Uncle, let little Johnny ride away on your massive shoulders to recover his green kingdom, where the steam rollers are as friendly as the farm dogs and it would never become necessary to look over one's left shoulder or clench one's right fist in one's pocket. You cannot miss it. Black currant bushes hide the ruined opera house where badgers are said to breed in great numbers; an old horse-tramway winds away westward through suave foothills crowned with stone circles—follow it and by nightfall one would come to a large good-natured waterwheel—to the north, beyond a forest inhabited by charcoal burners, one can see the Devil's Bedposts quite distinctly, to the east the museum where for sixpence one can touch the ivory chessmen. O Cupid, Cupid, howls the whole dim chorus, take us home. We have never felt really well in this climate of distinct ideas; we have never been able to follow the regulations properly; Business, Science, Religion, Art, and all the other fictitious immortal persons who matter here have, frankly, not been very kind. We're so, so tired, the rewarding soup is stone cold, and over our blue wonders the grass grew long ago. O take us home with you, strong and swelling One, home to your promiscuous pastures where the minotaur of authority is just a roly-poly ruminant and nothing is at stake, those purring sites and amusing vistas where the fluctuating arabesques of sound, the continuous eruption of colours and scents, the whole rich incoherence of a nature made up of gaps and asymmetrical events plead beautifully and bravely for our undistress."

And in that very moment when you so cry for deliverance from any and every anxious possibility, I shall have no option but to be faithful to my oath of service and instantly transport you, not indeed to any cathedral town or mill town or harbour or hillside or jungle or other specific Eden which your memory necessarily but falsely conceives of as the ultimately liberal condition, which in point of fact you have never known yet, but directly to that downright state itself. Here you are. This is it. Directly overhead a full moon casts a circle of dazzling light without any penumbra, exactly circumscribing its desolation in which every object is extraordinarily still and sharp. Cones of extinct volcanos rise up abruptly from the lava plateau fissured by chasms and pitted with hot springs from which steam rises without interruption straight up into the windless rarefied atmosphere. Here and there a geyser erupts without warning, spouts furiously for a few seconds and as suddenly subsides. Here, where the possessive note is utterly silent and all events are tautological repetitions and no decision will ever alter the secular stagnation, at long last you are, as you have asked to be, the only subject. Who, When, Why, the poor tired little historic questions fall wilting into a hush of utter failure. Your tears splash down upon clinkers which will never be persuaded to recognise a neighbour and there is really and truly no one to appear with tea and help. You have indeed come all the way to the end of your bachelor's journey where Liberty stands with her hands behind her back, not caring, not minding *anything*. Confronted by a straight and snubbing stare to which mythology is bosh, surrounded by an infinite passivity and purely arithmetical disorder which is only open to perception, and with nowhere to go on to, your existence is indeed free at last to choose its own meaning, that is, to plunge headlong into despair and fall through silence fathomless and dry, all fact your single drop, all value your pure alas.

*   *   *

But what of that other, smaller but doubtless finer group among you, important persons at the top of the ladder, exhausted lions of the season, local authorities with their tense tired faces, elderly hermits of both sexes living gloomily in the delta of a great fortune, whose *amour propre* prefers to turn for help to my more spiritual colleague.

"O yes," you will sigh, "we have had what once we would have called success. I moved the vices out of the city into a chain of re-conditioned lighthouses. I introduced statistical methods into the Liberal Arts. I revived the country dances and installed electric stoves in the mountain cottages. I saved democracy by buying steel. I gave the caesura its freedom. But this world is no better and it is now quite clear to us that there is nothing to be done with such a ship of fools, adrift on a sugarloaf sea in which it is going very soon and suitably to founder. Deliver us, dear Spirit, from the tantrums of our telephones and the whispers of our secretaries conspiring against Man; deliver us from these helpless agglomerations of dishevelled creatures with their bed-wetting, vomiting, weeping bodies, their giggling, fugitive, disappointing hearts, and scrawling, blotted, misspelt minds, to whom we have so foolishly tried to bring the light they did not want; deliver us from all the litter of *billets-doux,* empty beer bottles, laundry lists, directives, promissory notes and broken toys, the terrible mess that this particularised life, which we have so futilely attempted to tidy, sullenly insists on leaving behind it; translate us, bright Angel, from this hell of inert and ailing matter, growing steadily senile in a time for ever immature, to that blessed realm, so far above the twelve impertinent winds and the four unreliable seasons, that Heaven of the Really General Case where, tortured no longer by three dimensions and immune from temporal vertigo, Life turns into Light, absorbed for good into the permanently stationary, completely self-sufficient, absolutely reasonable One."

Obliged by the terms of His contract to gratify this other request of yours, the wish for freedom to transcend *any* condition, for direct unentailed power without *any*, however secretly immanent, obligation to inherit or transmit, what can poor shoulder-shrugging Ariel do but lead you forthwith into a nightmare which has all the wealth of exciting action and all the emotional poverty of an adventure story for boys, a state of perpetual emergency and everlasting improvisation where all is need and change.

All the phenomena of an empirically ordinary world are given. Extended objects appear to which events happen— old men catch dreadful coughs, little girls get their arms twisted, flames run whooping through woods, round a river bend, as harmless looking as a dirty old bearskin rug, comes the gliding fury of a town-effacing wave, but these are merely elements in an allegorical landscape to which mathematical measurement and phenomenological analysis have no relevance.

All the voluntary movements are possible—crawling through flues and old sewers, sauntering past shop-fronts, tiptoeing through quicksands and mined areas, running through derelict factories and across empty plains, jumping over brooks, diving into pools or swimming along between banks of roses, pulling at manholes or pushing at revolving doors, clinging to rotten balustrades, sucking at straws or wounds; all the modes of transport, letters, oxcarts, canoes, hansom cabs, trains, trolleys, cars, aeroplanes, balloons, are available, but any sense of direction, any knowledge of where on earth one has come from or where on earth one is going to is completely absent.

Religion and culture seem to be represented by a catholic

belief that something is lacking which must be found, but as to what that something is, the keys of heaven, the missing air, genius, the smells of childhood, or a sense of humour, why it is lacking, whether it has been deliberately stolen, or accidentally lost or just hidden for a lark, and who is responsible, our ancestors, ourselves, the social structure, or mysterious wicked powers, there are as many faiths as there are searchers, and clues can be found behind every clock, under every stone, and in every hollow tree to support all of them.

Again, other selves undoubtedly exist, but though everyone's pocket is bulging with birth certificates, insurance policies, passports and letters of credit, there is no way of proving whether they are genuine or planted or forged, so that no one knows whether another is his friend disguised as an enemy or his enemy disguised as a friend (there is probably no one whose real name is Brown), or whether the police who here as elsewhere are grimly busy, are crushing a criminal revolt or upholding a vicious tyranny, any more than he knows whether he himself is a victim of the theft, or the thief, or a rival thief, a professionally interested detective or a professionally impartial journalist.

Even the circumstances of the tender passion, the long-distance calls, the assignation at the aquarium, the farewell embrace under the fish-tail burner on the landing, are continually present, but since, each time it goes through its performance, it never knows whether it is saving a life, or obtaining secret information, or forgetting or spiting its real love, the heart feels nothing but a dull percussion of conceptual foreboding. Everything, in short, suggests Mind but, surrounded by an infinite extension of the adolescent difficulty, a rising of the subjective and subjunctive to ever steeper, stormier heights, the panting frozen expressive gift has collapsed under the strain of its communicative anxiety, and contributes nothing by way of meaning but a series of staccato barks or a delirious gush of glossolalia.

And from this nightmare of public solitude, this everlasting Not Yet, what relief have you but in an ever giddier collective gallop, with bisson eye and bevel course, toward the grey horizon of the bleaker vision, what landmarks but the four dead rivers, the Joyless, the Flaming, the Mournful, and the Swamp of Tears, what goal but the black stone on which the bones are cracked, for only there in its cry of agony can your existence find at last an unequivocal meaning and your refusal to be yourself become a serious despair, the love nothing, the fear all?

*   *   *

Such are the alternative routes, the facile glad-handed highway or the virtuous averted track, by which the human effort to make its own fortune arrives all eager at its abruptly dreadful end. I have tried—the opportunity was not to be neglected—to raise the admonitory forefinger, to ring the alarming bell, but with so little confidence of producing the right result, so certain that the open eye and attentive ear will always interpret any sight and any sound to their advantage, every rebuff as a consolation, every prohibition as a rescue—that is what they open and attend for—that I find myself almost hoping, for your sake, that I have had the futile honour of addressing the blind and the deaf.

Having learnt his language, I begin to feel something of the serio-comic embarrassment of the dedicated dramatist, who, in representing to you your condition of estrangement from the truth, is doomed to fail the more he succeeds, for the more truthfully he paints the condition, the less clearly can he indicate the truth from which it is estranged, the brighter his revelation of the truth in its order, its justice, its joy, the fainter shows his picture of your actual condition

399

in all its drabness and sham, and, worse still, the more sharply he defines the estrangement itself—and, ultimately, what other aim and justification has he, what else exactly *is* the artistic gift which he is forbidden to hide, if not to make you unforgettably conscious of the ungarnished offended gap between what you so questionably are and what you are commanded without any question to become, of the unqualified No that opposes your every step in any direction? —the more he must strengthen your delusion that an awareness of the gap is in itself a bridge, your interest in your imprisonment a release, so that, far from your being led by him to contrition and surrender, the regarding of your defects in his mirror, your dialogue, using his words, with yourself about yourself, becomes the one activity which never, like devouring or collecting or spending, lets you down, the one game which can be guaranteed, whatever the company, to catch on, a madness of which you can only be cured by some shock quite outside his control, an unpredictable misting over of his glass or an absurd misprint in his text.

Our unfortunate dramatist, therefore, is placed in the unseemly predicament of having to give all his passion, all his skill, all his time to the task of "doing" life—consciously to give anything less than all would be a gross betrayal of his gift and an unpardonable presumption—as if it lay in *his* power to solve this dilemma—yet of having at the same time to hope that some unforeseen mishap will intervene to ruin his effect, without, however, obliterating your disappointment, the expectation aroused by him that there was an effect to ruin, that, if the smiling interest never did arrive, it must, through no fault of its own, have got stuck somewhere; that, exhausted, ravenous, delayed by fog, mobbed and mauled by a thousand irrelevancies, it has, nevertheless, not forgotten its promise but is still trying desperately to get a connection.

Beating about for some large loose image to define the original drama which aroused his imitative passion, the first performance in which the players were their own audience, the worldly stage on which their behaving flesh was really sore and sorry—for the floods of tears were not caused by onions, the deformities and wounds did not come off after a good wash, the self-stabbed heroine could not pick herself up again to make a gracious bow nor her seducer go demurely home to his plain and middle-aged spouse—the fancy immediately flushed is of the greatest grandest opera rendered by a very provincial touring company indeed.

Our performance—for Ariel and I are, you know this now, just as deeply involved as any of you—which we were obliged, all of us, to go on with and sit through right to the final dissonant chord, has been so indescribably inexcusably awful. Sweating and shivering in our moth-eaten ill-fitting stock costumes which with only a change of hat and re-arrangement of safety-pins, had to do for the *landsknecht* and the Parisian art-student, bumping into, now a rippling palace, now a primeval forest full of holes, at cross purposes with the scraping bleating orchestra we could scarcely hear for half the instruments were missing and the cottage piano which was filling-out must have stood for too many years in some damp parlour, we floundered on from fiasco to fiasco, the schmalz tenor never quite able at his big moments to get right up nor the ham bass right down, the stud contralto gargling through her maternal grief, the ravished coloratura trilling madly off-key and the re-united lovers half a bar apart, the knock-kneed armies shuffling limply through their bloody battles, the unearthly harvesters hysterically entangled in their honest fugato.

Now it is over. No, we have not dreamt it. Here we really stand, down stage with red faces and no applause; no effect, however simple, no piece of business, however unimportant, came off; there was not a single aspect of our whole production, not even the huge stuffed bird of happiness, for which a kind word could, however patronisingly, be said.

Yet, at this very moment when we do at last see ourselves as we are, neither cozy nor playful, but swaying out on the ultimate wind-whipped cornice that overhangs the unabiding void—we have never stood anywhere else,—when our reasons are silenced by the heavy huge derision,—There is nothing to say. There never has been,—and our wills chuck in their hands— There is no way out. There never was,— it is at this moment that for the first time in our lives we hear, not the sounds which, as born actors, we have hitherto condescended to use as an excellent vehicle for displaying our personalities and looks, but the real Word which is our only *raison d'etre*. Not that we have improved; everything, the massacres, the whippings, the lies, the twaddle, and all their carbon copies are still present, more obviously than ever; nothing has been reconstructed; our shame, our fear, our incorrigible staginess, all wish and no resolve, are still, and more intensely than ever, all we have: only now it is not in spite of them but with them that we are blessed by that Wholly Other Life from which we are separated by an essential emphatic gulf of which our contrived fissures of mirror and proscenium arch—we understand them at last —are feebly figurative signs, so that all our meanings are reversed and it is precisely in its negative image of Judgment that we can positively envisage Mercy; it is just here, among the ruins and the bones, that we may rejoice in the perfected Work which is not ours. Its great coherences stand out through our secular blur in all their overwhelmingly righteous obligation; its voice speaks through our muffling banks of artificial flowers and unflinchingly delivers its authentic molar pardon; its spaces greet us with all their grand old prospect of wonder and width; the working charm is the full bloom of the unbothered state; the sounded note is the restored relation.

Postscript

(*Ariel to Caliban. Echo by the Prompter*)

Weep no more but pity me,
Fleet persistent shadow cast
By your lameness, caught at last,
Helplessly in love with you,
Elegance, art, fascination,
   Fascinated by
   Drab mortality;
Spare me a humiliation,
   To your faults be true:
I can sing as you reply
         . . . *I*

Wish for nothing lest you mar
The perfection in these eyes
Whose entire devotion lies
At the mercy of your will;
Tempt not your sworn comrade,—only
   As I am can I
   Love you as you are—
For my company be lonely
   For my health be ill:
I will sing if you will cry
         . . . *I*

Never hope to say farewell,
For our lethargy is such
Heaven's kindness cannot touch
Nor earth's frankly brutal drum;
This was long ago decided,
    Both of us know why,
    Can, alas, foretell,
When our falsehoods are divided,
    What we shall become,
One evaporating sigh
                    . . . ♪

Part IX

FOR THE TIME BEING

A Christmas Oratorio

IN MEMORIAM

CONSTANCE ROSALIE AUDEN

1870-1941

*What shall we say then? Shall we continue
in sin, that grace may abound? God forbid.*
ROMANS VI.

Advent

I

Chorus

Darkness and snow descend;
The clock on the mantelpiece
Has nothing to recommend,
Nor does the face in the glass
Appear nobler than our own
As darkness and snow descend
On all personality.
Huge crowds mumble—"Alas,
Our angers do not increase,
Love is not what she used to be";
Portly Caesar yawns—"I know";
He falls asleep on his throne,
They shuffle off through the snow:
Darkness and snow descend.

Semi-Chorus

Can great Hercules keep his
Extraordinary promise
To reinvigorate the Empire?
Utterly lost, he cannot
Even locate his task but
Stands in some decaying orchard
Or the irregular shadow
Of a ruined temple, aware of
Being watched from the horrid mountains
By fanatical eyes yet
Seeing no one at all, only hearing
The silence softly broken
By the poisonous rustle
Of famishing Arachne.

Chorus

Winter completes an age
With its thorough levelling;
Heaven's tourbillions of rage
Abolish the watchman's tower
And delete the cedar grove.
As winter completes an age,
The eyes huddle like cattle, doubt
Seeps into the pores and power
Ebbs from the heavy signet ring;
The prophet's lantern is out
And gone the boundary stone,
Cold the heart and cold the stove,
Ice condenses on the bone:
Winter completes an age.

Semi-Chorus

Outside the civil garden
Of every day of love there
Crouches a wild passion
　　To destroy and be destroyed.
O who to boast their power
Have challenged it to charge? Like
Wheat our souls are sifted
　　And cast into the void.

Chorus

The evil and armed draw near;
The weather smells of their hate
And the houses smell of our fear;
Death has opened his white eye
And the black hole calls the thief
As the evil and armed draw near.
Ravens alight on the wall,

Our plans have all gone awry,
The rains will arrive too late,
Our resourceful general
Fell down dead as he drank
And his horses died of grief,
Our navy sailed away and sank;
The evil and armed draw near.

II

Narrator

If, on account of the political situation,
There are quite a number of homes without roofs, and men
Lying about in the countryside neither drunk nor asleep,
If all sailings have been cancelled till further notice,
If it's unwise now to say much in letters, and if,
Under the subnormal temperatures prevailing,
The two sexes are at present the weak and the strong,
That is not at all unusual for this time of year.
If that were all we should know how to manage. Flood, fire,
The desiccation of grasslands, restraint of princes,
Piracy on the high seas, physical pain and fiscal grief,
These after all are our familiar tribulations,
And we have been through them all before, many, many times.
As events which belong to the natural world where
The occupation of space is the real and final fact
And time turns round itself in an obedient circle,
They occur again and again but only to pass
Again and again into their formal opposites,
From sword to ploughshare, coffin to cradle, war to work,
So that, taking the bad with the good, the pattern composed
By the ten thousand odd things that can possibly happen
Is permanent in a general average way.

Till lately we knew of no other, and between us we seemed

To have what it took—the adrenal courage of the tiger,
The chameleon's discretion, the modesty of the doe,
Or the fern's devotion to spatial necessity:
To practise one's peculiar civic virtue was not
So impossible after all; to cut our losses
And bury our dead was really quite easy: That was why
We were always able to say: "We are children of God,
And our Father has never forsaken His people."

   But then we were children: That was a moment ago,
Before an outrageous novelty had been introduced
Into our lives. Why were we never warned? Perhaps we were.
Perhaps that mysterious noise at the back of the brain
We noticed on certain occasions—sitting alone
In the waiting room of the country junction, looking
Up at the toilet window—was not indigestion
But this Horror starting already to scratch Its way in?
Just how, just when It succeeded we shall never know:
We can only say that now It is there and that nothing
We learnt before It was there is now of the slightest use,
For nothing like It has happened before. It's as if
We had left our house for five minutes to mail a letter,
And during that time the living room had changed places
With the room behind the mirror over the fireplace;
It's as if, waking up with a start, we discovered
Ourselves stretched out flat on the floor, watching our shadow
Sleepily stretching itself at the window. I mean
That the world of space where events re-occur is still there,
Only now it's no longer real; the real one is nowhere
Where time never moves and nothing can ever happen:
I mean that although there's a person we know all about
Still bearing our name and loving himself as before,
That person has become a fiction; our true existence
Is decided by no one and has no importance to love.

That is why we despair; that is why we would welcome
The nursery bogey or the winecellar ghost, why even
The violent howling of winter and war has become
Like a juke-box tune that we dare not stop. We are afraid
Of pain but more afraid of silence; for no nightmare
Of hostile objects could be as terrible as this Void.
This is the Abomination. This is the wrath of God.

III

Chorus

Alone, alone, about a dreadful wood
Of conscious evil runs a lost mankind,
Dreading to find its Father lest it find
The Goodness it has dreaded is not good:
Alone, alone, about our dreadful wood.

Where is that Law for which we broke our own,
Where now that Justice for which Flesh resigned
Her hereditary right to passion, Mind
His will to absolute power? Gone. Gone.
Where is that Law for which we broke our own?

The Pilgrim Way has led to the Abyss.
Was it to meet such grinning evidence
We left our richly odoured ignorance?
Was the triumphant answer to be this?
The Pilgrim Way has led to the Abyss.

We who must die demand a miracle.
How could the Eternal do a temporal act,
The Infinite become a finite fact?
Nothing can save us that is possible:
We who must die demand a miracle.

IV

Recitative

If the muscle can feel repugnance, there is still a false move to
    be made;
If the mind can imagine tomorrow, there is still a defeat
    to remember;
As long as the self can say "I," it is impossible not to rebel;
As long as there is an accidental virtue, there is a necessary vice:
And the garden cannot exist, the miracle cannot occur.

For the garden is the only place there is, but you will not find it
Until you have looked for it everywhere and found nowhere that
    is not a desert;
The miracle is the only thing that happens, but to you it will not
    be apparent,
Until all events have been studied and nothing happens that
    you cannot explain;
And life is the destiny you are bound to refuse until you have
    consented to die.

Therefore, see without looking, hear without listening, breathe
    without asking:
The Inevitable is what will seem to happen to you purely
    by chance;
The Real is what will strike you as really absurd;
Unless you are certain you are dreaming, it is certainly a dream
    of your own;
Unless you exclaim—"There must be some mistake"—you must
    be mistaken.

V

Chorus

O where is that immortal and nameless Centre from which our
    points of

Definition and death are all equi-distant? Where
The well of our wish to wander, the everlasting fountain
    Of the waters of joy that our sorrow uses for tears?
O where is the garden of Being that is only known in Existence
    As the command to be never there, the sentence by which
Alephs of throbbing fact have been banished into position,
    The clock that dismisses the moment into the turbine of time?

O would I could mourn over Fate like the others, the resolute
        creatures,
    By seizing my chance to regret. The stone is content
With a formal anger and falls and falls; the plants are indignant
    With one dimension only and can only doubt
Whether light or darkness lies in the worse direction; and
        the subtler
    Exiles who try every path are satisfied
With proving that none have a goal: why must Man
        also acknowledge
    It is not enough to bear witness, for even protest is wrong?

Earth is cooled and fire is quenched by his unique excitement,
    All answers expire in the clench of his questioning hand,
His singular emphasis frustrates all possible order:
    Alas, his genius is wholly for envy; alas,
The vegetative sadness of lakes, the locomotive beauty
    Of choleric beasts of prey, are nearer than he
To the dreams that deprive him of sleep, the powers that compel
        him to idle,
    To his amorous nymphs and his sanguine athletic gods.

How can his knowledge protect his desire for truth from illusion?
    How can he wait without idols to worship, without
Their overwhelming persuasion that somewhere, over the
        high hill,
    Under the roots of the oak, in the depths of the sea,

Is a womb or a tomb wherein he may halt to express
    some attainment?
  How can he hope and not dream that his solitude
Shall disclose a vibrating flame at last and entrust him forever
  With its magic secret of how to extemporise life?

The Annunciation

I

The Four Faculties

Over the life of Man
We watch and wait,
The Four who manage
His fallen estate:
We who are four were
Once but one,
Before his act of
Rebellion;
We were himself when
His will was free,
His error became our
Chance to be.
Powers of air and fire,
Water and earth,
Into our hands is given
Man from his birth:

Intuition

As a dwarf in the dark of
His belly I rest;

Feeling
A nymph, I inhabit
The heart in his breast;

Sensation
A giant, at the gates of
His body I stand;

Thought
His dreaming brain is
My fairyland.

Tutti
Invisible phantoms,
The forms we assume are
Adapted to each
Individual humour,
Beautiful facts or true
Generalisations,
Test cases in Law or
Market quotations:
As figures and formulae
Chemists have seen us,
Who to true lovers were
Putti of Venus.

Ambiguous causes
Of all temptation,
We lure men either
To death or salvation:
We alone may look over
The wall of that hidden
Garden whose entrance
To him is forbidden;

415

Must truthfully tell him
What happens inside,
But what it may mean he
Alone must decide.

II

Thought

The garden is unchanged, the silence is unbroken.
Truth has not yet intruded to possess
Its empty morning nor the promised hour
Shaken its lasting May.

Intuition

The human night,
Whose messengers we are, cannot dispel
Its wanton dreams, and they are all we know.

Sensation

My senses are still coarse
From late engrossment in a fair. Old tunes
Reiterated, lights with repeated winks,
Were fascinating like a tic and brought
Whole populations running to a plain,
Making its lush alluvial meadows
One boisterous preposter. By the river
A whistling crowd had waited many hours
To see a naked woman swim upstream;
Honours and reckless medicines were served
In booths where interest was lost
As easily as money; at the back,
In a wet vacancy among the ash cans,
A waiter coupled sadly with a crow.

Feeling

I have but now escaped a raging landscape:
There woods were in a tremor from the shouts
Of hunchbacks hunting a hermaphrodite;
A burning village scampered down a lane;
Insects with ladders stormed a virgin's house;
On a green knoll littered with picnics
A mob of horses kicked a gull to death.

Intuition

Remembrance of the moment before last
Is like a yawning drug. I have observed
The sombre valley of an industry
In dereliction. Conduits, ponds, canals,
Distressed with weeds; engines and furnaces
At rust in rotting sheds; and their strong users
Transformed to spongy heaps of drunken flesh.
Deep among dock and dusty nettle lay
Each ruin of a will; manors of mould
Grew into empires as a westering sun
Left the air chilly; not a sound disturbed
The autumn dusk except a stertorous snore
That over their drowned condition like a sea
Wept without grief.

Thought

My recent company
Was worse than your three visions. Where I was,
The haunting ghosts were figures with no ground,
Areas of wide omission and vast regions
Of passive colour; higher than any squeak,
One note went on for ever; an embarrassed sum

Stuck on the stutter of a decimal,
And points almost coincident already
Approached so slowly they could never meet.
There nothing could be stated or constructed:
To Be was an archaic nuisance.

Intuition

Look. There is someone in the garden.

Feeling

The garden is unchanged, the silence is unbroken
For she is still walking in her sleep of childhood:
Many before
Have wandered in, like her, then wandered out
Unconscious of their visit and unaltered,
The garden unchanged, the silence unbroken:
None may wake there but One who shall be woken.

The Angel Gabriel

Wake.

III

Gabriel

Mary, in a dream of love
Playing as all children play,
For unsuspecting children may
Express in comic make-believe
The wish that later they will know
Is tragic and impossible;
Hear, child, what I am sent to tell:
Love wills your dream to happen, so
Love's will on earth may be, through you,
No longer a pretend but true.

418

Mary

What dancing joy would whirl
My ignorance away?
Light blazes out of the stone,
The taciturn water
Burst into music,
And warm wings throb within
The motionless rose:
What sudden rush of Power
Commands me to command?

Gabriel

When Eve, in love with her own will,
Denied the will of Love and fell,
She turned the flesh Love knew so well
To knowledge of her love until
Both love and knowledge were of sin:
What her negation wounded, may
Your affirmation heal today;
Love's will requires your own, that in
The flesh whose love you do not know,
Love's knowledge into flesh may grow.

Mary

My flesh in terror and fire
Rejoices that the Word
Who utters the world out of nothing,
As a pledge of His word to love her
Against her will, and to turn
Her desperate longing to love,
Should ask to wear me,
From now to their wedding day,
For an engagement ring.

Gabriel

Since Adam, being free to choose,
Chose to imagine he was free
To choose his own necessity,
Lost in his freedom, Man pursues
The shadow of his images:
Today the Unknown seeks the known;
What I am willed to ask, your own
Will has to answer; child, it lies
Within your power of choosing to
Conceive the Child who chooses you.

IV

Solo and Chorus

Let number and weight rejoice
In this hour of their translation
Into conscious happiness:
For the whole in every part,
The truth at the proper centre
(*There's a Way. There's a Voice.*)
Of language and distress
Is recognised in her heart
Singing and dancing.

Let even the great rejoice.
Though buffeted by admirers
And arrogant as noon,
The rich and the lovely have seen
For an infinitesimal moment
(*There's a Way. There's a Voice.*)
In another's eye till their own
Reflection came between,
Singing and dancing.

Let even the small rejoice
Though threatened from purple rostra
And dazed by the soldier's drum
Proclaiming total defeat,
The general loquacious Public
(*There's a Way. There's a Voice.*)
Have been puzzled and struck dumb,
Hearing in every street
Singing and dancing.

Let even the young rejoice
Lovers at their betrayal
Weeping alone in the night,
Have fallen asleep as they heard,
Though too far off to be certain
(*There's a Way. There's a Voice.*)
They had not imagined it,
Sounds that made grief absurd,
Singing and dancing.

Let even the old rejoice
The Bleak and the Dim, abandoned
By impulse and regret,
Are startled out of their lives;
For to footsteps long expected
(*There's a Way. There's a Voice.*)
Their ruins echo, yet
The Demolisher arrives
Singing and dancing.

The Temptation of St. Joseph

I

Joseph

My shoes were shined, my pants were
           cleaned and pressed,

And I was hurrying to meet
  My own true Love:
But a great crowd grew and grew
Till I could not push my way through,
  Because
A star had fallen down the street;
  When they saw who I was,
The police tried to do their best.

Chorus [*off*]

Joseph, you have heard
What Mary says occurred;
Yes, it may be so.
Is it likely? No.

Joseph

The bar was gay, the lighting well-designed,
And I was sitting down to wait
  My own true Love:
A voice I'd heard before, I think,
Cried: "This is on the House. I drink
  To him
Who does not know it is too late";
  When I asked for the time,
Everyone was very kind.

Chorus [*off*]

Mary may be pure,
But, Joseph, are you sure?
How is one to tell?
Suppose, for instance . . . Well . . .

Joseph

Through cracks, up ladders, into waters deep,
I squeezed, I climbed, I swam to save

My own true Love:
Under a dead apple tree
I saw an ass; when it saw me
   It brayed;
A hermit sat in the mouth of a cave;
   When I asked him the way,
He pretended to be asleep.

Chorus [off]

Maybe, maybe not.
But, Joseph, you know what
Your world, of course, will say
About you anyway.

Joseph

Where are you, Father, where?
Caught in the jealous trap
Of an empty house I hear
As I sit alone in the dark
Everything, everything,
The drip of the bathroom tap,
The creak of the sofa spring,
The wind in the air-shaft, all
Making the same remark
Stupidly, stupidly,
Over and over again.
Father, what have I done?
Answer me, Father, how
Can I answer the tactless wall
Or the pompous furniture now?
Answer them . . .

Gabriel

                    No, you must.

Joseph

How then am I to know,
Father, that you are just?
Give me one reason.

Gabriel

                    No.

Joseph

All I ask is one
Important and elegant proof
That what my Love had done
Was really at your will
And that your will is Love.

Gabriel

No, you must believe;
Be silent, and sit still.

II

Narrator

   For the perpetual excuse
Of Adam for his fall—"My little Eve,
God bless her, did beguile me and I ate,"
   For his insistence on a nurse,
All service, breast, and lap, for giving Fate
Feminine gender to make girls believe
That they can save him, you must now atone,
   Joseph, in silence and alone;
While she who loves you makes you shake with fright,
Your love for her must tuck you up and kiss good night.

For likening Love to war, for all
The pay-off lines of limericks in which
The weak resentful bar-fly shows his sting,
   For talking of their spiritual
Beauty to chorus-girls, for flattering
The features of old gorgons who are rich,
For the impudent grin and Irish charm
   That hides a cold will to do harm,
Today the roles are altered; you must be
The Weaker Sex whose passion is passivity.

   For those delicious memories
Cigars and sips of brandy can restore
To old dried boys, for gallantry that scrawls
   In idolatrous detail and size
A symbol of aggression on toilet walls,
For having reasoned—"Woman is naturally pure
Since she has no moustache," for having said,
   "No woman has a business head,"
You must learn now that masculinity,
To Nature, is a non-essential luxury.

   Lest, finding it impossible
To judge its object now or throatily
Forgive it as eternal God forgives,
   Lust, tempted by this miracle
To more ingenious evil, should contrive
A heathen fetish from Virginity
To soothe the spiritual petulance
   Of worn-out rakes and maiden aunts,
Forgetting nothing and believing all,
You must behave as if this were not strange at all.

   Without a change in look or word,
You both must act exactly as before;

Joseph and Mary shall be man and wife
  Just as if nothing had occurred.
There is one World of Nature and one Life;
Sin fractures the Vision, not the Fact; for
The Exceptional is always usual
  And the Usual exceptional.
To choose what is difficult all one's days
As if it were easy, that is faith. Joseph, praise.

III

Semi-Chorus
  Joseph, Mary, pray for those
  Misled by moonlight and the rose,
  For all in our perplexity.
  Lovers who hear a distant bell
  That tolls from somewhere in their head
  Across the valley of their dream—
  "All those who love excessively
  Foot or thigh or arm or face
  Pursue a louche and fatuous fire
  And stumble into Hell"—
  Yet what can such foreboding seem
  But intellectual talk
  So long as bodies walk
  An earth where Time and Space
  Turn Heaven to a finite bed
  And Love into desire?
  Pray for us, enchanted with
  The green Bohemia of that myth
  Where knowledge of the flesh can take
  The guilt of being born away,
  Simultaneous passions make
  One eternal chastity:
  Pray for us romantics, pray.

Joseph, Mary, pray for us,
Independent embryos who,
Unconscious in another, do
Evil as each creature does
In every definite decision
To improve; for even in
The germ-cell's primary division
Innocence is lost and sin,
Already given as a fact,
Once more issues as an act.

Semi-Chorus

Joseph, Mary, pray for all
The proper and conventional
Of whom this world approves.
Pray for us whose married loves
Acquire so readily
The indolent fidelity
Of unaired beds, for us to whom
Domestic hatred can become
A habit-forming drug, whose will
To civil anarchy,
Uses disease to disobey
And makes our private bodies ill.
O pray for our salvation
Who take the prudent way,
Believing we shall be exempted
From the general condemnation
Because our self-respect is tempted
To incest not adultery:
O pray for us, the bourgeoisie.

Boys' Semi-Chorus

Joseph, Mary, pray

For us children as in play
Upon the nursery floor
We gradually explore
Our members till our jealous lives
Have worked through to a clear
But trivial idea
Of that whence each derives
A vague but massive feel
Of being individual.
O pray for our redemption; for
The will that occupies
Our sensual infancy
Already is mature
And could immediately
Beget upon our flesh far more
Expressions of its disbelief
Than we shall manage to conceive
In a long life of lies.

Chorus

Blessed Woman,
Excellent Man,
Redeem for the dull the
Average Way,
That common ungifted
Natures may
Believe that their normal
Vision can
Walk to perfection.

The Summons

I

Star of the Nativity

I am that star most dreaded by the wise,

For they are drawn against their will to me,
Yet read in my procession through the skies
The doom of orthodox sophrosyne:
I shall discard their major preservation,
All that they know so long as no one asks;
I shall deprive them of their minor tasks
In free and legal households of sensation,
Of money, picnics, beer, and sanitation.

Beware. All those who follow me are led
Onto that Glassy Mountain where are no
Footholds for logic, to that Bridge of Dread
Where knowledge but increases vertigo:
Those who pursue me take a twisting lane
To find themselves immediately alone
With savage water or unfeeling stone,
In labyrinths where they must entertain
Confusion, cripples, tigers, thunder, pain.

The First Wise Man

To break down Her defences
    And profit from the vision
That plain men can predict through an
    Ascesis of their senses,
With rack and screw I put Nature through
    A thorough inquisition:
But She was so afraid that if I were disappointed
I should hurt Her more that Her answers were disjointed—
    I did. I didn't. I will. I won't.
She is just as big a liar, in fact, as we are.
    To discover how to be truthful now
    Is the reason I follow this star.

The Second Wise Man

My faith that in Time's constant
    Flow lay real assurance

Broke down on this analysis—
    At any given instant
All solids dissolve, no wheels revolve,
    And facts have no endurance—
And who knows if it is by design or pure inadvertence
That the Present destroys its inherited self-importance?
    With envy, terror, rage, regret,
We anticipate or remember but never are.
    To discover how to be living now
    Is the reason I follow this star.

The Third Wise Man

Observing how myopic
    Is the Venus of the Soma,
The concept Ought would make, I thought,
    Our passions philanthropic,
And rectify in the sensual eye
    Both lens-flare and lens-coma:
But arriving at the Greatest Good by introspection
And counting the Greater Number, left no time for affection,
    Laughter, kisses, squeezing, smiles:
And I learned why the learned are as despised as they are.
    To discover how to be loving now
    Is the reason I follow this star.

The Three Wise Men

The weather has been awful,
    The countryside is dreary,
Marsh, jungle, rock; and echoes mock,
    Calling our hope unlawful;
But a silly song can help along
    Yours ever and sincerely:
At least we know for certain that we are three old sinners,
That this journey is much too long, that we want our dinners,

And miss our wives, our books, our dogs,
But have only the vaguest idea why we are what we are.
   To discover how to be human now
   Is the reason we follow this star.

Star of the Nativity

Descend into the fosse of Tribulation,
Take the cold hand of Terror for a guide;
Below you in its swirling desolation
Hear tortured Horror roaring for a bride:
O do not falter at the last request
But, as the huge deformed head rears to kill,
Answer its craving with a clear I Will;
Then wake, a child in the rose-garden, pressed
Happy and sobbing to your lover's breast.

II

Narrator

Now let the wife look up from her stove, the husband
Interrupt his work, the child put down its toy,
That His voice may be heard in our Just Society
   Who under the sunlight
Of His calm, possessing the good earth, do well. Pray
Silence for Caesar: stand motionless and hear
In a concourse of body and concord of soul
   His proclamation.

Recitative

CITIZENS OF THE EMPIRE, GREETING. ALL MALE PERSONS WHO
SHALL HAVE ATTAINED THE AGE OF TWENTY-ONE YEARS OR OVER
MUST PROCEED IMMEDIATELY TO THE VILLAGE, TOWNSHIP, CITY,
PRECINCT OR OTHER LOCAL ADMINISTRATIVE AREA IN WHICH
THEY WERE BORN AND THERE REGISTER THEMSELVES AND THEIR

431

Narrator

You have been listening to the voice of Caesar
Who overcame implacable Necessity
By His endurance and by His skill has subdued the
   Welter of Fortune.
It is meet, therefore, that, before dispersing
In pious equanimity to obey His orders,
With well-tuned instruments and grateful voices
   We should praise Caesar.

III

Fugal-Chorus

Great is Caesar: He has conquered Seven Kingdoms.
The First was the Kingdom of Abstract Idea:
Last night it was Tom, Dick and Harry; tonight it is S's with P's;
Instead of inflexions and accents
There are prepositions and word-order;
Instead of aboriginal objects excluding each other
There are specimens reiterating a type;
Instead of wood-nymphs and river-demons,
There is one unconditioned ground of Being.
Great is Caesar: God must be with Him.

Great is Caesar: He has conquered Seven Kingdoms.
The Second was the Kingdom of Natural Cause:
Last night it was Sixes and Sevens; tonight it is One and Two;
Instead of saying, "Strange are the whims of the Strong,"
We say, "Harsh is the Law but it is certain";
Instead of building temples, we build laboratories;

432

Instead of offering sacrifices, we perform experiments;
Instead of reciting prayers, we note pointer-readings;
Our lives are no longer erratic but efficient.
Great is Caesar: God must be with Him.

Great is Caesar; He has conquered Seven Kingdoms.
The Third was the Kingdom of Infinite Number:
Last night it was Rule-of-Thumb, tonight it is To-a-T;
Instead of Quite-a-lot, there is Exactly-so-many;
Instead of Only-a-few, there is Just-these;
Instead of saying, "You must wait until I have counted,"
We say, "Here you are. You will find this answer correct";
Instead of a nodding acquaintance with a few integers
The Transcendentals are our personal friends.
Great is Caesar: God must be with Him.

Great is Caesar: He has conquered Seven Kingdoms.
The Fourth was the Kingdom of Credit Exchange:
Last night it was Tit-for-Tat, tonight it is C.O.D.;
When we have a surplus, we need not meet someone with
    a deficit;
When we have a deficit, we need not meet someone with
    a surplus;
Instead of heavy treasures, there are paper symbols of value;
Instead of Pay at Once, there is Pay when you can;
Instead of My Neighbour, there is Our Customers;
Instead of Country Fair, there is World Market.
Great is Caesar: God must be with Him.

Great is Caesar; He has conquered Seven Kingdoms.
The Fifth was the Kingdom of Inorganic Giants:
Last night it was Heave-Ho, tonight it is Whee-Spree;
When we want anything, They make it;
When we dislike anything, They change it;
When we want to go anywhere, They carry us;

When the Barbarian invades us, They raise immovable shields;
When we invade the Barbarian, They brandish
    irresistible swords;
Fate is no longer a fiat of Matter, but a freedom of Mind.
Great is Caesar: God must be with Him.

Great is Caesar: He has conquered Seven Kingdoms.
The Sixth was the Kingdom of Organic Dwarfs:
Last night it was Ouch-Ouch, tonight it is Yum-Yum;
When diseases waylay us, They strike them dead;
When worries intrude on us, They throw them out;
When pain accosts us, They save us from embarrassment;
When we feel like sheep, They make us lions;
When we feel like geldings, They make us stallions;
Spirit is no longer under Flesh, but on top.
Great is Caesar: God must be with Him.

Great is Caesar: He has conquered Seven Kingdoms.
The Seventh was the Kingdom of Popular Soul:
Last night it was Order-Order, tonight it is Hear-Hear;
When he says, You are happy, we laugh;
When he says, You are wretched, we cry;
When he says, It is true, everyone believes it;
When he says, It is false, no one believes it;
When he says, This is good, this is loved;
When he says, That is bad, that is hated.
Great is Caesar: God must be with Him.

IV

Narrator

These are stirring times for the editors of newspapers:
History is in the making; Mankind is on the march.
The longest aqueduct in the world is already

434

Under construction; the Committees on Fen-Drainage
And Soil-Conservation will issue very shortly
Their Joint Report; even the problems of Trade Cycles
And Spiralling Prices are regarded by the experts
As practically solved; and the recent restrictions
Upon aliens and free-thinking Jews are beginning
To have a salutary effect upon public morale.
True, the Western seas are still infested with pirates,
And the rising power of the Barbarian in the North
Is giving some cause for uneasiness; but we are fully
Alive to these dangers; we are rapidly arming; and both
Will be taken care of in due course: then, united
In a sense of common advantage and common right,
Our great Empire shall be secure for a thousand years.

    If we were never alone or always too busy,
Perhaps we might even believe what we know is not true:
But no one is taken in, at least not all of the time;
In our bath, or the subway, or the middle of the night,
We know very well we are not unlucky but evil,
That the dream of a Perfect State or No State at all,
To which we fly for refuge, is a part of our punishment.

    Let us therefore be contrite but without anxiety,
For Powers and Times are not gods but mortal gifts from God;
Let us acknowledge our defeats but without despair,
For all societies and epochs are transient details,
Transmitting an everlasting opportunity
That the Kingdom of Heaven may come, not in our present
And not in our future, but in the Fullness of Time.
Let us pray.

V

Chorale

Our Father, whose creative Will
Asked Being for us all,

Confirm it that Thy Primal Love
May weave in us the freedom of
The actually deficient on
    The justly actual.

Though written by Thy children with
    A smudged and crooked line,
The Word is ever legible,
Thy Meaning unequivocal,
And for Thy Goodness even sin
    Is valid as a sign.

Inflict Thy promises with each
    Occasion of distress,
That from our incoherence we
May learn to put our trust in Thee,
And brutal fact persuade us to
    Adventure, Art, and Peace.

The Vision of the Shepherds

I

The First Shepherd

The winter night requires our constant attention,
    Watching that water and good-will,
Warmth and well-being, may still be there in the morning.

The Second Shepherd

For behind the spontaneous joy of life
There is always a mechanism to keep going,

The Third Shepherd

And someone like us is always there.

The First Shepherd

We observe that those who assure us their education

436

And money would do us such harm,
How real we are just as we are, and how they envy us,
   For it is the centreless tree
And the uncivilised robin who are the truly happy,
   Have done pretty well for themselves:

The Second Shepherd

Nor can we help noticing how those who insist that
   We ought to stand up for our rights,
And how important we are, keep insisting also
   That it doesn't matter a bit
If one of us gets arrested or injured, for
   It is only our numbers that count.

The Third Shepherd

In a way they are right,

The First Shepherd

        But to behave like a cogwheel
When one knows one is no such thing,

The Second Shepherd

Merely to add to a crowd with one's passionate body,
   Is not a virtue.

The Third Shepherd

        What is real
About us all is that each of us is waiting.

The First Shepherd

   That is why we are able to bear
Ready-made clothes, second-hand art and opinions
   And being washed and ordered about;

437

The Second Shepherd
That is why you should not take our conversation
   Too seriously, nor read too much
Into our songs;

The Third Shepherd
   Their purpose is mainly to keep us
From watching the clock all the time.

The First Shepherd
For, though we cannot say why, we know that something
   Will happen:

The Second Shepherd
   What we cannot say,

The Third Shepherd
Except that it will not be a reporter's item
   Of unusual human interest;

The First Shepherd
That always means something unpleasant.

The Second Shepherd
                         But one day or
The next we shall hear the Good News.

II

The Three Shepherds
   Levers nudge the aching wrist;
      "You are free
      Not to be,
      Why exist?"
Wheels a thousand times a minute
      Mutter, stutter,

438

"End the self you cannot mend,
Did you, friend, begin it?"
   And the streets
   Sniff at our defeats.
Then who is the Unknown
Who answers for our fear
As if it were His own,
So that we reply
Till the day we die;
"No, I don't know why,
But I'm glad I'm here"?

III

Chorus of Angels

Unto you a Child,
A Son is given.
Praising, proclaiming
The ingression of Love,
Earth's darkness invents
The blaze of Heaven,
And frigid silence
Meditates a song;
For great joy has filled
The narrow and the sad,
While the emphasis
Of the rough and big,
The abiding crag
And wandering wave,
Is on forgiveness:
Sing Glory to God
And good-will to men,
All, all, all of them.
Run to Bethlehem.

Shepherds

Let us run to learn
How to love and run;
Let us run to Love.

Chorus

Now all things living,
Domestic or wild,
With whom you must share
Light, water, and air,
And suffer and shake
In physical need,
The sullen limpet,
The exuberant weed,
The mischievous cat,
And the timid bird,
Are glad for your sake
As the new-born Word
Declares that the old
Authoritarian
Constraint is replaced
By His Covenant,
And a city based
On love and consent
Suggested to men,
All, all, all of them.
Run to Bethlehem.

Shepherds

Let us run to learn
How to love and run;
Let us run to Love.

Chorus

The primitive dead
Progress in your blood,
And generations
Of the unborn, all
Are leaping for joy
In your reins today
When the Many shall,
Once in your common
Certainty of this
Child's lovableness,
Resemble the One,
That after today
The children of men
May be certain that
The Father Abyss
Is affectionate
To all Its creatures,
All, all, all of them.
Run to Bethlehem.

At the Manger

I

Mary

O shut your bright eyes that mine must endanger
With their watchfulness; protected by its shade
Escape from my care: what can you discover
From my tender look but how to be afraid?
Love can but confirm the more it would deny.
    Close your bright eye.

Sleep. What have you learned from the womb that bore you
But an anxiety your Father cannot feel?

Sleep. What will the flesh that I gave do for you,
Or my mother love, but tempt you from His will?
Why was I chosen to teach His Son to weep?
    Little One, sleep.

Dream. In human dreams earth ascends to Heaven
Where no one need pray nor ever feel alone.
In your first few hours of life here, O have you
Chosen already what death must be your own?
How soon will you start on the Sorrowful Way?
    Dream while you may.

II

First Wise Man

Led by the light of an unusual star,
We hunted high and low.

Second Wise Man

                        Have travelled far,
For many days, a little group alone
With doubts, reproaches, boredom, the unknown.

Third Wise Man

Through stifling gorges.

First Wise Man

                    Over level lakes,

Second Wise Man

Tundras intense and irresponsive seas.

Third Wise Man

In vacant crowds and humming silences,

First Wise Man

By ruined arches and past modern shops,

Second Wise Man

Counting the miles,

Third Wise Man
And the absurd mistakes.

The Three Wise Men
O here and now our endless journey stops.

First Shepherd
We never left the place where we were born,

Second Shepherd
Have only lived one day, but every day,

Third Shepherd
Have walked a thousand miles yet only worn
The grass between our work and home away.

First Shepherd
Lonely we were though never left alone.

Second Shepherd
The solitude familiar to the poor
Is feeling that the family next door,
The way it talks, eats, dresses, loves, and hates,
Is indistinguishable from one's own.

Third Shepherd
Tonight for the first time the prison gates
Have opened.

First Shepherd
Music and sudden light

Second Shepherd
Have interrupted our routine tonight,

Third Shepherd
And swept the filth of habit from our hearts.

The Three Shepherds
O here and now our endless journey starts.

Wise Men
Our arrogant longing to attain the tomb,

Shepherds
Our sullen wish to go back to the womb,

Wise Men
To have no past.

Shepherds
No future,

Tutti
                              Is refused.
And yet, without our knowledge, Love has used
Our weakness as a guard and guide.
                              We bless

Wise Men
Our lives' impatience.

Shepherds
                    Our lives' laziness,

Tutti
And bless each other's sin, exchanging here

444

Wise Men

Exceptional conceit

Shepherds

> With average fear.

Tutti

Released by Love from isolating wrong,
Let us for Love unite our various song,
Each with his gift according to his kind
Bringing this child his body and his mind.

III

Wise Men

Child, at whose birth we would do obsequy
For our tall errors of imagination,
Redeem our talents with your little cry.

Shepherds

Clinging like sheep to the earth for protection,
We have not ventured far in any direction:
   Wean, Child, our ageing flesh away
   From its childish way.

Wise Men

Love is more serious than Philosophy
Who sees no humour in her observation
That Truth is knowing that we know we lie.

Shepherds

When, to escape what our memories are thinking,
We go out at nights and stay up drinking,
   Stay then with our sick pride and mind
   The forgetful mind.

Wise Men

Love does not will enraptured apathy;
Fate plays the passive role of dumb temptation
To wills where Love can doubt, affirm, deny.

Shepherds

When, chafing at the rule of old offences,
We run away to the sea of the senses,
   On strange beds then O welcome home
   Our horror of home.

Wise Men

Love knows of no somatic tyranny;
For homes are built for Love's accommodation
By bodies from the void they occupy.

Shepherds

When, exhausting our wills with our evil courses,
We demand the good-will of cards and horses,
   Be then our lucky certainty
   Of uncertainty.

Wise Men

Love does not fear substantial anarchy,
But vividly expresses obligation
With movement and in spontaneity.

Shepherds

When, feeling the great boots of the rich on our faces,
We live in the hope of one day changing places,
   Be then the truth of our abuse
   That we abuse.

446

Wise Men

The singular is not Love's enemy;
Love's possibilities of realisation
Require an Otherness that can say *I*

Shepherds

When in dreams the beasts and cripples of resentment
Rampage and revel to our hearts' contentment,
  Be then the poetry of hate
  That replaces hate.

Wise Men

Not In but With our time Love's energy
Exhibits Love's immediate operation;
The choice to love is open till we die.

Shepherds

O Living Love, by your birth we are able
Not only, like the ox and ass of the stable,
  To love with our live wills, but love,
  Knowing we love.

Tutti

O Living Love replacing phantasy,
O Joy of life revealed in Love's creation;
Our mood of longing turns to indication:
Space is the Whom our loves are needed by,
Time is our choice of How to love and Why.

The Meditation of Simeon

Simeon

As long as the apple had not been entirely digested, as long as there remained the least understanding between Adam and the stars, rivers and horses with whom he had once known complete intimacy, as long as Eve could share in any way with the moods of the rose or the ambitions of the swallow, there was still a hope that the effects of the poison would wear off, that the exile from Paradise was only a bad dream, that the Fall had not occurred in fact.

Chorus

When we woke, it was day; we went on weeping.

Simeon

As long as there were any roads to amnesia and anaesthesia still to be explored, any rare wine or curiosity of cuisine as yet untested, any erotic variation as yet unimagined or unrealised, any method of torture as yet undevised, any style of conspicuous waste as yet unindulged, any eccentricity of mania or disease as yet unrepresented, there was still a hope that man has not been poisoned but transformed, that Paradise was not an eternal state from which he had been forever expelled, but a childish state which he had permanently outgrown, that the Fall had occurred by necessity.

Chorus

We danced in the dark, but were not deceived.

Simeon

As long as there were any experiments still to be undertaken in restoring that order in which desire had once rejoiced to be reflected, any code of equity and obligation upon which some society had not yet been founded, any species of property of which the value had not yet been appreciated, any talent that had not yet won private devotion and public honour, any rational concept of the Good or intuitive feeling for the Holy that had not yet found its precise and beautiful expression, any technique of contemplation or ritual of sacrifice and praise that had not yet been properly conducted, any faculty of mind or body that had not yet been thoroughly disciplined, there was still a hope that some antidote might be found, that the gates of Paradise had indeed slammed to, but with the exercise of a little patience and ingenuity would be unlocked, that the Fall had occurred by accident.

Chorus

Lions came loping into the lighted city.

Simeon

Before the Positive could manifest Itself specifically, it was necessary that nothing should be left that negation could remove; the emancipation of Time from Space had first to be complete, the Revolution of the Images, in which the memories rose up and cast into subjection the senses by Whom hitherto they had been enslaved, successful beyond their wildest dreams, the mirror in which the Soul expected to admire herself so perfectly polished that her natural consolation of vagueness should be utterly withdrawn.

Chorus

We looked at our Shadow, and, Lo, it was lame.

Simeon

Before the Infinite could manifest Itself in the finite, it was necessary that man should first have reached that point along his road to Knowledge where, just as it rises from the swamps of Confusion onto the sunny slopes of Objectivity, it forks in opposite directions towards the One and the Many; where, therefore, in order to proceed at all, he must decide which is Real and which only Appearance, yet at the same time cannot escape the knowledge that his choice is arbitrary and subjective.

Chorus

Promising to meet, we parted forever.

Simeon

Before the Unconditional could manifest Itself under the conditions of existence, it was necessary that man should first have reached the ultimate frontier of consciousness, the secular limit of memory beyond which there remained but one thing for him to know, his Original Sin, but of this it is impossible for him to become conscious because it is itself what conditions his will to knowledge. For as long as he was in Paradise he could not sin by any conscious intention or act: his as yet unfallen will could only rebel against the truth by taking flight into an unconscious lie; he could only eat of the Tree of the Knowledge of Good and Evil by forgetting that its existence was a fiction of the Evil One, that there is only the Tree of Life.

Chorus

The bravest drew back on the brink of the Abyss.

Simeon

From the beginning until now God spoke through His prophets. The Word aroused the uncomprehending depths of their flesh to a witnessing fury, and their witness was this:

that the Word should be made Flesh. Yet their witness could only be received as long as it was vaguely misunderstood, as long as it seemed either to be neither impossible nor necessary, or necessary but not impossible, or impossible but not necessary; and the prophecy could not therefore be fulfilled. For it could only be fulfilled when it was no longer possible to receive, because it was clearly understood as absurd. The Word could not be made Flesh until men had reached a state of absolute contradiction between clarity and despair in which they would have no choice but either to accept absolutely or to reject absolutely, yet in their choice there should be no element of luck, for they would be fully conscious of what they were accepting or rejecting.

Chorus
The eternal spaces were congested and depraved.

Simeon
But here and now the Word which is implicit in the Beginning and in the End is become immediately explicit, and that which hitherto we could only passively fear as the incomprehensible I AM, henceforth we may actively love with comprehension that THOU ART. Wherefore, having seen Him, not in some prophetic vision of what might be, but with the eyes of our own weakness as to what actually is, we are bold to say that we have seen our salvation.

Chorus
Now and forever, we are not alone.

Simeon
By the event of this birth the true significance of all other events is defined, for of every other occasion it can be said that it could have been different, but of this birth it is the case that it could in no way be other than it is. And by the

existence of this Child, the proper value of all other existences is given, for of every other creature it can be said that
it has extrinsic importance but of this Child it is the case
that He is in no sense a symbol.

Chorus

We have right to believe that we really exist.

Simeon

By Him is dispelled the darkness wherein the fallen will
cannot distinguish between temptation and sin, for in Him
we become fully conscious of Necessity as our freedom to
be tempted, and of Freedom as our necessity to have faith.
And by Him is illuminated the time in which we execute
those choices through which our freedom is realised or prevented, for the course of History is predictable in the degree
to which all men love themselves, and spontaneous in the
degree to which each man loves God and through Him his
neighbour.

Chorus

The distresses of choice are our chance to be blessed.

Simeon

Because in Him the Flesh is united to the Word without
magical transformation, Imagination is redeemed from promiscuous fornication with her own images. The tragic conflict of Virtue with Necessity is no longer confined to the
Exceptional Hero; for disaster is not the impact of a curse
upon a few great families, but issues continually from the
hubris of every tainted will. Every invalid is Roland defending the narrow pass against hopeless odds, every stenogra-
pher Brunnhilde refusing to renounce her lover's ring which
came into existence through the renunciation of love.

Nor is the Ridiculous a species any longer of the Ugly; for since of themselves all men are without merit, all are ironically assisted to their comic bewilderment by the Grace of God. Every Cabinet Minister is the woodcutter's simple-minded son to whom the fishes and the crows are always whispering the whereabouts of the Dancing Water or the Singing Branch, every heiress the washerwoman's butter-fingered daughter on whose pillow the fairy keeps laying the herb that could cure the Prince's mysterious illness.

Nor is there any situation which is essentially more or less interesting than another. Every tea-table is a battlefield littered with old catastrophes and haunted by the vague ghosts of vast issues, every martyrdom an occasion for flip cracks and sententious oratory.

Because in Him all passions find a logical In-Order-That, by Him is the perpetual recurrence of Art assured.

Chorus

Safe in His silence, our songs are at play.

Simeon

Because in Him the Word is united to the Flesh without loss of perfection, Reason is redeemed from incestuous fixation on her own Logic, for the One and the Many are simultaneously revealed as real. So that we may no longer, with the Barbarians, deny the Unity, asserting that there are as many gods as there are creatures, nor, with the philosophers, deny the Multiplicity, asserting that God is One who has no need of friends and is indifferent to a World of Time and Quantity and Horror which He did not create, nor, with Israel, may we limit the co-inherence of the One and the Many to a special case, asserting that God is only concerned with and of concern to that People whom out of all that He created He has chosen for His own.

For the Truth is indeed One, without which is no salvation, but the possibilities of real knowledge are as many as are the creatures in the very real and most exciting universe that God creates with and for His love, and it is not Nature which is one public illusion, but we who have each our many private illusions about Nature.

Because in Him abstraction finds a passionate For-The-Sake-Of, by Him is the continuous development of Science assured.

Chorus

Our lost Appearances are saved by His love.

Simeon

And because of His visitation, we may no longer desire God as if He were lacking: our redemption is no longer a question of pursuit but of surrender to Him who is always and everywhere present. Therefore at every moment we pray that, following Him, we may depart from our anxiety into His peace.

Chorus

Its errors forgiven, may our Vision come home.

The Massacre of the Innocents

I

Herod

Because I am bewildered, because I must decide, because my decision must be in conformity with Nature and Necessity, let me honour those through whom my nature is by necessity what it is.

To Fortune—that I have become Tetrarch, that I have
escaped assassination, that at sixty my head is clear and
my digestion sound.

To my Father—for the means to gratify my love of travel
and study.

To my Mother—for a straight nose.

To Eva, my coloured nurse—for regular habits.

To my brother, Sandy, who married a trapeze-artist and
died of drink—for so refuting the position of the
Hedonists.

To Mr. Stewart, nicknamed The Carp, who instructed
me in the elements of geometry through which I came
to perceive the errors of the tragic poets.

To Professor Lighthouse—for his lectures on The Pelo-
ponnesian War.

To the stranger on the boat to Sicily—for recommending
to me Brown on Resolution.

To my secretary, Miss Button—for admitting that my
speeches were inaudible.

There is no visible disorder. No crime—what could be
more innocent than the birth of an artisan's child? Today
has been one of those perfect winter days, cold, brilliant,
and utterly still, when the bark of a shepherd's dog carries
for miles, and the great wild mountains come up quite close
to the city walls, and the mind feels intensely awake, and
this evening as I stand at this window high up in the citadel
there is nothing in the whole magnificent panorama of plain
and mountains to indicate that the Empire is threatened by
a danger more dreadful than any invasion of Tartars on
racing camels or conspiracy of the Praetorian Guard.

Barges are unloading soil fertiliser at the river wharves.
Soft drinks and sandwiches may be had in the inns at reasonable prices. Allotment gardening has become popular.

The highway to the coast goes straight up over the mountains and the truck-drivers no longer carry guns. Things are beginning to take shape. It is a long time since anyone stole the park benches or murdered the swans. There are children in this province who have never seen a louse, shopkeepers who have never handled a counterfeit coin, women of forty who have never hidden in a ditch except for fun. Yes, in twenty years I have managed to do a little. Not enough, of course. There are villages only a few miles from here where they still believe in witches. There isn't a single town where a good bookshop would pay. One could count on the fingers of one hand the people capable of solving the problem of Achilles and the Tortoise. Still it is a beginning. In twenty years the darkness has been pushed back a few inches. And what, after all, is the whole Empire, with its few thousand square miles on which it is possible to lead the Rational Life, but a tiny patch of light compared with those immense areas of barbaric night that surround it on all sides, that incoherent wilderness of rage and terror, where Mongolian idiots are regarded as sacred and mothers who give birth to twins are instantly put to death, where malaria is treated by yelling, where warriors of superb courage obey the commands of hysterical female impersonators, where the best cuts of meat are reserved for the dead, where, if a white blackbird has been seen, no more work may be done that day, where it is firmly believed that the world was created by a giant with three heads or that the motions of the stars are controlled from the liver of a rogue elephant?

Yet even inside this little civilised patch itself, where, at the cost of heaven knows how much grief and bloodshed, it has been made unnecessary for anyone over the age of twelve to believe in fairies or that First Causes reside in mortal and finite objects, so many are still homesick for that disorder wherein every passion formerly enjoyed a frantic licence. Caesar flies to his hunting lodge pursued by ennui;

in the faubourgs of the Capital, Society grows savage, corrupted by silks and scents, softened by sugar and hot water, made insolent by theatres and attractive slaves; and everywhere, including this province, new prophets spring up every day to sound the old barbaric note.

I have tried everything. I have prohibited the sale of crystals and ouija-boards; I have slapped a heavy tax on playing cards; the courts are empowered to sentence alchemists to hard labour in the mines; it is a statutory offence to turn tables or feel bumps. But nothing is really effective. How can I expect the masses to be sensible when, for instance, to my certain knowledge, the captain of my own guard wears an amulet against the Evil Eye, and the richest merchant in the city consults a medium over every important transaction?

Legislation is helpless against the wild prayer of longing that rises, day in, day out, from all these households under my protection: "O God, put away justice and truth for we cannot understand them and do not want them. Eternity would bore us dreadfully. Leave Thy heavens and come down to our earth of waterclocks and hedges. Become our uncle. Look after Baby, amuse Grandfather, escort Madam to the Opera, help Willy with his home-work, introduce Muriel to a handsome naval officer. Be interesting and weak like us, and we will love you as we love ourselves."

Reason is helpless, and now even the Poetic Compromise no longer works, all those lovely fairy tales in which Zeus, disguising himself as a swan or a bull or a shower of rain or what-have-you, lay with some beautiful woman and begot a hero. For the Public has grown too sophisticated. Under all the charming metaphors and symbols, it detects the stern command, "Be and act heroically"; behind the myth of divine origin, it senses the real human excellence that is a reproach to its own baseness. So, with a bellow of rage, it kicks Poetry downstairs and sends for Prophecy. "Your sister has just insulted me. I asked for a God who should be as like me as possible. What use to me is a God whose divinity consists in doing difficult things that I cannot do or saying clever things that I cannot understand? The God I want and intend to get must be someone I can recognise immediately without having to wait and see what he says or does. There must be nothing in the least extraordinary about him. Produce him at once, please. I'm sick of waiting."

Today, apparently, judging by the trio who came to see me this morning with an ecstatic grin on their scholarly faces, the job has been done. "God has been born," they cried, "we have seen him ourselves. The World is saved. Nothing else matters."

One needn't be much of a psychologist to realise that if this rumour is not stamped out now, in a few years it is capable of diseasing the whole Empire, and one doesn't have to be a prophet to predict the consequences if it should.

Reason will be replaced by Revelation. Instead of Rational Law, objective truths perceptible to any who will undergo the necessary intellectual discipline, and the same for all, Knowledge will degenerate into a riot of subjective visions—feelings in the solar plexus induced by under-nourishment, angelic images generated by fevers or drugs, dream warnings inspired by the sound of falling water. Whole cosmogonies will be created out of some forgotten personal resentment, complete epics written in private languages, the daubs of school children ranked above the greatest masterpieces.

Idealism will be replaced by Materialism. Priapus will only have to move to a good address and call himself Eros to become the darling of middle-aged women. Life after death will be an eternal dinner party where all the guests are twenty years old. Diverted from its normal and wholesome outlet in patriotism and civic or family pride, the need

458

of the materialistic Masses for some visible Idol to worship will be driven into totally unsocial channels where no education can reach it. Divine honours will be paid to silver teapots, shallow depressions in the earth, names on maps, domestic pets, ruined windmills, even in extreme cases, which will become increasingly common, to headaches, or malignant tumours, or four o'clock in the afternoon.

Justice will be replaced by Pity as the cardinal human virtue, and all fear of retribution will vanish. Every corner-boy will congratulate himself: "I'm such a sinner that God had to come down in person to save me. I must be a devil of a fellow." Every crook will argue: "I like committing crimes. God likes forgiving them. Really the world is admirably arranged." And the ambition of every young cop will be to secure a death-bed repentance. The New Aristocracy will consist exclusively of hermits, bums, and permanent invalids. The Rough Diamond, the Consumptive Whore, the bandit who is good to his mother, the epileptic girl who has a way with animals will be the heroes and heroines of the New Tragedy when the general, the statesman, and the philosopher have become the butt of every farce and satire.

Naturally this cannot be allowed to happen. Civilisation must be saved even if this means sending for the military, as I suppose it does. How dreary. Why is it that in the end civilisation always has to call in these professional tidiers to whom it is all one whether it be Pythagoras or a homicidal lunatic that they are instructed to exterminate. O dear, Why couldn't this wretched infant be born somewhere else? Why can't people be sensible? I don't want to be horrid. Why can't they see that the notion of a finite God is absurd? Because it is. And suppose, just for the sake of argument, that it isn't, that this story is true, that this child is in some inexplicable manner both God and Man, that he grows up, lives, and dies, without committing a single sin? Would that make life any better? On the contrary it would make it far, far worse. For it could only mean this; that once having shown them how, God would expect every man, whatever his fortune, to lead a sinless life in the flesh and on earth. Then indeed would the human race be plunged into madness and despair. And for me personally at this moment it would mean that God had given me the power to destroy Himself. I refuse to be taken in. He could not play such a horrible practical joke. Why should He dislike me so? I've worked like a slave. Ask anyone you like. I read all official dispatches without skipping. I've taken elocution lessons. I've hardly ever taken bribes. How dare He allow me to decide? I've tried to be good. I brush my teeth every night. I haven't had sex for a month. I object. I'm a liberal. I want everyone to be happy. I wish I had never been born.

II

Soldiers

When the Sex War ended with the slaughter of
    the Grandmothers,
They found a bachelor's baby suffocating under them;
Somebody called him George and that was the end of it:
    They hitched him up to the Army.
    George, you old debutante,
    How did you get in the Army?

In the Retreat from Reason he deserted on his
    rocking-horse
And lived on a fairy's kindness till he tired of kicking her;
He smashed her spectacles and stole her check-book
    and mackintosh
    Then cruised his way back to the Army.
    George, you old numero,
    How did you get in the Army?

Before the Diet of Sugar he was using razor-blades
And exited soon after with an allergy to maidenheads;
He discovered a cure of his own, but no one would
  patent it,
 So he showed up again in the Army.
 George, you old flybynight,
 How did you get in the Army?

When the Vice Crusades were over he was hired by
  some Muscovites
Prospecting for deodorants among the Eskimos;
He was caught by a common cold and condemned to the
  whiskey mines,
 But schemozzled back to the Army.
 George, you old Emperor,
 How did you get in the Army?

Since Peace was signed with Honour he's been minding
  his business;
But, whoops, here comes His Idleness, buttoning
  his uniform;
Just in tidy time to massacre the Innocents;
 He's come home to roost in the Army.
 George, you old matador,
 Welcome back to the Army.

III

Rachel

On the Left are grinning dogs, peering down into a solitude
  too deep to fill with roses.
On the Right are sensible sheep, gazing up at a pride where
  no dream can grow.
Somewhere in these unending wastes of delirium is a lost
  child, speaking of Long Ago in the language of wounds.
Tomorrow, perhaps, he will come to himself in Heaven.

But here Grief turns her silence, neither in this direction,
nor in that, nor for any reason.
And her coldness now is on the earth forever.

The Flight into Egypt

I

Joseph

Mirror, let us through the glass
No authority can pass.

Mary

Echo, if the strong should come,
Tell a white lie or be dumb.

Voices of the Desert

It was visitors' day at the vinegar works
In Tenderloin Town when I tore my time;
A sorrowful snapshot was my sinful wage:
Was that why you left me, elusive bones?
  Come to our bracing desert
  Where eternity is eventful,
    For the weather-glass
    Is set at Alas,
  The thermometer at Resentful.

Mary

The Kingdom of the Robbers lies
Between Time and our memories;

Joseph

Fugitives from Space must cross
The waste of the Anonymous.

Voices of the Desert

How should he figure my fear of the dark?
The moment he can he'll remember me,
The silly, he locked in the cellar for fun,
And his dear little doggie shall die in his arms.
   Come to our old-world desert
   Where everyone goes to pieces;
     You can pick up tears
     For souvenirs
   Or genuine diseases.

Joseph

Geysers and volcanoes give
Sudden comical relief;

Mary

And the vulture is a boon
On a dull hot afternoon.

Voices of the Desert

All Father's nightingales knew their place,
The gardens were loyal: look at them now.
The roads are so careless, the rivers so rude,
My studs have been stolen; I must speak to the sea.
   Come to our well-run desert
   Where anguish arrives by cable,
     And the deadly sins
     May be bought in tins
   With instructions on the label.

Mary

Skulls recurring every mile
Direct the thirsty to the Nile;

Joseph

And the jackal's eye at night
Forces Error to keep right.

Voices of the Desert

In a land of lilies I lost my wits,
Nude as a number all night I ran
With a ghost for a guest along green canals;
By the waters of waking I wept for the weeds.
  Come to our jolly desert
  Where even the dolls go whoring;
    Where cigarette-ends
    Become intimate friends,
  And it's always three in the morning.

Joseph and Mary

Safe in Egypt we shall sigh
For lost insecurity;
Only when her terrors come
Does our flesh feel quite at home.

II

Recitative

Fly, Holy Family, from our immediate rage,
That our future may be freed from our past; retrace
    The footsteps of law-giving
  Moses, back through the sterile waste,

Down to the rotten kingdom of Egypt, the damp
Tired delta where in her season of glory our
    Forefathers sighed in bondage;
  Abscond with the Child to the place

That their children dare not revisit, to the time
They do not care to remember; hide from our pride
    In our humiliation;
  Fly from our death with our new life.

464

III

Narrator

Well, so that is that. Now we must dismantle the tree,
Putting the decorations back into their cardboard boxes—
Some have got broken—and carrying them up to the attic.
The holly and the mistletoe must be taken down and burnt,
And the children got ready for school. There are enough
Left-overs to do, warmed-up, for the rest of the week—
Not that we have much appetite, having drunk such a lot,
Stayed up so late, attempted—quite unsuccessfully—
To love all of our relatives, and in general
Grossly overestimated our powers. Once again
As in previous years we have seen the actual Vision and failed
To do more than entertain it as an agreeable
Possibility, once again we have sent Him away,
Begging though to remain His disobedient servant,
The promising child who cannot keep His word for long.
The Christmas Feast is already a fading memory,
And already the mind begins to be vaguely aware
Of an unpleasant whiff of apprehension at the thought
Of Lent and Good Friday which cannot, after all, now
Be very far off. But, for the time being, here we all are,
Back in the moderate Aristotelian city
Of darning and the Eight-Fifteen, where Euclid's geometry
And Newton's mechanics would account for our experience,
And the kitchen table exists because I scrub it.
It seems to have shrunk during the holidays. The streets
Are much narrower than we remembered; we had forgotten
The office was as depressing as this. To those who have seen
The Child, however dimly, however incredulously,
The Time Being is, in a sense, the most trying time of all.
For the innocent children who whispered so excitedly
Outside the locked door where they knew the presents to be
Grew up when it opened. Now, recollecting that moment

We can repress the joy, but the guilt remains conscious;
Remembering the stable where for once in our lives
Everything became a You and nothing was an It.
And craving the sensation but ignoring the cause,
We look round for something, no matter what, to inhibit
Our self-reflection, and the obvious thing for that purpose
Would be some great suffering. So, once we have met the Son,
We are tempted ever after to pray to the Father;
"Lead us into temptation and evil for our sake."
They will come, all right, don't worry; probably in a form
That we do not expect, and certainly with a force
More dreadful than we can imagine. In the meantime
There are bills to be paid, machines to keep in repair,
Irregular verbs to learn, the Time Being to redeem
From insignificance. The happy morning is over,
The night of agony still to come; the time is noon:
When the Spirit must practise his scales of rejoicing
Without even a hostile audience, and the Soul endure
A silence that is neither for nor against her faith
That God's Will will be done, that, in spite of her prayers,
God will cheat no one, not even the world of its triumph.

IV
Chorus

He is the Way.
Follow Him through the Land of Unlikeness;
You will see rare beasts, and have unique adventures.

He is the Truth.
Seek Him in the Kingdom of Anxiety;
You will come to a great city that has expected your return
     for years.

He is the Life.
Love Him in the World of the Flesh;
And at your marriage all its occasions shall dance for joy.